THE NEW SPACE

THE NEW SPACE

MOVEMENT AND EXPERIENCE IN VIENNESE MODERN ARCHITECTURE

Christopher Long

Photographs by Wolfgang Thaler

YALE UNIVERSITY PRESS NEW HAVEN AND LONDON

Published with assistance from the Martin S. Kermacy Endowment, School of Architecture, University of Texas at Austin, and a publication grant from the Office of the Vice President for Research, University of Texas at Austin.

yalebooks.com/art

Designed by Jena Sher
Set in Locator and Elena type
by Mary Gladue
Printed in China by Regent Publishing
Services Limited

Library of Congress Control Number: 2015956228
ISBN: 978-0-300-21828-2

A catalogue record for this book is available from the British Library.

This paper meets the requirements of ANSI/NISO Z39.48-1992 (Permanence of Paper).

10 9 8 7 6 5 4 3 2 1

Frontispiece: Josef Frank, Beer House (detail of fig. 155)

Page vi: Adolf Loos, Goldman & Salatsch Building (detail of fig. 33)

Jacket illustrations: (front) Josef Frank, Beer House (detail of fig. 157); *(back)* Adolf Loos, Villa Müller (detail of fig. 188)

FOR GIA

CONTENTS

ACKNOWLEDGMENTS

This book has been with me for a long time—indeed, for more than two decades. I first thought about writing something along these lines while I was working on my dissertation on Josef Frank in the early 1990s. Since then, I have touched on the issues of space and experience in Viennese modernism on sundry occasions in articles, in lectures, or in other books, though, admittedly, never in a fully sustained way. My musings about the architectural "paths" in the works of Loos, Strnad, and Frank were stimulated by repeated trips to their buildings over many years. Each time I entered and strolled through these structures, they refreshed—and sometimes compelled me to revise—my ideas.

IX

I wrote most of this book in the summer of 2014, while recovering from surgery to repair a torn ligament in my left ankle. The fact that I could not walk forced me to contemplate and rehearse in my mind the routes in each of the buildings I discuss. That I had to rely on a series of mental constructs—which were still vivid for me—was not a handicap but just the reverse. It pushed me to ponder with great care my memory of each architectural moment, each sensation, bringing all into sharper relief than had I simply been ambling through the buildings. I had preserved the visual and physical sensations—many, many of them—just as the three architects had intended.

My guides and helpers through this journey have been many, and I am indebted to them all. One of the largest debts I owe is to Nicolas Allinder, who produced the redrawn plans in this book. Nic, one of my former graduate students at the University of Texas at Austin, had the brilliant idea of using drawings of the paths as a series of linked and continuous plans as a way of making them fully manifest. It is the perfect medium for telling this story, and I am especially grateful to him.

And I owe no less of a debt to Wolfgang Thaler, whose splendid new photography of these remarkable buildings provides a second, visual text in the book, without which the techniques and effects of these unique structures would be nigh impossible to convey. Traveling with Wolfgang to these sites of wonder has been the best form of research I can imagine.

I also want to thank Christine Gloggengiesser, who worked with the many house owners and institutions to arrange permission for the buildings to be photographed; Markus Kristan, curator of the architecture collection and Ingrid Kastel in the documentation department at the Grafische Sammlung Albertina, Vienna, who fielded my questions and helped me with access to the Loos and Frank archives; and Eric Anderson, Rhode Island School of Design, who answered some important questions about Jakob von Falke and his ideas. I also owe thanks to Ruth Hansich (Dortmund and Vienna), Erich Hubmann and Andreas Vass (Vienna), Claudia Mazanek (Vienna), Iris Meder (Vienna), and Georg Riesenhuber (Brussels) for thoughtfully sharing materials, sources, and ideas with me.

I am especially grateful to the homeowners and institutions that graciously provided access to their properties: Tano Bojankin and Dr. Johannes Strohmayer (Beer House); Johannes Holländer (Scheu House); Gun Jacobson (Tolvekarna); Familie Steiner (Villa Khuner); Reinhard Pühringer and the Raiffeisenbank, Vienna (Looshaus); Dr. Dieter Sponer (Hock House); Gemeindeamt Pernitz (Kinderheim, Ortmann); Vera Fraunbaum and the Israeli embassy in Austria (Villa Moller); and Maria Szadkowska and the Muzeum Hlavního Města Prahy (Villa Müller).

In addition, I would like to express my thanks to the librarians, archivists, and staff members at the Architecture and Design Collection, Art, Design and Architecture Museum, University of California, Santa Barbara, especially Jocelyn Gibbs; Architektur Zentrum Wien; Gerd Zillner, Kiesler Stiftung, Vienna; Museum für angewandte Kunst / Gegenwartskunst, Vienna; Museum für Gestaltung, Bauhaus-Archiv, Berlin; Plan- und Schriftenkammer der Magistratsamt (MA 37), Vienna; Österreichische Nationalbibliothek—Bildarchiv, Vienna; and the Wien Bibliothek, Vienna. Once more, I am thankful to the staff of the Architecture and Planning Library at the University of Texas at Austin, especially Martha Gonzáles Palacios, Beth Dodd, Kathryn Pierce Meyer, and Daniel Orozco, for their gracious and expert assistance.

Peter Duniecki, Brigitte Groihofer, and Monika Platzer, all in Vienna, have aided me in a variety of ways over the years. Steve Cadman kindly allowed me to use his photograph of the Richard Norman Shaw House in Hampstead, London. Vera Berkman (Tucson, Arizona) and Susanne Eisenkolb (Berlin) kindly gave me their permission to translate and reproduce the texts, respectively, of Oskar Strnad and Josef Frank. Maru Bing and the Kulka estate in New Zealand graciously granted permission to quote from Heinrich Kulka's 1931 monograph on Loos (see appendix). The Kulka estate also generously gave permission to reproduce several of Kulka's drawings and his model of the Baker House. My many lunchtime conversations with my colleague Francesco Passanti helped clarify a number of issues for me, especially regarding Le Corbusier and his concept of the *promenade architecturale*. I would also like to thank the anonymous peer reviewers for the book, whose suggestions were especially useful. I am also grateful to Todd S. Cronan and R. Scott Gill who read the manuscript and offered many useful suggestions.

A grant from the Martin S. Kermacy Endowment at the University of Texas at Austin helped to cover the cost of the photographs, and a second grant from the same fund helped to offset the production costs for the book. I am grateful to Frederick Steiner, dean of the School of Architecture, for his continued support. I must also acknowledge a generous subvention grant from the Office of the Vice President for Research at the University of Texas at Austin that covered the remainder of the book's production costs.

I had the great privilege of working once more with the wonderful staff of the Art Workshop at Yale University Press. I want especially to thank Katherine Boller, Deborah Bruce-Hostler, Heidi Downey, Mary Mayer, Tamara Schechter, and Jena Sher for their efforts in making this book a reality.

Finally, I want to thank my father, Harry Long, and my wife, Gia Marie Houck, for their unceasing support and love.

Detail of Figure 50

INTRODUCTION

"In Vienna the interesting battles [were] waged on the surface. A concern for façade, symbol, and decoration—exactly those things the Viennese most aggressively claimed to have left in the past—was their precise contribution to modernism."[1] So wrote Kirk Varnedoe in 1986. Varnedoe was then curator of painting and sculpture at the Museum of Modern Art in New York, and this passage appears in one of his essays in the catalogue for the exhibition *Vienna 1900: Art, Architecture & Design*, which the museum mounted that year.

Varnedoe was always an astute seer. He was undeniably right about the architecture of the generation of Vienna "around 1900." For roughly a decade and a half, from around 1894 to 1910 (or, to put it slightly differently in the context of time, from the time when Otto Wagner commenced his personal design revolution until the waning of the Jugendstil at the end of the first decade of the new century), Viennese modernism was in its essence about the reconsideration and remaking of ornament and symbol—and, ultimately, as it would turn out, their rejection. Joseph Maria Olbrich, Josef Hoffmann, and the other young Secessionists of the fin de siècle were consumed with the problem of finding—or better, contriving—a modernist expression. Long into the 1920s, and even into the 1930s, the quest for a style remained a preoccupation for some of the Viennese.

But around 1910 it all began to change. The fundamental shift came in the work of a group of younger architects and designers who had been educated in the first years of the new century and who came onto the scene just as the Secessionist movement was fading away. Led by Oskar Strnad and Josef Frank, they posed questions not about style, but about lifestyle—about how one should live, work, and dwell in modern times. They saw the call to modernism as a deeper cultural problem, not a matter of mere appearances.

They took their cues in great measure from Adolf Loos. Loos was nearly a full decade older than Strnad (he was, in fact, born the same year as Hoffmann) and fifteen years older than Frank; he belonged temporally to the fin-de-siècle generation, but he would remain apart from it. He would come, in any event, to have far more in common with the younger *revoltés*. He, too, had always believed that modernism was about culture, not style per se, about how cultivated people should comport themselves and reside in the new age. Loos's starting point was to discern where the culture was, what was culturally appropriate, and what that meant for his time. Only then, by fastidiously sorting through everything that modern life brought and everything that had survived from the past that still had relevance, he believed, could one discern what was truly modern.

What emerged from this round of cultural questioning was the direction that would define Viennese modernism for the next two decades, until Hitler and the Nazis devoured Austria in 1938. It came to be known as the *Wiener Wohnkultur*—the Viennese living culture—and it was an effort to assemble a lifestyle of comfort and ease, a way of being in the modern world while simultaneously finding refuge from it. For Loos and these younger Viennese, the idea was never quite about making a purified modernism—for they did not exclude forms and objects from history in their designs—but about locating their precise position within a new urban and urbane world. Their design language was not so much au courant as it was comfortably and properly of the moment. It was the antipode of what came to be characterized as European "functionalism"; it was a denial of the ideal of purposeful appearance and an embrace of a cozy here and now.

What ran in parallel to this inquiry into splendid and gracious living was a concern about how we inhabit architectural space itself. It was, to cast it precisely, not merely about how to frame architectural spaces, but how to make spaces that fit the new way of being in the world.

This book is about this new spatial conception. It is an attempt at an alternative reading of the story of Viennese modernism—or, at least, one of its central chapters. It is, as the book's title suggests, about architectural space, but not space as a fixed element or space as a wholly abstract concept. Rather, it is about how a few Viennese modernists— Loos, Strnad, and Frank—explored the experience of space and how architecture might elicit perceptions or emotions. And, ultimately, it is about how they thought space could be utilized to stimulate or enhance lived experience.

Loos and—to a lesser extent—Frank are now recognized for their spatial inquiries, Loos for his notion of what came to be known as the *Raumplan*, or space plan (which, very simply, had it that space could be expanded in modern buildings not only horizontally but also vertically by cutting through the floors and arranging the spaces on multiple, interlocking levels, connected by stairs), and Frank for his play of volumes and movement, his idea of "Das Haus als Weg und Platz" (the house as path and place), which was in a sense both an expansion and relaxation of Loos's Raumplan idea. Over the years, a good deal has been written about the concept of space in the works of Loos and Frank—and even a little about Strnad, whose spatial ideas, while mostly overlooked, were of nearly equal import—examining how they assembled rooms within a volume and the complex ways in which they connected these spaces.[2]

My project, however, is an effort to suggest a different reading of their spatial programs, one that does not entirely replace the old one, but seeks to offer a significant amendment: that a core part of the spatial explorations of all three architects had to do not only with the design or configuration of spaces, but the ways in which the experience of space through movement might affect the viewer or inhabitant. It is in a sense about what Le Corbusier, later and independently, would call the *promenade architecturale*, the architectural promenade.[3]

The term appears for the first time in Le Corbusier's description of the Villa Savoye at Poissy.[4] He writes: "In this house occurs a veritable promenade architecturale, offering aspects constantly varied, unexpected and sometimes astonishing."[5] For Le Corbusier, the architectural promenade was, in part, as Flora Samuel has written, "designed to resensitise people to their surroundings."[6] In Le Corbusier's well-known formulation: "You enter: the architectural spectacle at once offers itself to the eye. You follow an itinerary and the perspectives develop with great variety."[7] But Le Corbusier was interested not merely in optical or emotional effects: the promenade became, as Armando Rabaça has succinctly and eloquently described it, "a manifestation of Le Corbusier's code of ordering spaces and organizing the world, through which he invested them with a symbolic dimension and philosophical world view."[8] It was, in other words, about a means for his grand project of bringing together man and his world that played out over and over again in his designs.[9] It was as much a statement about his own ambitious vision as it was a means for engaging those who inhabited his spaces.

What our three Viennese aimed at was different. They were concerned directly with how an involvement with architecture could vitalize the rituals of daily living. They wanted to investigate the patterns of living—almost exclusively in the domestic sphere. But, even more, they sought to examine how fostering new varieties of space could frame our actions and our emotions, and, beyond that, how spatial engagement might make domestic life pleasurable and meaningful. They were interested in how experiences of space and place might stimulate our memories and sentimentality, how architecture could become "internalized" for us.

The origins of their notions of space and experience extend back to the late nineteenth century, to the debate among philosophers and art theorists in Germany concerning the mechanisms of how we perceive and "feel" works of art. The key figures here include Robert Vischer, who investigated notions of empathy or aesthetic sympathy; Theodor Lipps, who expanded Vischer's ideas and supported the principle of subconscious perception and direct experience; and sculptor Adolf von Hildebrand, who was concerned with how we see an object in three dimensions. For these Viennese, though, the most important of these theorists was the art historian August Schmarsow, who argued that architecture was, in the end, about space and space-making. Schmarsow's work overturned previous beliefs about architecture as the shaping and articulation of structural form; he claimed instead that "the essence of architecture" lay in the framing of spaces. And he would go on to insist that good architecture was spatially affective—that to move through a building was to grasp the space with our senses and to feel something. The proper role of the architect, thus, was to forge profound spatial experiences.

This book is about how our three protagonists—Strnad, Loos, and Frank—sought to set this idea—literally and figuratively—into motion.

A brief summing up of the structure of this work may be helpful here. The first chapter explores the ideas of Schmarsow and other German theorists of his time. The second investigates how Strnad initially sought to translate their ideas into built form. The remaining chapters carry the story forward chronologically over roughly four decades, alternating between discussions of the evolving ideas and works of Loos and Frank. The last chapter extends the narrative to the World War II period and into the 1950s, when Frank, by that time living and working in Sweden, sought to push the concept of dynamic space to its very limits. In one sense, these latter chapters form a sort of dialectic, a running dialogue between Loos and Frank about the framing of spaces and movement. But there is not always a demonstrable push and pull between Loos and Frank: rather, the discussion is about how the two architects undertook parallel, if sometimes interrelated, experiments in the new spatial ordering—and how they would ultimately come to conceive distinctive, powerful, and highly personal constructs and experiences.

Unless otherwise noted, all translations are my own. I should also add here a note on terminology. Throughout the book, I have avoided the term "promenade" in order to make clear the differences between what the Viennese and Le Corbusier were seeking to achieve. The word I have used instead is "path," which is the closest English equivalent to *Weg*, the term that Frank and Strnad employed most often to describe a planned and directed "ambulatory." Although it is less poetic than "promenade," it conveys well the nature of what they sought to make: routes into and through dwellings that would be traversed over and over—moments of ordinary daily living that could also be extraordinary.

CHAPTER ONE

The Essence of Architectural Creation

Figure 1 August Schmarsow (1853–1936), ca. 1910. From *Zeitschrift für Kunstfreunde und Kunstsamm-lungen,* vol. II, no. 3/4 (Leipzig 1911).

opposite Detail of Figure 8

For much of the nineteenth century, it was an established rite of passage for newly appointed German professors to present an *Antrittsrede*—an inaugural address. Custom held that the scholar in question would explicate his agenda, laying out his basic views and aims concerning the discipline in which he would teach and perform research. The ritual held within it the potential for moments of true originality and revelation. In practice, though, the results more often than not were disappointing. Only rarely, so seldom indeed that examples scarcely come to mind, do these talks now merit more than a token footnote. But on 8 November 1893, in the *Aula* or great assembly hall of the University of Leipzig, August Hannibal Schmarsow, lately named to the chair of the Institute of Art History, presented an address that—though almost no one fully appreciated it at the time—would come to have great and durable import.

Schmarsow was then forty years old (fig. 1). He had made a swift and spectacular ascent in the rarified world of German academia. Born in the tiny village of Schildfeld in the flatlands of Mecklenburg between Hamburg and Schwerin, he completed his secondary schooling at a Gymnasium in Rostock. He hoped to study with the Swiss cultural and art historian Jakob Burkhardt at the University of Basel, but because of an illness and on the advice of his doctor, he was compelled to abandon the idea. He instead undertook studies in art history, philosophy, and literature at the universities of Bonn, Strasbourg, and Zurich before completing his *Habilitation* in art history at the University of Göttingen, writing on the Renaissance painters Raphael and Pinturicchio.[1]

Schmarsow's appointment in Leipzig had not been without controversy, for among the candidates for the position were the rising Swiss-born art historian Heinrich Wölfflin and the well-regarded philosopher of aesthetics Robert Vischer.[2]

Wölfflin only a few years before had published his landmark book *Renaissance und Barock* (Renaissance and Baroque).[3] The work, an effort to argue for the continuity of the two epochs (previous writers had always asserted that the Baroque was a decidedly misguided break from the purity of Renaissance classical forms) and reclaim a proper place for the later style in the canon of Western architecture, had gathered considerable attention. It was a groundbreaking new view, one that would spawn a long lineage of scholars and writings, and it was among the first solid contributions to the new methodology of formalism, an approach that sought above all to find the style characteristic of a culture or epoch in works of art.

Vischer, too, was a rising academic star. Two decades earlier in his doctoral thesis he had explored the idea of aesthetic empathy, which raised the possibility of combining psychology and art history to examine how we react to works of art—an idea that would come to influence many scholars in the field.

Schmarsow was not without his own achievements. Like Wölfflin, he had been a pioneer on issues of style, both the individual style of the artist and the way in which the collective styles of groups of artists captured the particular expression of an age. But his interests were more far-reaching. He was known to search broadly for meaning in art, delving into an extensive array of approaches and periods. Disconcertingly for many, however, Schmarsow often did so via rather eccentric means, relying on lengthy discourses (and tedious calculations) on the minutiae of proportion or symmetry; and, not infrequently, he ignored other, larger aesthetic questions. His approach drew decidedly mixed reviews. Werner Weisbach, one of his students at the turn of the century, was typical of his detractors. Weisbach thought his teacher pedantic and too heatedly intellectual. He criticized Schmarsow's use of mathematical formulas, which he believed was symptomatic of a "shallow feeling for art."[4] Schmarsow's professional colleagues were also at times disparaging. Franz Wickhoff, the eminent professor of art history in Vienna and the founder of the famed Vienna School of Art Historians, once called him a "blight on the profession," and he cast doubt on Schmarsow's "grasp of history and the basic questions it poses."[5]

Schmarsow had launched his career in 1878 when he accepted a position at the Prussian engraving collection, the Kupferstichkabinett in Berlin. There he began building a photographic collection—one of the first of its kind. He left after a short time to take up a teaching position at Göttingen. He soon grew unhappy after becoming embroiled in a dispute with two other scholars, Anton Springer and Giovanni Morelli, over the authenticity of a Renaissance sketchbook, and he departed on less than rosy terms. In 1885 he was invited to succeed Vischer at the University of Breslau. But almost immediately he again became enmeshed in controversy. The local archbishop forbade the university's theological students from attending Schmarsow's lectures because he had adopted a "scientific approach" that all but ignored the religious questions of medieval architecture. Faced with intractable opposition, he resigned and took several of his best students to Florence. It was there that he accomplished one of the things he is now most noted for: he worked to found the Deutsches Kunsthistorisches Institut (German Art Historical Institute), based on the model of the German Archeological Institute in Rome.[6] Among his first students were Aby Warburg and Max J. Friedländer, both soon to become redoubtable figures in the field.

By 1893, notwithstanding his very evident successes, Schmarsow had developed a reputation in some quarters for being a crank and a malcontent. It was whispered in academic hallways around Germany that he was brilliant but unpredictable and stroppy. None of this seemed to dissuade the authorities in Leipzig, however. Despite misgivings (and with the backing of Karl Lamprecht, one of the other art historians there, who admired Schmarsow's wide-ranging interests), they issued the call for him to take up the chair for art history. (Schmarsow and Lamprecht, perhaps predictably, would later have a bitter falling out over their differing views of how to pursue the study of art history.)[7]

Figure 2 Title page from Schmarsow's published address, *Das Wesen der architektonischen Schöpfung* (Leipzig: Karl W. Hiersemann, 1894). Bayerische Staatsbibliothek, Munich.

Thus it was that in the late autumn of 1893 Schmarsow came to present his inaugural lecture (fig. 2).[8] He strode confidently to the podium and, without fanfare, began a talk that must have stunned and dismayed most of those attending, who no doubt were expecting a more or less regular discourse on art history.

The start was alarming enough: Schmarsow commenced with a general demolition of the architecture of his day. For the first several minutes what he said in effect amounted to a baying critique of all that plagued late nineteenth-century architectural practice. He complained that most contemporary architects regarded their practice merely "as the art of dressing" (*Bekleidungskunst*), a not very subtle dig at the great Gottfried Semper, who had championed the idea at midcentury. He characterized their doings as little more than superficial composition of a purely technical and decorative kind: "the pasting together of inherited styles on the framework of a functional construction, a process for which even the best of them is at a loss to summon up any creative enthusiasm"—in short, they were accomplishing no more than perfunctory decorating. And of those who claimed that architecture was synonymous with tectonics—which is to say, with structure or the expression of structural form—Schmarsow carped that they were confusing "technical achievement" with making an original and creative statement. Instead, he asked—his true agenda only slowly becoming manifest—"Is it not time at last to inquire into the origin and innermost essence of architecture?"[9]

Schmarsow then commenced a full-blown assault on his fellow art historians. He insisted that it made little sense to go on studying buildings "from outside" that is, merely imposing aesthetic judgments. (This was plainly also a full-frontal assault on historicism, with its stress on façade and style.) Such judgments, he claimed, were never more than shallow and artificial. Rather, he continued, the only sensible course was to examine architecture from "within," to attempt to understand its own "internal" logic—its essence. But of what did this essence consist, and how might one get at it?

It was at this point that he revealed the first of several brilliant insights. Architecture, Schmarsow said, was not, as nearly everyone had always assumed, about the act of building or about the material substance of an architectural construct; it was about our interaction with it: "Do the mass of purposely hewn stone, the well-made beam or the securely made arched vaults constitute the architectural work of art, or does the work of art only come into being when human aesthetic reflection begins to transpose itself into the whole and to understand and appreciate all the parts with a pure and free vision?"[10]

The answer, of course, was implicit in the question. It is our experience—our sensory involvement, acting upon the imagination—that gives reality and significance to architecture.

Schmarsow's shifting of the wellspring of architectural meaning from aesthetics to experience was groundbreaking. But it was not wholly unprecedented. Already in the later eighteenth century, the French architect Nicolas Le Camus de Mézières had made a plea for a phenomenological understanding of architecture—for a sensationalist exploration of form and its sentimental or expressive value. But what Le Camus de Mézières was after was how we experience the substance of a building—its walls, ceilings, floors, and, more particularly, its symbols and ornament.[11]

Schmarsow's psycho-physiological theory of architecture instead was most indebted to several other figures from within the very snug orbit of German art historians and philosophers at the end of the nineteenth century, among them Vischer and Wölfflin. All were concerned in some way with the role of the viewer in relationship to works of art. The discussion, which reached its apex around the time of Schmarsow's inaugural address, had grown out of an earlier discourse about how we see and understand the world around us.

Toward the end of the eighteenth century, Immanuel Kant had suggested that the perception of space arose in the perceiving subject. It would take more than fifty years for scientists and observers to work out precisely how this happened. Initially, as in Johann Wolfgang von Goethe's study *Zur Farbenlehre* (Theory of Colors), the process of understanding subjective vision involved empirical studies in optics and physiological psychology.[12] By midcentury, in the experiments and writings of Hermann von Helmholtz, Johann Friedrich Herbart, Gustav Theodor Fechner, Ernst Wilhelm von Brücke, Wilhelm Wundt, and others, there were attempts to understand the relationship between the physiology of vision and our subjective experience of seeing—how, for example, we construct our conception of the world using our full sensory apparatus.[13] It became increasingly apparent that we use a variety of processes—both sensory and mental—to form a picture in our minds. Over time what emerged were various dynamic theories of perception and cognition suggesting that we "compose" a mental image from an assembly of views, like a series of snapshots. Or put another way: we "see" by accumulating individual views in our minds and then piece them together to form a single impression.

The next decisive step, defining how subjective feeling conditions our perception of form, came in the work of Vischer. In his 1873 dissertation, *Über das optische Formgefühl: Ein Beitrag zur Aesthetik* (On the Optical Sense of Form: A Contribution to Aesthetics), Vischer argued that when we set eyes on a work of art we undergo physical, emotional, and psychological experiences—experiences that ultimately affect and transform us in one fashion or another.[14] The term he uses is *Einfühlung*, literally "to feel into"—or, as we would put it in English simply but not precisely with the same full meaning, empathy.

The term *Einfühlung* was an older one, first employed, it seems, by Johann Gottfried Herder and developed in the writings of a number of other nineteenth-century thinkers, including Friedrich Nietzsche and Vischer's own father, the novelist, poet, and writer on the philosophy of art Friedrich Theodor Vischer.[15] The elder Vischer's aesthetic writings had been focused very largely on symbols and the way in which symbols in art provoke emotional transferences.[16] But the younger Vischer undertook a far more radical course. He suggested that the experience of an object or of space could have direct bodily effects— that we can "feel" a work of art or architecture. And what we might feel is not merely optical. Indeed, we might literally experience a visceral response. "We can often observe in ourselves," he wrote, "the curious fact that a visual stimulus is experienced not so much with our eyes as with a different sense in another part of the body."[17] Goosebumps or shivers were one form of such a response, but it was also possible to sense an object or a work of art more deeply—even, as we might say colloquially, to be "shaken to the core." "The whole body is involved," Vischer contended, "the entire physical being is moved."[18] This is possible because as we observe something we sense it not only visually but also through the processes of imagination, emotion, and spatial understanding. Ultimately, it can even happen for us to go a step further and begin to reshape creatively what we see and sense in our minds through a process of "artistic" regeneration. Einfühlung, for Vischer, was thus more than casual transference of emotion to an artistic object. It was an urge to unite with the world around us.

Vischer explained that much of this experience of Einfühlung occurred through our responses to simple natural or geometric forms, though it was also possible that three-dimensional objects, such as flowers or sculptures, could trigger the same effects. But the fact that according to Vischer nonrepresentational forms might elicit equally powerful responses set the stage for the later advent of visual abstraction in art.[19] He contends, for instance, that the reason for this tendency toward abstract understanding is due partly to our mental makeup and normal understanding of the world around us: "In general, we find all regular forms pleasing because our organs and their functional forms are regular. Irregular forms bother us . . . like 'an unfulfilled expectation.' The eye is pained to find no trace of the laws that govern organization and movement."[20]

Vischer recognized that movement itself could be understood in the same physical and psychological manner. But he thought most tellingly that it might be purely a product of the mind: "A kinesthetic stimulus does not always and necessarily lead to actual movement but always to the idea of it. Imagination is an act by which we mentally simulate something that previously existed as a vague content of our sensations as sensuous, concrete form. . . . Our concern henceforth is thus with mental activity."[21]

This could work in another way, too. We might imagine ourselves in a place or in motion: "When I visualize in my mind my own body, I am performing a subjective—shall we say—imaging of the self."[22] In suggesting that there could be a direct linkage between movement, self, and imagination, Vischer established one of the bases of Schmarsow's later spatial theories.

The concept of Einfühlung also influenced Wölfflin's early writings. In his 1886 dissertation, *Prologemena zu einer Psychologie der Architektur* (Prologemena to a Psychology of Architecture), Wölfflin asserted that the idea of a psychology of vision could be most fruitfully applied to the study of architecture.[23] He wanted very much to discard physiological explanations, preferring instead to stress psychological factors. He followed Vischer's lead in seeking to analyze how different forms express moods or emotions, and he argued similarly that the reason we can discern such moods and emotions has to do with the fact that we use more than our vision to understand and react to the world around us: "*Physical forms possess a character only because we ourselves possess a body* [emphasis in the original]. If we were purely visual beings, we would always be denied an aesthetic judgment of the physical world. But as human beings with a body that teaches us the nature of gravity, contraction, strength, and so on, we gather experience that enables us to identify with the conditions of other forms."[24] Wölfflin's idea that bodily involvement was crucial to the experience of architecture undoubtedly also influenced Schmarsow's thinking (though it should be added that Schmarsow was eager to shake off Wölfflin's concern with stylistic issues). But two other thinkers, Conrad Fiedler and Adolf von Hildebrand, probably had a greater impact on him.

Fiedler, who spent many years as an art historian and theorist in Munich, had suggested that architecture could find a new beginning by emphasizing spatial formation. In "Bemerkungen über Wesen und Geschichte der Baukunst" (Observations on the Nature and History of Architecture), an essay published in 1878, Fiedler muses on the possibilities of future architecture and suggests that the basis for a new style might best be founded not on the Renaissance, which was derived from extravagant Roman forms, or the Gothic, with its exaggerated construction, but on the Romanesque and its "simple and formally unelaborated notion of a vaulted enclosure of space."[25] The implication that Schmarsow apparently took from this was that architecture might be thought of as the establishment of spatial boundaries, the "wrapping" and delimiting of spaces.

Hildebrand (who, it should be noted, had drawn extensively from Helmholtz's earlier treatise on optics), almost certainly had an even more pronounced influence on Schmarsow's thinking. Picking up on Wölfflin's ideas about bodily involvement, he maintained that we see and understand objects in a spatial field—that we are inherently mobile creatures and, thus, the process of perception could never be static: "Since we do not view nature simply as a visual being tied to a single vantage point, but, rather, with all our senses at

5

once, in perpetual change and motion, we live and weave a spatial consciousness into the nature that surrounds us." And this awareness of space persists, he noted, "even when we close our eyes."[26] Hildebrand was a sculptor; the book from which this quotation is taken, *Das Problem der Form in der bildenden Kunst* (The Problem of Form in the Fine Arts), concerns mostly how we view sculptures in three dimensions. Yet he was aware that much of his language could be applied equally to works of architecture.

Hildebrand writes, for example, about how objects become reference points for spatial understanding: "Objects thus have to be used to build up a total space and create what one could call a kinesthetic framework, which—though discontinuous—nevertheless suggests a continuous total volume."[27] Repeatedly, he underscores the dynamic nature of our spatial conception—how only through "roving" and moving our heads and eyes do we form complete mental images of what we see. With movement we acquire a series of successive impressions, which we bring together in our minds to create a complete image. Extending this idea to buildings, he asserts: "Notwithstanding all the stylistic distinctions that architecture displays, its task remains to unify its forms as an effect of relief. Only in this way does a building achieve artistic unity. If we understand a building as an organism of stylistic forms, it is comparable to an object in nature; its forms achieve artistic unity only through the idea of relief."[28]

That Hildebrand's book appeared in 1893, a short time before Schmarsow presented his inaugural address, says much. In one obvious sense, Schmarsow's address may be understood as his response to Hildebrand's concepts of movement and perception, along with an expansion of the earlier ideas of Helmholtz, Fiedler, Wölfflin, and Vischer.[29] But what Schmarsow aimed at was altogether different. Art historians before had thought primarily about the relation of space to objects—art pieces, sculpture, or buildings. Schmarsow declared that the true medium of architecture was not structure or mass (or indeed anything on the surface), but space itself. In the address he put this clearly and succinctly: "From the troglodyte's cave to the Arab's tent; from the long processional paths of Egyptian pilgrimage temples to the splendid column-borne roofs of the Greek god; from the Caribbean hut to the [German] Reichstag building—we can say in the most general terms that they are all without exception *spatial constructs* [*Raumgebilde*]."[30] Buildings, so Schmarsow now claimed, were fundamentally spatial creations. And what mattered were the spaces, not their surrounding "envelopes."

Here, too, it must be said that Schmarsow's thoughts were not wholly without precedent. Others before him had proposed ideas about the import of architectural space. In the two generations before Schmarsow's, there had been repeated references to the notion that space formed a vital part of architecture. The German architect Richard Lucae, who would become the director of the Berlin Bauakademie, had proposed in an article in 1869 that the way we experience spaces in buildings is a "powerful" aspect of architecture.[31] And before him, Semper himself had suggested "spatial creation" as a means of overcoming the "art of dressing" that Schmarsow had criticized (though Schmarsow says nothing about Semper's spatial idea in his address).[32] Hans Wilhelm Auer, one of Semper's former students in Zurich, some years later put forward the notion that space had an indispensable role in architecture—in his word, it was the "soul" of architectural creation—and thus was a generative force in the evolution of architectural forms.[33]

And the discourse about space extended even further back. German architects and theorists Heinrich Hübsch and Carl Bötticher had noted that the creation of space was a central task of architecture, and they argued that there was a close relationship between space and stylistic development. For Bötticher, like Semper, the spatial qualities of a building were more important than the decorative and had a role in determining its construction.[34]

What was novel in Schmarsow's reading was the idea that space was fully autonomous. Earlier thinkers had asserted that it acquired its meaning through its function, arising usually from social utility, the style of the building, or in relation to a structure's constitutive elements—its walls, floor, and ceiling. What mattered for Schmarsow, though, was not the function of a space or the enclosing mass but its reality and how we "feel" it.[35] Our sense of space, he said (echoing and expanding on Vischer), "which surrounds us wherever we may be," consists of "the residues of sensory experience, including the muscular sensation of our bodies, the sensitivity of our skin, and the structure of our bodies—all these contribute to what we call our spatial understanding."[36] For Schmarsow, this sense of space, once actuated, becomes the operating force behind the making of architecture: "Our ever-active imagination takes this germ [of sensual knowledge] and develops it according to the directional axes inherent in even the tiniest nucleus of every spatial idea—from this small acorn a tree grows, a whole world that surrounds us. Our sense of space [*Raumgefühl*] and spatial imagination [*Raumphantasie*] press toward spatial creation [*Raumgestaltung*], and they seek their satisfaction in art. We call this art architecture. . . ."[37] Accordingly, Schmarsow asserted, architecture is about our subjective experience of space, about the ways in which we "grasp" and inhabit it, and that, in turn, is directly related to the process of forming it. In this way, our experience is directly related to architectural design.

It was a profound alteration in understanding, a revolution in architectural thinking nearly Copernican in its reach. Still, it must be said again that almost everything Schmarsow had argued up to this point had been anticipated, and in some instances explicitly posited, in the writings of Vischer, Hildebrand, and others. Some years ago, the Czech architectural historian Jindřich Vybíral described Schmarsow as a "capable combiner," rather than a truly original thinker.[38] That is very nearly right, though it must also be said that Schmarsow was surely very good at taking the seeds of others' ideas, fusing them together, and wresting another meaning out of the process. But Schmarsow would add two essentially new and seminal ideas about the relationship of space and architecture.

The first appeared in his inaugural address. Near the end of his speech, he suggested that ideas of space had evolved over time. If, he reasoned, space is at the heart of what architecture is, then such alterations had meaning for historical understanding: "*The history of architecture is the history of the sense of space* [*eine Geschichte des Raumgefühls*] and thus consciously or unconsciously it is a basic constituent in the history of *worldviews*" [emphasis in the original].[39] A number of later historians would adopt this concept and develop it, most notably perhaps the Prague-born art historian Paul Frankl, who in his 1914 book *Die Entwicklungsphasen der neueren Baukunst* (The Developmental Phases of the New Architecture) would seek to give a systematic reading to the evolution of architectural space from the time of the Renaissance to the nineteenth century.[40]

The second idea, however, Schmarsow would develop only gradually over the next dozen years. He began formulating it in another talk he gave in 1896, "Über den Werth der Dimensionen im menschlichen Raumgebilde" (On the Importance of Dimensions in Human Spatial Creation); he would further advance it in his 1905 book *Grundbegriffe der Kunstwissenschaft* (Basic Concepts of Art Historical Studies); and it would culminate in an essay he published in 1914, "Raumgestaltung als Wesen der architektonischen Schöpfung" (Spatial Formation as the Essence of Architectural Creation).[41] It was a deceptively simple thought, but one with far-reaching consequences. It began with the observation (again drawn no doubt from Vischer and Hildebrand) that it is only when we *move* through a space that we are able to grasp it fully. Schmarsow, continuing this line of thinking, argued that our senses—especially sight and touch—must be engaged for us to develop spatial consciousness, and this process functions most fully when we move from place to place in the third dimension. Our spatial understanding accordingly results from kinetic bodily engagement with our surroundings.[42] He further emphasized that the spatial form of architecture is a direct response to the requirements of human activities. The function of architecture is to make boundaries—enclosed spaces in which people could make free and purposive movements. Everything else in architecture—the façade, the interior fittings, the ornament, the structure—is secondary, subordinate to spatial requirements.[43] This had been true throughout time. "[T]he enclosing of space [*Raumumschließung*]," he wrote, "of the moving subject was the first important concern of architecture...."[44] And the best architecture, he suggested, was that which featured lively spaces, whose outlines were shaped directly by the requirements of active human life.[45]

Such ideas, based on a new calculus of functionality, would gain currency with the advent of modernism a few decades hence and soon come to rest at the core of the new architecture. A few observers recognized the importance of what Schmarsow was saying and what it might mean for the new way of building. A year after his address was published, the German architect Bruno Specht wrote that Schmarsow's insights about the primacy of space and spatial experience "could contribute much to the healthy development of modern building."[46]

Mostly, though, Schmarsow faced abrasive criticism, if not wholesale rejection.[47] The Munich-based architectural historian and critic Richard Streiter, for example, rebuffed Schmarsow's assertion that spatial form determined style: "In the great majority of cases the organization of space [*Raumbildung*] alone is not enough to arrive at a characterization of artistic inspiration, that which can be described as the style of an epoch."[48] The Viennese art historian Alois Riegl similarly attacked him, asserting that spatial ideas, though important, were not the only drivers of architectural development: "Schmarsow has recently declared the formation of space to be the primary purpose of all architecture. If this were true, the Egyptians would never have developed architecture at all, because they fundamentally rejected space. But in fact the Egyptians laid the groundwork for all monumental architecture. This makes plain that architecture and the formation of space were not originally identical. An architecture of space did exist, but it arose only in a later stage of development, as people prepared to make the transition from normal to distant viewing."[49]

In previous writings, his *Stilfragen* (Questions of Style, 1893) and *Die spätrömische Kunstindustrie* (The Late Roman Art Industry, 1901), Riegl had contended that the history of architecture was an evolutionary progression from haptic methods of perception to optical ones. Egyptian temples, he wrote, were fundamentally about a search for materiality; the Egyptians lacked interest in spatiality. Only with the rise of the Greek temple in the fifth century, Riegl maintained, did optical modes of perception begin to emerge, and only with the mature architecture of the Romans—in the Pantheon, most notably—did they reach full expression.[50]

Schmarsow countered that it was the changing forms of space that drove the development of architecture. And he would go on to contend in later writings that such a reading was the only way to understand the history of building.

But after 1905, fewer and fewer people listened. Schmarsow would continue to promote his views for another two and a half decades. His influence, though—at least in art history circles—would slowly fade. Over time, he was viewed increasingly as an eccentric and difficult figure—"exceedingly self-confident," as one observer put it, "but given to crude scholarly formulations."[51] Although some of his students found in him an inspiring teacher, many more complained of his idiosyncratic teaching methods and his autocratic manner. In 1919 he was forced to resign from his position in Leipzig after accusations—which he never refuted—that he had plagiarized the work of one of his students. Not a single member of the faculty tried to defend him.[52] He lived on until 1936, still occasionally publishing small studies.

To the end, Schmarsow persisted in his belief that the subjective viewer, reliant in large measure on optical and somatic perception, had been present in every epoch. In his *Grundbegriffe der Kunstwissenschaft* (which was in part a searing critique of Riegl's views), he had attacked the latter's assertion that the Egyptians relied mostly on haptic sensing, pointing to the complex spatial progressions of Egyptian pilgrimage temples: "The whole of the ancient Egyptian temple is a spatial composition for a long temporal sequence of impressions, which can only be compared to musical or epic and dramatic compositions, i.e., a series of acts—even if the performance of experiences takes place in no other venue than within the human breast."[53]

Schmarsow hinted that his argument about buildings as spatial compositions "for a long temporal sequence of impressions" might apply to buildings across time. But he never took the next step, of developing fully the notion of the "architectural promenade." What he had accomplished was to push the philosophical and physiological problem of how we perceive space to a new place, for inherent in his call for a dynamic experience of architecture was an understanding that to move attentively through an architectural construct would lead to greater appreciation—and delight—in form and space. Implicit in this idea was the possibility of exploiting artistically pure space as an entity unto itself—and the notion that to do so would necessarily arouse a reaction on the part of the viewer.

It is exactly here that we come to the thought that would drive the experiments of our three Viennese modernists: buildings could be understood as spatial sequences arrayed to elicit specific sensual and emotional responses. The role of the architect accordingly was to frame spaces in such a way that movement through them would become a subjective spectacle.

Each of our three protagonists would seek innovative strategies for fashioning such spatial journeys.

9

CHAPTER TWO

Thoughts on Designing
a Ground Plan

It was the young Oskar Strnad—architect, designer, educator, and sometime theorist—
who would undertake the first full investigation of the possibilities of the new spatial
ordering in Vienna. And he would do so in ways that would determine a great deal of
what came after.

Strnad is now a mostly forgotten figure, even in Austria; at least his name does not
prompt the same degree of recognition as Adolf Loos or, even, Josef Frank. At the time,
though, just at the end of the first decade of the new century, Strnad was regarded as one
of the prodigies of the generation that followed after the Secessionists, and his promise
seemed very great indeed.

He was then only a few years removed from his architectural studies. Born in Vienna
in 1879, the son of a Jewish estate manager, he lived for long stretches of his youth in
Györ, in what is now Hungary, and in Saalfelden, in Salzburg province, where his father
oversaw the interests of various properties. He was a lively and willful child, with two
abiding interests: riding horses—he won several prizes for his expert horsemanship—
and, more decisively, art. Once, at age thirteen, he undertook a trip alone to Dresden to
see the famed Madonna di San Sisto by Raphael, without informing anyone of his plans
and using money he had earned himself. And he was so consumed with drawing and
painting that he sometimes neglected his studies; he had to repeat his sixth year at the
Realschule. But he persisted, and after completing his *Matura* in 1900, he entered the architecture faculty of the Vienna Technische Hochschule, studying there with Carl König,
Max Ferstel, and Karl Mayreder.[1]

It was from König that Strnad would derive the most important lessons. Holder of
the university's chair for Classical and Renaissance architecture, König was a formidable
figure of the old school. He had been the prime mover behind the introduction of the
neo-Baroque in Vienna in the 1880s, and he remained an unwavering opponent of modern-

ism (and of Otto Wagner and the Secessionists) until his death in 1915. Strnad, however, admired König for his immense erudition, for his surpassing knowledge of history, and, especially, for his pointed questioning about the workings of architecture, its formal logic, and its inner rationales.[2] In impromptu lectures, König asked after the meaning of specific design strategies, and he did so with direct and piercing questions: How precisely should a door appear? What is the best form for a vestibule? How high should a window-sill be? How should one enter a room? König's questioning was propelled by an abiding concern with issues of form, meaning, and use—and, even more so, the relationships among them. He wanted his students to think about how one engaged a building, what was involved, for example, in the act of grasping and turning a door handle, ascending a staircase, or sitting in a room. He thought that the answers to these questions more often than not should come directly from history. König's own inaugural address in 1901 had been a plea for the maintenance of historicism and the rejection of modern reform ideas. But the mere act of posing such questions offered his students a method for thinking about how to fashion architecture at its most basic level, one many would soon use to more radical ends.[3] From König, Strnad absorbed a highly charged and critical view of architecture. It would become the basis of his own questioning and his own design strategies.

After finishing his architecture degree, the young Strnad took the highly unusual step of staying on to complete a doctorate with König, writing a dissertation on early Christian art and architecture, which he illustrated with his own exquisitely made watercolors. He handed in the work in 1904, but for nearly two years afterward he labored as an ordinary draftsman in the offices of Friedrich Ohmann and theater specialists Ferdinand Fellner and Hermann Helmer. Twice in this period he also undertook protracted trips to Italy, scrutinizing the architecture of classical antiquity, supporting himself through grants or by making fine renderings.[4]

In 1906 Strnad established his own practice, soon joining with another of his former classmates from the Technische Hochschule, Oskar Wlach. Over the next several years, mostly in collaboration with Wlach, he completed an array of projects. These included competition entries for the new War Ministry building on the Ringstrasse, a theater in Aussig (Ústí nad Labem), a church in Wiener Neustadt, and a chamber of commerce in Troppau (Opava). All would remain unbuilt. But the two men were able to execute a few projects, including several apartment interiors and the Strnad family grave marker in Vienna. One of their early designs stands out: an apartment building, the so-called Miethaus Hörandner on Stückgasse in Vienna, completed in 1911. It is a prescient and notable statement of the language of functionalism, with assertive massing and lean, simplified façades.

By the time the Hörandner building was on the boards, Strnad was already involved in two new endeavors. In 1909, at the behest of Alfred Roller, director of the Vienna Kunstgewerbeschule (School of Applied Arts), and with the support of Josef Hoffmann, who taught at the school, he received a call to take up a teaching position there, assuming the class for basic design.[5] Halfway through his first year of teaching he began work on a villa on Cobenzlgasse at the northwestern edge of the city.

The client for the new house was Oskar Hock, director of the Lenzinger paper factory, and his wife Kathrina née Poppovič. The site was on a steep hillside, with commanding views of the surrounding hills and vineyards. Early on, Strnad worked on the project with Viktor Lurje, another of his former classmates from the Technische Hochschule. But part-way through the design process he was joined by Wlach, and Lurje left to pursue other

projects. The product in the end, though, was unmistakably Strnad's—and more essentially so was its underlying concept.[6]

The siting of the house was an adroit response to the problem of building on such a challenging plot of land. The terrain rose sharply about fifteen meters from the street, then leveled off partway up the hill. Strnad opted to put the main living areas on what was effectively the third floor, positioning the mass of the house so that the main upper façade faced onto a garden (figs. 3, 4). On the south-facing side, he added a four-columned portico, which led into—or out of—the large living area on what was functionally the piano nobile (figs. 5, 6).

In stylistic terms, the house belonged to the then-current revival of neoclassicism— and more directly, to the neo-Biedermeier—that had begun to displace the Jugendstil in Vienna by that time. Its surfaces, however, were markedly reduced, with plain window and door surrounds constituting the only ornament. There were a few eccentric features as well, including five strangely attenuated attic dormers (two on one side, three on the other), which extended down to the roof cornice, and some rather unconventional fenestration (especially on the street side façade, where the windows do not align).

In the original plans, the house was even more unconventional. Strnad had first decided on an asymmetrical placement of the portico (with two dormers on one side, one on the other), which made for a strangely unbalanced composition. The peculiar look of the house nearly prevented its completion. The local authorities, alarmed by the prospect of Strnad's odd-duck design sitting at the edge of the Wienerwald, the city's great urban forest (in what was then still a largely unbuilt area), sought to deny an occupancy permit on the basis of "gross disfigurement of the cityscape."[7] It was only after a protracted fight (and the fact that the city was forced to pay for the Hock family's stay at the nearby, pricey Cobenzl Hotel) that the controversy was finally resolved. Strnad agreed to make several changes, and the authorities relented.[8]

Although the house's appearance drew the greater part of the attention at the time, what set it decidedly apart was the winding processional path leading up from the street to the main living spaces. Strnad took advantage of the hillside setting to create a highly unusual entry sequence.

The approach commences at the street-side gate then follows a straight line to the right-hand corner of the house. Directly ahead is an arched opening (fig. 7). To the left, set within a small loggia, is a door leading to the lower service areas of the house. But the main processional path continues to the right, through another arched opening and immediately onto an external stair. (Later, a garage would be added just to the right of the walkway). Strnad's routing of the staircase was determined in part by an old cherry tree, which was situated halfway up the climb (fig. 8). The extended stair wraps around the tree but follows an irregular course, necessitating a series of abrupt turns. The flights of the stair are also of differing lengths, making the experience of climbing notably varied. (Along the way, on the first level above the street, is a terrace extending along the front of the house.)

It is only after this protracted ascent that one comes to the main door, situated on the second level. Here one enters the house (nowadays through a small, two-columned portico, which Strnad added in the early 1930s at the owner's request) (fig. 9). Inside is a vestibule; originally, the kitchen and pantry were directly ahead. But the principal route requires a sharp turn to the right and another ascent up a short flight of four more steps (fig. 10). At this point, in a second anteroom, the path splits. Straight ahead is an additional flight of stairs, the main route up for the owners and guests; to the right is a metal service

15

Figure 9 Hock House, exterior stair.

Figure 10 Hock House, interior stair sequence from the vestibule.

opposite **Figure 11** Hock House, anteroom, with main stair (right) and service stair.

stair, which connects all of the levels of the house (figs. 11, 12). After one more full ninety-degree turn, this time to the left, one arrives on the main living floor—the goal of this protracted, winding, and arduous climb.

Strnad explained the guiding ideas behind the house in two undated theoretical essays—both written, it seems, around 1913, not long after the house's completion.[9] One of the pieces, "Einiges Theoretische zur Raumgestaltung" (A Few Theoretical Thoughts on the Arrangement of Space), deals mostly with the practical aspects of "marking" spaces in order to make them readily graspable to the viewer (see appendix). He writes, for example: "To make conscious spatial images, which enable a unified understanding of the sort that produces a clear, steady spatial sense, the elements that allow us to get the measure of a space with our eyes must be grouped in a way—regularly and simply—so that we can take them in at one time. Only when this is possible is our spatial impression convincing and natural."[10]

This and other of his observations in the text almost certainly borrowed from the same late nineteenth-century German theorists who had influenced Schmarsow, most importantly Hildebrand, who had put great stress on how such reference points allow one to gain his or her bearings. That Strnad would have absorbed and made use of such ideas is hardly surprising. By the end of the first decade of the new century, Hildebrand's ideas—and for that matter, Schmarsow's—about how we sense and comprehend the world around us were slowly being assimilated into the discourse about architecture in the German-speaking technical universities, including those in Austria.[11] Strnad expands on these ideas in the essay, discussing, for example, how we see space in natural settings.

> Think, for example, of a meadow in which some trees stand. The trees offer us the possibility of assessing the space before us. Unconsciously we count one, two, three, four trees, and so on, and develop a solid idea of the space we perceive before us. The more trees there are in the meadow, the more our spatial impression changes. The broad dimensions of the meadow become smaller and smaller until at last we see the trees and not the forest. Which is to say: rather than the original broad spatial impression, we have almost no spatial impression at all. Nothing as far as the space goes has changed, but the spatial effect for us is wholly remade. The forest now offers us no spatial idea, although we still have our spatial awareness. This is a result, however, of our spatial consciousness at that moment, from our ability to move; we know that we can walk forward into the forest, we recognize that our forward motion will alter the relationship of one tree to the next, in that we move through the space.[12]

This is more or less a direct reassertion of Hildebrand's argument. But Strnad also recognized, as Hildebrand had, that natural forms do not necessarily allow for complex artistic representation. Hildebrand had written: "Since nature does not always display the gestural signs that we need to arouse our sympathy, and since our imagination derives them—as an actor does—from our cumulative past together with our immediate bodily feeling, the artist will not bind himself slavishly to the actual appearance presented to him by nature at any given time."[13]

Strnad's answer to this in architectural terms was to utilize conventional forms and structures, in regular patterns, to demarcate spaces and make them legible.

Thus, on a wall of a room there should be a clearly delineated line somewhere, which gives us a sure means to estimate the length of that wall. A completely white wall, with absolutely nothing on it, and which has no clearly defined upper edge and no ceiling, gives the eye no pause; the eye is not in a position to sense when it has nothing to take hold of. There must be something on the wall that offers the possibility to read it, to assess it, in order for us to be able to get a feeling for the depth of a room. The means to make a wall readable include all manner of things, such as windows, pilasters, chests, pictures, and so on. The way in which they relate to each other determines the effects that allow us to grasp the dimensions of a space. If they are spread out haphazardly, like the trees in the forest, then the spatial impression one has will be similar—all cut up—and we will not be able to see the forest for the trees.[14]

We can easily apprehend a simple rectangular space. But this is easier, Strnad notes, if there are spatial markers—the word he uses is *Raumwerte* (in English most nearly "spatial determinants")—to aid us in our effort to "read" the space. Among the examples he gives of such *Raumwerte* are windows, pilasters, columns, moldings, and floor or ceiling patterns. When these are absent, the process becomes more challenging. In point of fact, the whole look of the space is transformed when such "markers" are added: "Everyone knows from experience that an empty room will generally feel uncomfortable and that fully furnished rooms can have varied effects. Everyone will also have seen that a room with a different furniture arrangement will have a completely different spatial impact. That should make us ponder: the dimensions of the room have not changed at all but the spatial effect we sense is entirely new."[15]

Furnishings, so Strnad argues, may also contribute to this quality of legibility, but he recognized, as Hildebrand and Schmarsow had before him, that it was only when the viewing subject was in motion that she or he could grasp the full impact of a space. The significant lines come toward the end of the essay. Strnad writes: "An essential requirement for livable spaces is movement. The changing of one's position relative to various objects (which, by the way, is the stuff of all spatial consciousness) yields a progressive alteration of images, which we receive from the objects in the room. First the chair in front of the armoire is visible, then it is in front of the door, and finally it is by the window."[16] Which is to say that by moving from place to place and seeing an architectural work and the objects either outside or within it from multiple vantage points, one could begin to develop a full sense of both building and space. Indeed, it is only when the viewer is moving, Strnad insists, that his or her sensory apparatus is fully engaged. To move through an architectural scene heightens one's awareness of space. The ever-changing images—the countless "snapshots" one takes in with one's eyes—are processed in the brain into a set of three-dimensional images and, finally, into a complete mental map of the space in question. We are able to do this, he observes, because we have experienced it many times from our earliest days and come to do it well.[17]

But Strnad understood something that Schmarsow had not: that such viewing is never completely continuous. In places it may be interrupted, and our perception therefore may be altered or incomplete.

These points at which movement stops, changes, or moves from reading the surface to perceiving depth correspond in some sense with the hinges of the human body in that they provide an opportunity to carry out movement. Let us then call these "joints" [*Gelenke*]: in that way we are describing what one would normally understand as a

Figure 12 Hock House, service stair (detail).

capital, a foundation, or a cornice. With a finely attuned sensibility, one recognizes that there is an alteration here that has to be indicated, and the more precisely this indication is developed, the greater, the more elegant and refined is the whole impression. Instead of the joints of a farmer, those of an elegant lady; instead of the joints of an elephant, those of a gazelle. The forms of these joints, the recognition of their essential role in fostering affects and the possibilities they offer are the personal and special domain of the designer, and are among the designer's most challenging and sensitive tasks.[18]

What Strnad also understood, though he does not elaborate the idea in his essay, is that visual breaks of this sort could not only result from the combining or placement of architectonic elements, but also from the way in which rooms were joined or passages were routed. Abrupt changes in direction, forcing the viewing subject to turn suddenly or even unexpectedly, could compel her or him to have a very different sort of viewing experience. It would foster greater awareness of the space and the surrounding architectural frame, and create vivid experiences. The key statement of this notion comes in the essay's penultimate paragraph: "The more opportunities of movement [*Sich-Bewegen*] a space has, the more discontinuities [*Verschneidungen*] and displacements [*Verschiebungen*] there are to see, the richer the spatial creation [*Raumbildung*] will be."[19]

What precisely Strnad means by "discontinuities" or "displacements" he does not say. Based on what he inserts into the design of the Hock House it seems that what he was after were places where the architecture might deviate from what would be expected or conventional. A discontinuity could be a break in a path or a place where that path might be altered or distorted in some fashion (made broader or narrower, or lighter or darker, for example). A displacement could occur where conjoining spaces do not align horizontally (for instance, they might be shifted off axis) or vertically, with one higher or lower than the other. (Strnad would eventually incorporate this latter idea into some of his designs, but it was only later that Loos and Frank would experiment with the entire array of such possibilities.)

The other important idea has to do with "enriching" our mental image of a spatial creation. Strnad here is almost certainly cadging from Schmarsow. His reference to a "progressive alteration of images" and its relationship to spatial creation is an almost direct recitation of the Schmarsowian formula for architectural worth. But Strnad adds something novel and very important: Schmarsow had alluded to complex spatial progressions—those of the Egyptian New Kingdom temples, as we have seen—and he had suggested that they would enhance spatial experience; Strnad now began to attempt to work out precisely how such a complex spatial experience might be produced.

In fact, if one reads "A Few Theoretical Thoughts on the Arrangement of Space" carefully, it is clear that Strnad is primarily concerned with how to make the new spatial ideas into a practicable design strategy, one that might reform how architecture could be fashioned. Although the Hock House is not specifically discussed in the essay, he must have thought of it as an experiment in carrying out the new spatial precepts. Often patent are Strnad's efforts to employ legible markers in spaces. A splendid example of this in the Hock House's entry sequence is the old cherry tree, which is visible from nearly all points along the entry path. At nearly every moment during an ascent or descent, the tree would have served as a point of reference. Without it, the path would certainly have been less easy to comprehend; other, more distant markers would have had to serve the purpose. But because the path itself is highly complex—replete with discontinuities and disjunctures— the views of the tree operate to accentuate the path's strangeness, its otherness. The tree remains a constant even while everything around it—in terms of one's spatial experience—is changing. The entry path thus works in two ways: it is both disconcertingly complex and reassuring.

In the Hock House's interiors, Strnad utilized *Raumwerte* in a similar manner, though the markers here are mostly furnishings, openings (typically windows and doors), or patterns in the floor. He was ever attentive to the way, even where complex movements were introduced, that furnishings would provide easily perceived markers and convey a sense of normalcy through scale and position.

But Strnad was even more interested in how spatial progressions could force a new form of perceptual engagement. Toward the end of "A Few Theoretical Thoughts on the Arrangement of Space," where he introduces the idea of fostering discontinuities and displacements, he posits a very different way of designing spaces: he suggests that a movement sequence can be enriched by making it "difficult" yet understandable. The phrase he uses is "The unity of this displaced movement [*Verschiebungsbewegung*] will yield the sense of scale."[20]

Strnad does not explain directly why this is, but undoubtedly what he was after is the notion that a viewer can be compelled to "participate in" and "grasp" a work of architecture through the manipulation of the path. This can happen visually—the constant changes in one's orientation during the climb up to the piano nobile in the Villa Hock generate a rich set of optical stimuli—but it can also take place by provoking other sensory responses, our haptic sense, for example, or our auditory one. In the case of the exterior ascent of the Villa Hock, one's haptic sense might be activated when touching the railings or feeling a breeze; one's auditory senses might become involved through the sound of footfalls on the stairs.

Just as important for Strnad, though, is what happens to one's somatic sense. Bodily movement, especially strenuous bodily movement—the mere act of climbing up so many steps—or the repeated changes in direction during a winding climb, prompts for the subject an immediate and powerful awareness of architectonic reality. The building in this way becomes palpable and actual. Strnad manifestly shared the belief of a number of other thinkers and practitioners of the period that architecture had a greater potential than any other of the arts to evoke real emotion in us.

What is so plainly missing in his essay, however—beyond specific allusions to his own works—is any discussion of how Strnad came to these ideas. I have already alluded several times to the writings of Schmarsow and Hildebrand, which seem to be the most likely sources. But by 1909, when Strnad was at work on the Hock House, there were new voices in the fold. Vischer's first writings about Einfühlung in the 1870s had spawned an academic cottage industry focused on understanding the connection between perceptual experience and feeling. Several leading psychologists turned to the topic, most notably Munich professor Theodor Lipps.

In his book *Raumästhetik und geometrisch-optische Täuschungen* (Aesthetics of Space and Geometric-Optical Illusions), published in two parts in the 1890s, and other, later writings, Lipps, who became the most prominent of the many writers on empathy around the turn of the century, sought to forge a scientific theory of Einfühlung, one shorn of its more metaphysical aspects. He thought that we project ourselves completely into the objects we are contemplating—so completely that we lose a direct sense of our own sensory or bodily feelings and that we instead simply imagine what we perceive. The pleasure we derive comes from our sense of engagement. In terms of watching a dance performance, this might mean, as Harry Mallgrave has suggested, that we imagine the bodily sensations we would have if we ourselves were performing the dance.[21]

Lipps admitted that works of art allowed one to experience Einfühlung in its purest form, but any object, he contended, could arouse similar feelings, and our experience of them was equally worth study.[22] His writings, nonetheless, had a powerful and immediate impact on the development of architecture at and just after the turn of the century, influencing, for example, the ideas of Richard Streiter (who had been one of Lipps's students) and Henry van de Velde.[23] Ideas about empathy, indeed, had a distinct impact on a number of practitioners of the new Jugendstil, including, most conspicuously perhaps, Hermann Obrist and August Endell. Both subscribed to a concept derived from Vischer's original notion of Einfühlung, namely that encounters with artworks could be kinesthetic and thus elicit an unconscious and immediate effect of the musculature of the beholder—a sort of extreme physical version of empathy.[24]

For Strnad (and many others of his generation who had already rejected the Jugendstil as a failed experiment) what very probably mattered more were the evolving ideas of other progressive architects and thinkers. Discussions about architectural space and its primacy had begun to appear in the writings of other authorities. Hendrik Petrus Berlage, for example, in his book *Gedanken über Stil in der Baukunst* (Thoughts about Style in Building) in 1905, had restated Schmarsow's belief in the importance of space in architectural creation, arguing that the making of volumes rested at the heart of architecture and that they should be enclosed with the simplest means.[25]

Strnad's own developing notion of spatial planning, though, had less to do with space-making per se than with the making of spatial experience. Thus, the more significant sources for him were probably the then-emerging concepts of theatrical stagecraft and performance.

They would have been a natural and logical choice for him. Strnad was already besotted with the theater—in his later years it would become a near obsession—and he kept abreast of the newest developments in the field. He was assuredly aware of the ideas of Swiss stage designer Adolphe Appia, best known at the time for his many scenic designs for Richard Wagner's operas. What would have made Appia particularly appealing to Strnad was his insistence on dynamic and three-dimensional movements by the actors. Appia's stage sets were conceived in such a manner that the performers were constantly moving—up flights of stairs, across platforms, or through arches or doors—all of which were arranged so as to translate Wagner's operas into grand, action-filled spectacles.[26]

Strnad may have equally acquired inspiration from the pedagogical ideas of the Swiss composer and music educator Émile Jaques-Dalcroze. Dalcroze had first taught in Geneva, but he left in 1910 to establish his school in Hellerau, the experimental garden city near Dresden founded by entrepreneur and social reformer Karl Schmidt, with Richard Riemerschmid and Wolf Dohrn. There Dalcroze's rhythmic gymnastics, or "eurythmics," became widely renowned and celebrated. In those years just before the First World War, many leading artists and intellectuals, from Ebenezer Howard and Wölfflin to Walter Gropius and the future Le Corbusier, made the pilgrimage to see for themselves Dalcroze's innovative methods in practice.[27]

But even before Dalcroze made the move to Germany, his ideas had attracted wide notice. Traveling shows of his dancers and musicians had crisscrossed the continent, seizing the public's fancy and influencing the theatrical and artistic avant-garde. The driving notion of Dalcroze's technique was to tap into the body's natural rhythm and to use these movements as the basis for music and dance. He developed an elaborate system of rhythmical gymnastics, "plastic exercises," as he termed them, which would precede the actual learning of musical instruments. These specific bodily movements and marches, he stressed, were intended to allow students to find their own biological rhythm.[28]

What may have invited Strnad's notice was the possibility that such activity would not only stimulate somatic mindfulness, but also heighten one's awareness of one's surroundings. Moving in time was a means to compel engagement with the self *and* with the world. Strnad hinted in his writings that the reason such "embodiment" was possible was because we perceive what is around us through our own scale and our "occupation" of our surroundings.

Schmarsow had already suggested something of the sort. In his writings in the 1890s and after, he had developed a theory centered on the three major arts—painting, sculpture, and architecture—and the distinctions among them. In each instance, the differences, he asserted, were related to the human body and its basic axes.[29] The first dimension (vertical) was the province of sculpture; the second (horizontal) that of painting; and the third, which concerned direction and movement, was the realm of architecture. Schmarsow held that architecture was, accordingly, the most fully realized art because it involved our entire sensory apparatus (our whole bodies), and its realization, by extension, was the fullest reflection of who we are and how we inhabit the world.

It seems likely that Strnad intended in some fashion to bring the theories of these varied thinkers together. What he writes in "A Few Theoretical Thoughts on the Arrangement of Space" is a mélange of what was being said about space, experience, and movement in those years. Yet there are not enough specific clues in his texts to allow us to determine which admixture of thinkers and concepts went into shaping his ideas. He alludes to none of these figures by name: not Semper, Vischer, or Lipps, not Berlage, Appia, or Dalcroze— or, for that matter, any other theorist or practitioner. With the exception of Schmarsow and Hildebrand, whose writings Strnad appears at times to paraphrase, it is not evident which, if any, of these other thinkers' texts he may have actually read. It is entirely possible that he knew of some of them only from secondhand sources and others not at all.

The earliest example of Strnad's surviving writings about space and movement similarly mentions no sources, and it has to do not with late nineteenth-century theory or early twentieth-century performance but the architecture of classical antiquity. It comes in the form of a review he wrote in 1912 of a recent archeological study of the Palace of Diocletian in Split by the Austrian architect George Niemann.[30] Strnad's portrayal of the main entry into the palace is a perfect recital of his thoughts about spatial and architectural awareness: "Up a flight of stairs, one enters the foyer and then comes into the vestibule. A domed space. The prevailing semidarkness produces fear in those arriving. One stands here before the power of the emperor. A door leads into the throne room, a view of sea. Here is a long gallery that the emperor built in order to withdraw from the world. High above the water, along a placid, uniform, and windowless wall are monotonous arches. There is hardly a rhythm. Only a beginning, a middle, and an end; a barely perceptible scherzo, in the arches, a pliable architrave."[31]

The theoretical ingredients are all here: the importance of moving through a space and experiencing it; the way in which a space can induce emotion (here: fear); the personal or social intention of a space (power or withdrawal); and the way in which the form of an architectural element can foster or deny a visual sense of movement (for instance, a constructed scherzo, a "visual joke" in stone). What Strnad records in this passage is his belief that the elements of spatial form and emotion are embedded in architecture—deeply so for him in classical antiquity. Yet he also establishes a method of reading such spatial sequences, one that apparently arises out of his extending and reshaping of recent theory.

The problem is that without being able to pin down precisely Strnad's sources, it is nearly impossible to determine exactly what he means by certain terms. Words like

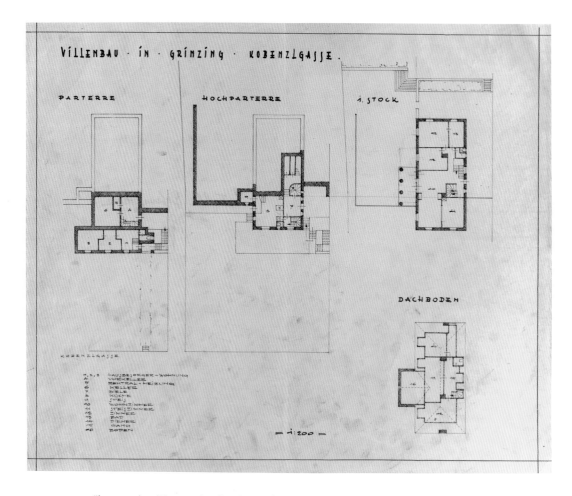

"impression," "sensation," or "experience" or phrases such as "appealing to the mind" that had frequently been used in philosophy, psychology, and aesthetic theory over the previous half-century, often with quite varied intentions and meanings, are applied seemingly haphazardly in Strnad's writings. He shows no interest in achieving closer definition; as is often the case with architects who adopt philosophical ideas, he is neither consistent nor particularly rigorous in how he uses his terms. His attention rests not in the epistemology of words, but in a more generalized understanding of architectural space and our experience of it.

In the second of the two essays from around 1913, "Gedanken beim Entwurf eines Grundrisses" (Thoughts on Designing a Ground Plan; see appendix), Strnad does describe in some detail what a design strategy intended to heighten spatial awareness might consist of. It sets out in logical order (albeit in rather staccato fashion) the thoughts that underlay his effort. "The first thought," he writes, "from disordered and uncontained surroundings, to find the beginning, the beginning of the path (forecourt, the first stage). The first stopping point (door, gate, portal). The continuation of the path and the establishment of barriers [*Widerständen*] in a rhythmical sequence. The establishment of all junctions [*Wegabzweigungen*] and all terminal points. The possibilities of such processional planning are endlessly varied."[32]

The second thought involves the architectonic features of a processional path: "The determination of the floor of this path in its full dimensions and the introduction of barriers, steps, doors, to form the boundaries of its dimensions (width and confinement, area and depth, and so on)."[33]

Both of these, he tells us, result from movement: "These two thoughts arise from our capacity for bodily movement and the sensations we have, and the sensation of the rhythm inherent in our movements (climbing stairs, as well as walking, turning, and the like)."[34]

Strnad then turns to the effects that the manipulation of light can have on the subject's journey and experience, and he explains how our other senses might be brought in. The central notion for him is that all the design efforts to provoke such responses must work in concert: "When creating a ground plan all of these sensations must be simultaneously weighed and satisfied. From them, harmonies must be fashioned. The concept of such a composition is similar to that of a musical score and consists of a plethora of notes and handwritten prompts about the lines of the ground plan, about the relationships between the various measurements, about the materials and how they are handled, and sketches concerning colors. The substance of a building, 'played' by the craftsman (which is to say translated into material reality), is in its totality what the architect experiences and puts down in his 'score,' and becomes a fully realized world."[35]

Foremost, though, Strnad asserts, is our subjective response. Architectural design above all is not about making an aesthetic statement but about reaching the imagination of those who inhabit the spaces.

> An architectural conception arises from the focused imagination as well as the possibilities we have for movement (as the absolute feeling for space), as well as the effects of light (the color of the material substance), of smell, of hearing, and of touch (of the material substance); not the superficial aspect of the material but also its soul must stand out. The treatment of the surface of the material on no account should be fashioned entirely with regard to aesthetic considerations, but also from the inexplicable spiritual ones. Only the architect is in the position to create from the material a special world in which this dead material can be experienced as a living organism. In this sense, the material is transparent, for it is not its surface that conveys an effect, but its independent existence.[36]

From this we can infer Strnad's intentions for the Villa Hock. The building is an effort to make the sensation of space as tangible as possible and to inspire contemplation about how we inhabit the world. Although he never uses the word, it is about "being"—being in a specific place and finding pleasure and joy in that fact. The whole of the path up and through the house is designed to reach the main living areas in a sensual manner.

Strnad's arrangement of the principal interior spaces is more straightforward, though it is also replete with spatial effects. In his original plans for the house (which still show the portico on the piano nobile—labeled "1. Stock" on the drawing—set off to one side), he specified a somewhat more complex arrangement, with the living room partially wrapping around the dining room and two small bedrooms and a bath on the west side (fig. 13). He modified this ordering in the final plans, setting the living room in the center, framed symmetrically on the outside by the portico, with the dining room to the east and the bedrooms to the west—a more classical composition.

The main route of penetration leads to the large living room, at the heart of the house. A turn in either direction, left or right, takes one into the rooms at either end, which constitute "terminal points" of the path. The living room itself, however, is the principal destination— a place to relax after the exertion of entry—though the path does go on—through the French doors on the garden side to the exterior on the opposite side of the house—or, by means of the continuation of the main stair, to the upstairs bedrooms.

25

Figures 14 and 15 Hock House door and door handle.

Figure 16 Oskar Strnad (with Oskar Wlach), Wassermann House, Vienna, 1912–15. MAK– Österreichisches Museum für angewandte Kunst / Gegenwartskunst, Vienna, K. I. 13850/3.

Strnad's efforts to enhance the experience of being in the house did not stop with the creation of these multiple paths, however. As he writes in "Thoughts on Designing a Ground Plan," he was also concerned with issues such as color and form. He considered, too, questions of solidity and transparency. The door into the main living areas, for example, has a small window in it, showing how the path continues and admitting light (fig. 14). It is both solid and open. He paid minute attention to places one might grasp—the haptic element—such as the door handles, which in Strnad's designs are always rounded-over and made to fit comfortably in the hand (fig. 15).

The interiors of the Hock House proved much less dramatic in spatio-formal terms than the exterior stair. Indeed, despite the relative openness of the main floor—a suggestion of the coming free-flowing spaces of modernism—the house was in most ways a conventional exercise. Its large, airy rooms were prescient but not unprecedented.

Strnad would investigate these ideas of movement and experience on the interior of another house, a villa for the writer Jakob Wassermann and his wife Julie (née Speyer), which he designed and built between 1912 and 1915 (fig. 16).[37]

Once again, he produced the work in collaboration with Wlach, though the arrangement of the spaces was probably entirely his. (Wlach, it appears, was responsible for some of the finishes and furnishings.) Like the Hock House, the Wassermann House was organized around the notion of a directed path. Strnad devised an extended axis leading from the street through a small vestibule and into a large L-shaped living area (*Halle*) (figs. 17–21). Along this main route of penetration (which Strnad indicated with a red line on the ground plan), he introduced various pavements and floorings, vistas, and lighting effects; the path also involved a gradual climb upward, with (if one counts the assorted stair landings) as many as nine different levels from the street to the hall.

He did not dispense fully with the concept of the winding stair as an integral element. But here he placed it inside the body of the house. Departing from the main axis through the villa is a "junction"—another path positioned midway, extending to and from the central hallway. Here is a stair joining the ground level with the upper-floor bedrooms

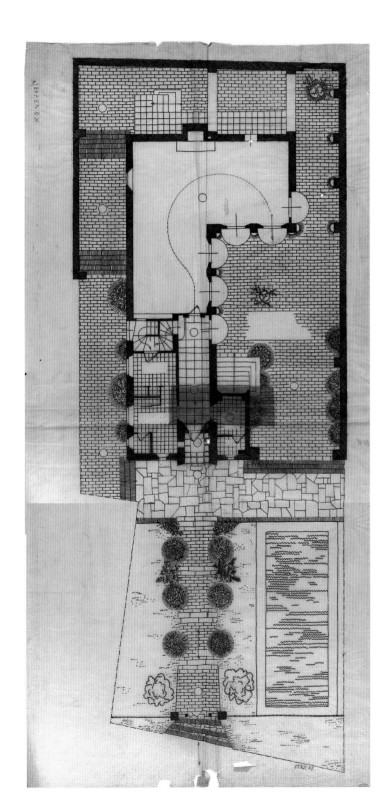

left **Figure 17** Wassermann House, ground-floor plan. MAK–Österreichisches Museum für angewandte Kunst / Gegenwartskunst, Vienna, K. I. 13915/1.

above **Figure 18** Wassermann House, detail of the exterior entry sequence. MAK–Österreichisches Museum für angewandte Kunst / Gegenwartskunst, Vienna, K. I. 13850/4.

Figure 19 Wassermann House, hallway. MAK–Österreichisches Museum für angewandte Kunst / Gegenwartskunst, Vienna, K. I. 13843/2.

Figure 20 Wassermann House, living and music room. MAK–Österreichisches Museum für angewandte Kunst / Gegenwartskunst, Vienna, K. I. 13834/1.

opposite **Figure 21** Wassermann House, Wassermann family in the living room. From *Innen-Dekoration* 29 (January–February 1918): 20.

(fig. 22). Although the serpentine staircase serves as a connector, it is also an elaborate spatial element, intended to enhance the inhabitant's perceptions, and, at the same time, to produce an experience of changing bodily sensations. In keeping with this effort to accentuate somatic and visual involvement, Strnad routed the stair so that it turned back on itself—rather than allowing it merely to spiral upward.

This scheme of walking and climbing is also repeated in the courtyard on the house's east side (fig. 23). In contrast to the Villa Hock, however, the winding exterior stair here presents only a secondary route of entry—a means to link the upstairs rooms directly with the garden. As a formal gesture, it suggests the spatial play of the interior, but it no longer has the primacy—or the ungainliness—of the Hock House's stairway.

In fact, the organization of the Villa Wassermann at first glance seems decidedly straightforward. The *Halle* and the other principal rooms are simple and open, interrupted only by a few casually placed pieces of furniture. But there is more to it than that. Margarete Schütte-Lihotzky, who studied with Strnad during the First World War, later recalled that he told her that the design of the villa was driven by two concerns:

> The first: It is of fundamental importance how one enters the house. One should go inside gradually and then be led to a center point. In the Wassermann House, Strnad himself demonstrated this to me. By means of a long hallway, which opens through glass doors out onto the garden, one arrives in the living room directly in front of the fireplace, where the family assembles. The second challenge: to fuse together architecture and nature, house and garden, so that the separation between the two will be dissolved as much as possible allowing much of the house, of the architecture, to be brought into nature, and, in the same way, to permit much of the natural world to enter the house, thereby fostering a gradual transition between them.[38]

The directness of the villa's plan, indeed, belies Strnad's precise manipulation of the experience of entering and moving through the house. He was especially attentive to the way in which the main paths were constituted. Both outside and inside, he made use

opposite **Figure 22** Wassermann House, stair. From *Innen-Dekoration* 29 (January–February 1918): 18.

Figure 23 Wassermann House, side terrace and stair. From *Innen-Dekoration* 29 (January–February 1918): 19.

33

of diverse paving materials—stone, brick, tile, wood—and he introduced subtle changes in level as a means to bolster the impression of variety. His emphasis on materiality, both its haptic qualities and visual textures, also enforced the interplay of architectural frame and space. Throughout the main path, the formal articulation of floor and wall produced a rhythmical sequence, not unlike music, as he had suggested in "Thoughts on Designing a Ground Plan."

For Strnad, these "musical" modulations went beyond the house's material substance. As essential for him, for example, was the drama of light and the coloristic effects one experienced while moving through the bounded volumes.[39] Each stimulus, each architectonic moment, contributed to the experience of the whole. To design a house was not merely to establish its spatial dimensions, but also to devise a full array of sensory stimuli.

When the house was completed in early February 1915, after the war had already devolved into a terrible and bloody deadlock, Jakob Wassermann wrote in his diary what for Strnad would have been a most satisfying assessment: "Three days ago we moved into my house in Kaasgraben. . . . [It] is beautiful, light, livable, and could make me happy if the times weren't so dark."[40]

If the idea of the path was Strnad's primary organizing idea, it was also, as he would claim, a means for overcoming the limitations of architecture itself. Several years after the war, in 1922, Strnad wrote in his essay, "Neue Wege in der Wohnraum-Einrichtung" (New Directions in the Design of Living Spaces): "Space is fate. To free one from fate is to 'build a path, delimit space.' Thus, not wall but path, experience the floor."[41]

"Experience" is the word that stands out, for as Strnad would have it, what matters is how we are involved with a building and what we "feel"—somatically, but especially psychologically. The true measure of architecture, he thought, should be our subjective response. Buildings existed to be seen, touched, heard, perhaps even smelled, but above all to reside as a set of impressions in the mind. The Villa Wassermann was a controlled experiment in generating such impressions—impressions no longer tied solely to style or pictorial effect.

Figure 24 Oskar Strnad, project for a theater for Max Reinhardt, 1921; section. From *Wasmuths Monatshefte* 6, no. 6 (1921): 186.

Figure 25 Reinhardt theater project, plan. From *Wasmuths Monatshefte* 6, no. 6 (1921): 185.

Yet there were limitations to what Strnad could make in this way. It is indicative that the title of his essay was "Thoughts on Designing a *Ground Plan*." Though stairs and landings play a great role in his design strategies, he continued to think mostly about space expanding (or moving) horizontally. This is wholly true throughout the main living areas of the Hoch House, though on the upper floor of the Wassermann House Strnad does vary the floor levels—a few steps up or down. Still, the possibilities of full three-dimensional planning remain largely unexplored.

After the war, however, Strnad had undertaken one more remarkable effort in space-making, in 1921: a theater project, originally conceived for the great Austrian impresario Max Reinhardt. He prepared three variants of the design, the last of which he previewed to a small audience at the Österreichisches Museum für Kunst und Industrie in late November.[42]

He had, he told those assembled, first started work on the project in 1917, for a site in Switzerland. The first version he had completed that year, the second in 1920. But he was unsatisfied. Too much of what was in the design, as he also recorded in a short article in *Wasmuths Monatshefte* afterward, was "architecture." "My spatial conception," he explained, "was unfulfilled; the spatial movement (*Raumbewegung*) in particular was not perfected." He then commenced work immediately on the third version.[43]

The idea for the project, he said, had come to him years before: "What moved me the entire time was less the theater itself than a dim conception of space. Space of and for itself. The desire to shape space formlessly. Or better said: not what is 'seen,' that which is usually termed architecture, but to grasp what is 'around me.' Most completely, I could describe my sense of this in the following way: to bring continuously moving endless space into conscious harmony" (*Das fortwährend Bewegte des unendlichen Raumes in bewußte Harmonie zu bringen*).[44]

With this in mind, Strnad began to sketch what he had envisioned, without even bothering to render a façade "for reasons," as he notes, "that are readily understood."[45]

This third version of the project, images of which he published in the same issue of *Wasmuths Monatshefte*, shows a highly unconventional arrangement. It is a large amphitheater, circular in shape, the roof supported by twelve piers, approximately fifty meters tall (fig. 24). The diameter is ninety meters, and Strnad tells us that he intended for it to seat around 3,600. The overall arrangement is similar to Hans Poelzig's Großes Schauspielhaus in Berlin, his renovation of the older Zirkus Schumann, which Poelzig also designed for Reinhardt in 1919. Stridently other, however, is Strnad's configuration of the stage. It consists of a great rotating ring, driven by a gearwheel system that extends around the periphery of the auditorium (fig. 25). On it are the individual sets, in series, but lacking many standard features: "The sets are not constructed in the usual sense. Only that which is necessary for the scenes. Without side wings, foliage borders, without ceilings, in partial darkness, which merge into 'endless' space. All of the sets are mounted onto the rotating ring, and those on which action is taking place are illuminated and within view of the audience."[46]

To switch from one set to the next would involve merely putting the rotating ring into motion, and the action could then continue without delay. Since the actors might enter the stage from any number of places, including from the auditorium itself, the whole could serve to foster a great sense of movement and variety. This effect could be further enhanced, Strnad explains, through the interventions of the lighting technician and the stage manager, who would be able to manipulate what the viewer would see through spotlighting and changing backdrops, yielding a dynamic spectacle.[47]

The dynamism of the stage sets was, of course, in part the result of the way in which the action—and the actors—transferred from place to place. But new here is that the space

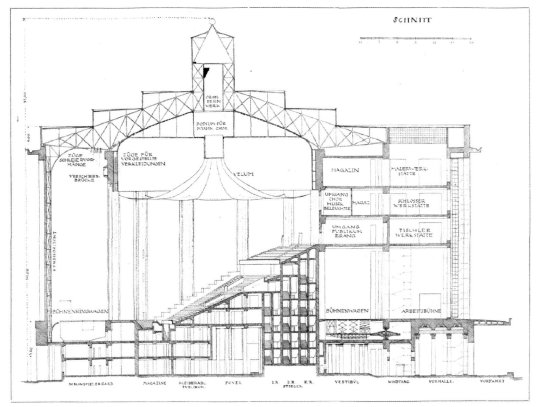

SCHNITT

Oskar Strnad, Wien

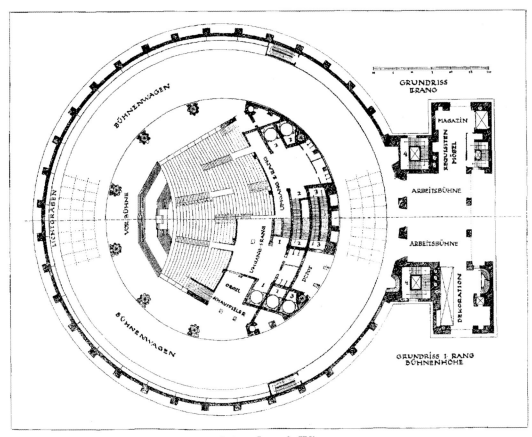

Oskar Strnad, Wien
Projekt für ein Schauspielhaus

itself is moving. The audience is seated and stationary; the visual movement that occurs is the consequence of the rotation of the outer stage ring. It is a possibility Schmarsow had not considered—that spaces themselves could become "active" and physically shifting. It was a potent idea, though one Strnad would not follow up on. At the time, he was more concerned with trying to convey the effect of spatial dynamism. He built a small model of the theater and stages, which he had photographed for the article. Each of the "vignettes" displays varied heights, multiple stairs, and plays on perspective—all meant to amplify his idea of "boundless space" (fig. 26).

In the end, he was disappointed. (In the photographs, he thought the special lighting effects were not discernible.) He wondered if it were possible at all to make the sort of spatial drama that he had conceived of. Even these efforts he thought too limited, too orthodox.

Not long afterward, he believed he had found the answer to how to improve and augment his spatial vision. While staying in a small town in the Gulf of Salerno in southern Italy, he at last discovered what he had wanted to create in his theater.

Here there is no architecture, no façade, no buildings (or what we call houses). There are only rocks and walls, grottoes and arcades, holes and windows, and intricately winding stairs and rock fissures. Built architecture looks as if created by nature, and nature appears to be built. Nature and "deliberateness" are one. Here the inexhaustible wealth of nature's spatial movements is not obstructed by petty order. Everything flows with the spatial movements and the creations of nature and reverberates them, even trees and flowers assume a spatial, three-dimensional presence (cacti, Japanese medlars, orange trees), full of the same rich movements as the rocks. Here one is not looking at a fixed picture. Unceasing turns and shifts. Everything is simultaneous: beside me . . . below me, and above me. Impossible to draw. During the first days of my stay here I felt dizzy because the accustomed "orientation," the regularity of our three-dimensional world was missing. It felt to me as if everything—mountain, street, stairway, house and tree—was revolving around me. This is similar to the spatial experience I want my theater project to convey. Great wealth of spatial movement, strong dynamics of space, light, and movement in front of me, beside me, below me, above me.[48]

Strnad had touched on something quite extraordinary: the idea of pure space, almost wholly removed from any linkage with materiality—architecture (or merely the world around us) as space and space alone, with only our experience to guide us and provide us with meaning. It was a notion of a psychic sense of being in a place without architectural intent, a profoundly original idea, but one neither he (nor, for that matter, Adolf Loos or Josef Frank, who declined to jettison their belief in the activism of architecture itself) would ever fully probe. Despite his conceptual advance, Strnad was never able to realize his dream—perhaps it was unrealizable, more a product of his imagination than any sort of grounded reality. He left the theater project unfinished. He would continue to make sets for theatrical productions for the remaining years of his life, until his early death in 1935, still musing from time to time about new ways of making space. But nothing he designed afterward ever equaled the brilliance or the promise of his early work.

By rights, Strnad should be remembered now as one of the early visionaries of a new spatial ordering, a prophet who laid down the foundations—in direct and definite fashion— of a new architecture of mind and body. But he was too early, and he stopped too soon, to collect credit for his advances. His mission to shape our experiences in concrete, brick, stone, and wood, to render a narrative of architectural awareness, was mostly lost to memory.

It was now up to two of his fellow Viennese architects, Loos and Frank, to continue the inquiry into the possibilities of space and movement.

CHAPTER THREE

Raumplan and Movement

The idea of a new architecture of space was remarkably present—if still mostly unspoken—in Vienna in 1911. That year the young R. M. Schindler, recently graduated from the Technische Hochschule (where he, too, had come under the influence of Carl König), had a great epiphany.

> In the summer of 1911, sitting in one of the earthbound peasant cottages on top of a mountain pass in Styria, a sudden realization of the meaning of space in architecture came to me. Here was the house, its heavy walls built of the stone of the mountain, plastered over by groping hands—in feeling and material nothing but an artificial reproduction of one of the many caverns in the mountainside.
>
> I saw essentially that all architecture of the past, whether Egyptian or Roman, was nothing but the work of a sculptor dealing with abstract forms. The architect's attempt really was—to gather and pile up masses of building material, leaving empty hollows for human use. . . .
>
> And stooping through the doorway of the bulky, spreading house, I looked up into the sunny sky. Here I saw the real medium of architecture—SPACE.
>
> This gives us a new understanding of the task of modern architecture. Its experiments serve to develop a new language, a vocabulary and syntax of space.[1]

By the time he sat down to write his space manifesto—probably in the summer of 1913—Schindler was under the influence of Otto Wagner (he had entered the Wagnerschule at the Academy of Fine Arts in 1910), and he would also attend classes in Adolf Loos's "Privatschule." Schindler rejected key features of their ideas, however. In particular, he dispensed with traditional notions of constructional style, monumentality, and comfort. He argued instead for space as a fully constitutive element.[2] Although he would not publish his

manifesto for more than two decades (and then in altered form), Schindler's space idea would aptly describe the modern architecture of coming years: it was to be, put plainly, about open, flowing spaces, their form determined and shaped by their function.

But absent in his conception are the two features that would define the Viennese architecture of our story: movement and subjective response. There were, however, other efforts taking place to mark out the new space. In the same year, 1911, Strnad's Villa Hock, then nearing completion, offered one formative view of the possibilities of the spatial path; the other came in Adolf Loos's Goldman & Salatsch Building on Michaelerplatz (fig. 27).

Loos had received the commission to design the building in the late summer of 1909. He was by that time already in his late thirties, and it was to be his first important building. He had spent the previous thirteen years, since his return from the United States, writing and carrying out commissions for interiors—most of them for friends and acquaintances.

The clients for the new structure, Leopold Goldman and his brother-in-law, Emanuel Aufricht, were the owners of an exclusive tailor and outfitter firm they had inherited from Leopold's father. The shop had originally been on the Graben, at the city's very center. In 1909 they purchased an eighteenth-century building a short distance away on Michaelerplatz, across the square from the Hofburg—the imperial palace—with the intention of moving the business there. They decided to tear down the old structure and erect a modern commercial and apartment building. Their new business was to occupy a portion of the ground floor and all of the second floor.

To select a design, they decided to hold a private competition, with all of the entrants determined by invitation. Loos had previously worked for the Goldman family (he had, in fact, designed the interiors for the first Goldman & Salatsch store, as well as the Aufricht family's apartment adjacent to it, and he had worked on a house for the younger Goldman and the grave marker for his father); he was asked to submit a design, along with eight others.[3]

The exact circumstances of the competition are now clouded. It seems that Loos first declined the invitation, stating that he had found that competitions rarely resulted in the choice of the best design.[4] But when the competition failed to produce a satisfactory concept, Loos sketched a plan, which he showed to Goldman. Goldman saw its merits and asked Loos to take over the project. Because Loos up to that time had never built a building and he was not then a licensed architect, Goldman asked another young but experienced architect, Ernst Epstein, to assist him. Over the next six months, the two men worked together closely to prepare the design.[5]

Loos's original plan for the shop (the remainder of the building was in some measure an afterthought) was probably made in July 1909 (fig. 28). It suggests a more or less conventional arrangement, with the Goldman & Salatsch store at the main entrance, flanked by four other ground-floor stores. But another drawing Loos made a short time later, this time of the upper portion of the shop on the mezzanine, reveals the revolutionary nature of his concept (fig. 29).

The space was to be shaped into multiple levels, the floors shifted up or down in relation to each other. The heights of each area, in what would be an intricate arrangement, are shown in the drawing. They are a first indication of his idea of employing a complex spatial plan—the Raumplan, as it would become known—of interlocking volumes of varied heights on different levels.

Loos would go on to develop and refine his idea, and when the building and shop within were finally completed in the late summer of 1911 what he had achieved was matchless and remarkable.[6] The entry into the original store was through a tetrastyle portico; it led directly into the large ground-floor showroom (figs. 30, 31). From there, one ascended to the upper floors by means of a central stairway (fig. 32). The shop was functionally divided. On the ground floor was the sales area for accessories—gloves, hats, ties, under-

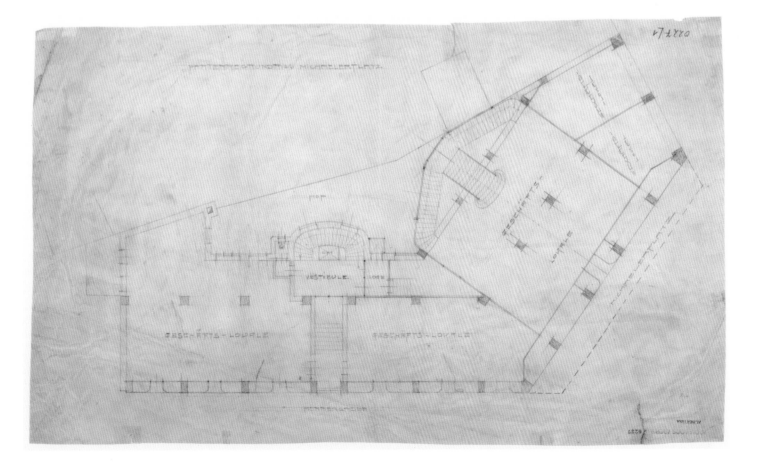

Figure 29 Loos, preliminary plan for the mezzanine floor of the Goldman & Salatsch Building, dated 11 August 1909. Grafische Sammlung Albertina, Vienna, ALA 519.

Figure 30 Goldman & Salatsch Building. Photo by Bruno Reiffenstein, ca. 1930. Bildarchiv der Österreichischen Nationalbibliothek, Vienna, I. N. R 8528-D.

opposite **Figure 31** Goldman & Salatsch Building, main stair within the store. Photo by Martin Gerlach Jr., ca. 1930. From Heinrich Kulka, *Adolf Loos: Das Werk des Architekten* (Vienna: Anton Schroll, 1931), plate 45.

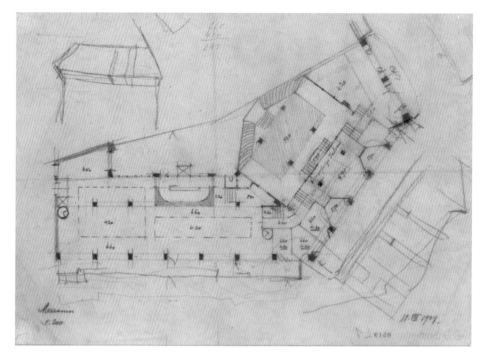

opposite **Figure 32** Goldman & Salatsch Building,
view of the stair leading to the mezzanine.

above **Figure 33** Goldman & Salatsch Building,
view of the mezzanine.

opposite

Figure 34 Goldman & Salatsch Building, reception space on the mezzanine.

Figure 35 Goldman & Salatsch Building, material storage and ordering area on the mezzanine. Photo from a promotional brochure for Goldman & Salatsch, ca. 1911. Grafische Sammlung Albertina, Vienna, ALA 1526/9.

below **Figure 36** Goldman & Salatsch Building, repair workshop on the lower mezzanine level. Photo from a promotional brochure for Goldman & Salatsch, ca. 1911. Grafische Sammlung Albertina, Vienna, ALA 1526/13.

wear, socks, and the like—while the upper floors were reserved for making suits, for consultations, fittings, and selecting materials. Housed in these upper spaces were all of the work areas for the tailors and a separate shirt-fabricating room.

It is on these upper floors where Loos's revolutionary concept is most fully evident. The mezzanine is essentially split into two levels, with a number of smaller subdivisions. One can see clearly the effect in a diagonal view of the space (fig. 33). The various areas are connected by means of short flights of stairs. In some places, as in the reception room, the ceilings are lowered (fig. 34). In others, such as the material storage and ordering area or the suit workshop, there are openings in the floors that allow a visual and physical connection between them (figs. 35–37). Some aspects of this design had precedents, but the overall concept was certainly new.

Here rests one of the great mysteries of Loos's work. Where did this idea come from? When precisely did he develop it?

One clue comes in the form of an undated drawing of another project, an atrium house, that Loos seems to have made the same year (fig. 38). It shows four stories of what appears to be a taller building with a tower. In the section on the right-hand side of the rendering is an indication of the same kind of spatial play. It is most evident in the transition from the office to the kitchen above, which are connected by a spiral staircase. The rooms are of assorted heights; one in the front (presumably the piano nobile) was taller, while the kitchen and office at the rear are lower—in keeping, it seems, with their less important functions.

Loos would later point specifically to his desire to build "economically" as the reason he adopted his volumetric scheme.[7] But here resides still another mystery. For an architect

47

who wrote a great deal—and especially well, for Loos was an exceptional writer, one of the very best writers on architecture of the last century—he penned only a few lines about his spatial idea. And most of what he did write comes in the form of a footnote. It appears in an essay on an entirely different topic, a eulogy for his favorite cabinetmaker, a man named Josef Veillich. The piece was written in 1929—long after Loos had developed and realized the Raumplan concept in various works. He mentions the Weissenhofsied-lung, the recent housing exhibition in Stuttgart mounted by the German Werkbund and overseen by Ludwig Mies van der Rohe, in which Loos had pointedly not been invited to take part. "I would have had something to exhibit," he writes with palpable bitterness, "namely the dissolving of the organization of living rooms into space, not on a level surface, story by story, as has been achieved heretofore. With this invention, I would have saved humanity a great deal of work and time in its development." His statement continues in the footnote: "Because this is the great revolution in architecture: the dissolving of a ground plan into space! Before Immanuel Kant people could not think spatially and architects were forced to make the toilet as high as the formal hall. Only by means of dividing the space in half could they succeed in making lower rooms. And just as we will one day play three-dimensional chess, so other architects will be able in the future to dissolve the ground plan into space."[8]

Loos's other major statement about the Raumplan idea appeared in late 1911 in a speech defending his design of the Goldman & Salatsch Building (or the Looshaus, as it would become universally known). Referring to the other competition designs (and why his scheme was superior), he said: "The plans [of the other architects] all took into account only the regular horizontal layering of the floors whereas, in my opinion, the architect should think in terms of space, in the form of the cube. Thus, I already had an advantage in the economical use of space. A toilet does not have to be as high as a formal hall. If one gives each room only the height it requires, he can build much more economically."[9]

opposite **Figure 37** Goldman & Salatsch Building, suit workshop. Photo from a promotional brochure for Goldman & Salatsch, ca. 1911. Grafische Sammlung Albertina, Vienna, ALA 1526/12.

Figure 38 Loos, drawing of an atrium house with tower, ca. 1909. Grafische Sammlung Albertina, Vienna, ALA 528.

That is effectively the entirety of what he left us about the Raumplan idea in his own words. There are only two other significant sources that offer insight into his thoughts. One comes in the book his assistant Heinrich Kulka wrote about him in 1931. In a section in the text titled "Der Raumplan," Kulka presents a longer and more complete version of Loos's idea.[10] This is the first time, remarkably, that the term appeared in print; Loos never used it in any of his own writings. Whether Kulka formulated the term or whether he took it over from Loos remains one of the undiscovered chapters of the emergence of the new space.

Kulka was then still working for Loos. He had studied with Loos around the end of World War I and began assisting him in the mid-1920s, overseeing many of his later projects. During the last years of Loos's life, Kulka spent a great deal of time with him, and he must

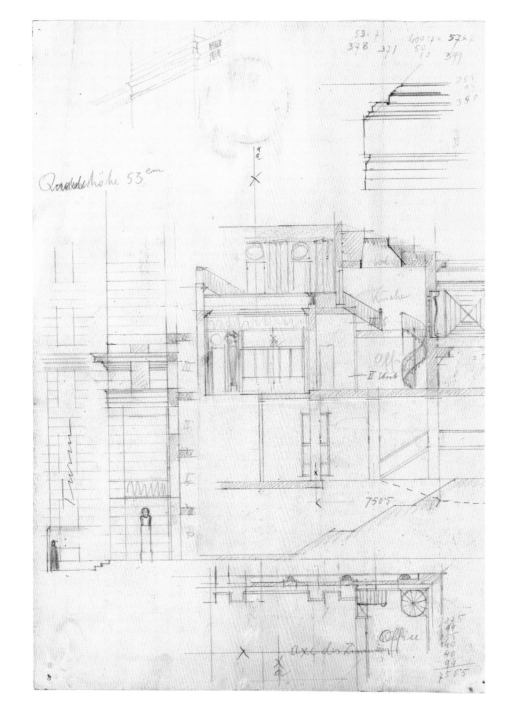

49

have conversed with him at length about his thoughts and motives concerning his designs. What Kulka writes thus must be a very largely, if not wholly, accurate version of Loos's space concept. Some of the language is even reminiscent of Loos's speech patterns, suggesting that Kulka may have partly transcribed—or remembered—a discussion or discussions he had with him.

Kulka at one point offers a capsule definition of the Raumplan, the only one we have from that time. It is, he writes, about "thinking freely in space, the planning of spaces resting at different heights and that are not joined to any regular system of the horizontal layering of floors, the composing of connected spaces into a harmonic and inseparable whole and a spatially economical entity."[11] He also repeats Loos's assertions about his desire to build "economically," arguing that Loos had mastered this technique.

> Depending on their purpose and importance, the spaces not only had varying sizes but also varying heights. Loos can use the same amount of building material to create more living space, because in this way in the same building envelope, the same foundation, under the same roof, inside the same exterior walls he can make more spaces. He makes the absolute most of the available building material and the building site.[12]

This adds little to what Loos himself had written. There is, though, one surprise in Kulka's text. He provides a brief description of how Loos purportedly had come to the Raumplan idea. It has to do with theaters. Loos had observed something (one assumes while he was attending a play or an opera) that was notable about such spaces: "Theaters had stacked galleries, each one floor high, or adjacent spaces (loggias) that were visibly linked to the various stories of the main space. Loos recognized that the ceilings of the loggias were uncomfortably low if one was not looking out into the large main space, that by means of a connection with a taller principal space one could save space with a lower adjacent space, and he used this insight in building houses."[13]

There are two distinct parts to this observation. One has to do with Loos's stated desire to use the Raumplan to "save space." Kulka observed that there was also a subjective element: the loggia spaces were "uncomfortably low," and this could be remedied by providing visual access to a larger volume. In the Goldman & Salatsch store, this design strategy seems to be present in multiple places. Along the edge of the reception space, for example, the lowered passage looks out onto the full-height portion of the mezzanine (fig. 39). Loos's desire to build economically is also easily readable, for instance, in the office space, which also has a lowered ceiling (fig. 40).

Yet Loos must have had other intentions, for the spaces are too unconventional and too specific to have been the product solely of his economical imperative or the notion that a lookout could redeem a lowered space. What is unavoidable to anyone now walking through these spaces is a realization that Loos, very much like Strnad, introduced a complex sequencing of visual and other sensory experiences to heighten one's awareness of the architecture. The Looshaus, like Strnad's Hock and Wassermann houses, was an effort at making what might be termed an "affective path."

"Affective" here—stirring moods or feelings—relates, of course, to the concept of empathy. It implies an experience of *something* and an accompanying emotional response. That it is linked to "path" is the second element—movement and how movement can heighten experience. That this feature is present and observable in many of Loos's Raumplan designs is indisputable. But his full intentions are much more difficult to get at, for he writes little about this idea.

Figure 39 Goldman & Salatsch Building,
upper mezzanine.

opposite **Figure 40** Goldman & Salatsch Building, view from the mezzanine office looking back toward the stair and the material storage area.

Figure 41 Loos, project for the War Ministry Building, Vienna; elevation. Grafische Sammlung Albertina, Vienna, ALA 376.

We have another source concerning Loos's Raumplan ideas, however, that sheds light on the issue. It comes from another of Loos's assistants, the Czech architect Karel Lhota, who worked for him in the late 1920s and early 1930s. He, too, quotes Loos on the Raumplan: "I do not design plans, façades, sections, I design space. Actually, in my work, there is no ground floor, upper floor, or cellar, there are only connected rooms, anterooms, and terraces. Every space requires a specific height—the dining room a different one from the pantry—and for that reason the ceilings lie at different heights."[14]

This is a bit different from what Loos had said or written before. What comes next provides an essential clue: "Accordingly, one must connect these rooms with each other so that the transition is imperceptible [*unmerklich*] and natural, but also as practicable as possible. That is, as I see it, for others a secret, for me obvious."[15]

The path thus, in this formulation, is about making "quiet" and intuitive linkages between spaces, which, at the same time, should be functional and sensible. Loos says nothing else, though, nothing that might have given us insight into his thinking or his strategies—other than that for him it was all "obvious."

In the quotation from Lhota, he goes on to describe the origins of his space idea: "I discovered this spatial solution [*raumlösung*] years ago for the Goldman & Salatsch store."[16] But it was already present, he continues, "in the competition project for the War Ministry building in Vienna, in which the middle portion was arranged into large rooms, with the offices with lower stories arrayed around them, an enormous saving of space—but no one noticed it."[17]

Loos had worked on his entry for the War Ministry competition in 1907 and 1908. The jury rejected it out of hand, because, as Loos's biographers Burkhardt Rukschcio and Roland Schachel would write later, "in general [it became] the target of a strong criticism, even derision" for its radically simplified massing and façades.[18] The submitted elevations, however, show precisely what Loos was describing: a three-story central tract, with six-story blocks on either side (fig. 41). It was an inauspicious beginning, but there are no earlier indications of a Raumplan in Loos's designs. His idea must indeed have had its genesis around 1907.

Loos's argument for the Raumplan, though, was firmly rooted at the outset in his claims for economical use of space. He says nothing at this time about the experience of the transitions from one space to another (those for his War Ministry entry seem to have been little more than perfunctory), nothing that would aid us in understanding the more complex movement sequences in the Goldman & Salatsch store, much less his later houses.

To argue, thus, for an intentional subjective aspect on Loos's part in the Raumplan is far from easy. Loos offers us little else to support such an assertion. But there is a related statement in the well-known passage from his essay "Architektur" about the "emotional" role of architecture: "Architecture awakens moods in people. The task of the architect

53

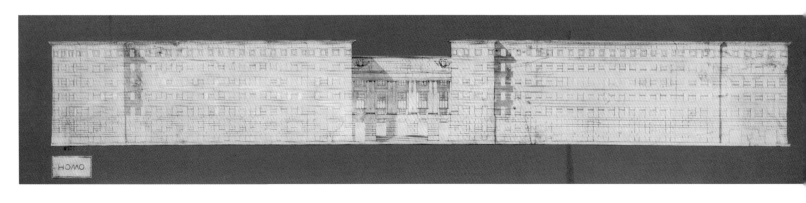

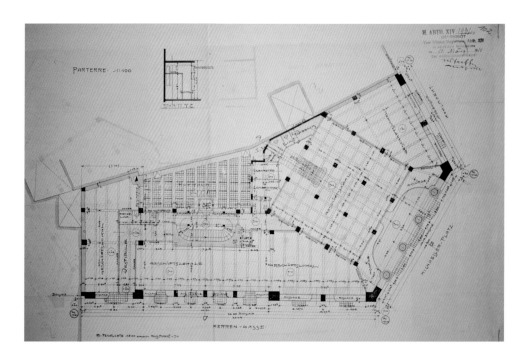

therefore is to emphasize these moods. A room should appear comfortable, a house livable. A court of justice should appear threatening to those harboring secret vices. A bank building must say: Here your money is well and safely kept by honest people."[19] In the same section, he goes on to acknowledge that many of these subjective associations are culturally or personally relative: "The architect can only achieve [these linkages] in those buildings if people are already predisposed to them."[20]

The wellspring of this notion of "architectural moods" extends further back in Loos's writings. It first appears in his essay "Das Prinzip der Bekleidung" (The Principle of Cladding), published in 1898.[21] He argues that the "task of the architect is to produce a warm, livable space." Only when this is understood should the architect create a constructive frame. Loos complains that in practice this necessary ordering of tasks is too often ignored: "There are architects who do this differently. They do not imagine rooms but walls. What is left over after building the walls are the rooms." But "the artist, the architect," he continues, "first feels the effect he thinks of producing, and he sees with his creative eye the spaces that he wants to create. The effect he wants the viewer to have, whether it is fear in the case of a prison, the fear of God for a church, fear of the state for a government building, piety for a grave, hominess for a house, gaiety for a drinking establishment—this effect will be fostered by means of the materials and the form."[22]

Loos's thinking here is almost assuredly derived not from Schmarsow but from Semper, and specifically from Semper's *Bekleidungstheorie*—his theory of cladding, which Semper had laid out most fully in *Der Stil*.[23] But Loos appends nothing else that offers insight into how he conceived of the connections in his Raumplan designs, nothing about what he wanted people to experience. Nowhere does he make mention, directly or indirectly, of Schmarsow, Vischer, Hildebrand, or any of the other German theorists of the previous generation—aside from Semper.

Was Loos aware of their ideas? By 1909, the year he began working on the design for the Looshaus, these theories, as we have seen, were beginning to permeate the world of architectural discourse in Vienna. It is even possible that Loos may have discussed them with Strnad since the two men were on friendly terms. But there are no sure indications either way.

opposite **Figure 42** Loos, submitted plans for the Goldman & Salatsch Building showing the ground floor, dated 11 March 1910. Plan- und Schriftenkammer der Magistratsamt (MA 37), Vienna.

Figure 43 Loos, submitted plans for the Goldman & Salatsch Building showing the mezzanine level, dated 11 March 1910. Plan- und Schriftenkammer der Magistratsamt (MA 37), Vienna.

The evidence for Loos's intention to foster an affective path in the Goldman & Salatsch store—the only good evidence—is visual, expressed in the building itself. It is not notably apparent in the original drawings. The set of renderings—all drawn, it seems, by Epstein—that Loos submitted to the building authorities only hints at the complex spatial ordering in the transition from the ground floor to the mezzanine level (figs. 42, 43). Redrawing these spaces in plan provides little additional indication of the nature of the spaces above or of the paths (figs. 44–46). And there are no sections surviving in either Loos's or Epstein's hands, which is in itself surprising. Loos seems to have designed the tangled plan as a mental image—without bothering to render it in section. Even in section, though, it is nearly impossible to grasp the effect. It is the sequencing of the spaces that is revealing: movement through the building itself is a document, a record of his intentions.

The main path commences at the entry. In the porch, Loos introduced large, curving sheets of glass below and smaller, beveled panes above to create a sparkling light effect (fig. 47). Inside, the main route leads up the central stair. The path at this point is compressed, framed by the pillars and vitrines. From there, the stair splits into two parts, winding up to the left or the right. Here the play of space and light becomes much richer (fig. 48). Made up of Luxfer prisms, the ceiling produces a glittering of light, which is amplified by the large mirrors at the rear.[24] The mirrors, in turn, offer a first glimpse of the mezzanine above, a preview of the intricate array of spatial impressions to come. Then, as the path continues along the first level of the mezzanine, the space and the view are reduced again, framed by the walls of the upper levels (fig. 49). At the end of this passageway the outlook opens up once more, granting the viewer a full sense of the myriad spatial possibilities (figs. 50, 51). Along one of the possible routes from this point one can first see the tailor's work area above and below (fig. 52).

Yet it is only through movement—through the act of walking and climbing, and by means of moving one's head to take in the different vistas—that the space begins to become understandable. A stationary observer cannot possibly grasp the full spatial ordering, just as a ground plan offers only a partial reading of the spaces.

The difficulty of representing in drawn form what is occurring is notable and revealing. For all the complexities of Strnad's two prewar villas—for all of their discontinuities and

55

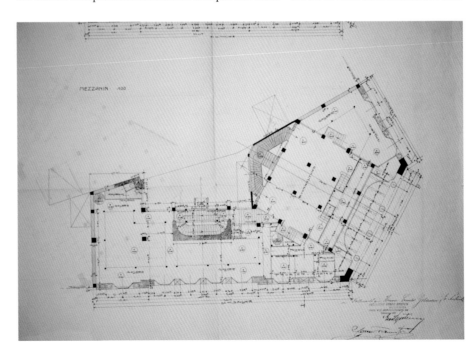

Figure 44 Goldman & Salatsch Building, ground-floor plan, 1:200. Drawing by Nicolas Allinder. 1. Main shop floor (men's outfits and accessories); 2. Retail space; 3. Courtyard.

Figure 45 Goldman & Salatsch Building, lower mezzanine plan, 1:200. Drawing by Nicolas Allinder. 1. Reception area for the tailor shop; 2. Accounting; 3. Fabrics; 4. Office; 5. Sewing workspace; 6. Ironing.

Figure 46 Goldman & Salatsch Building, upper mezzanine plan, 1:200. Drawing by Nicolas Allinder. 1. Lounge; 2. Fabrics; 3. Dressing rooms; 4. Tailor workspace.

opposite **Figure 47** Goldman & Salatsch Building, view of the porch.

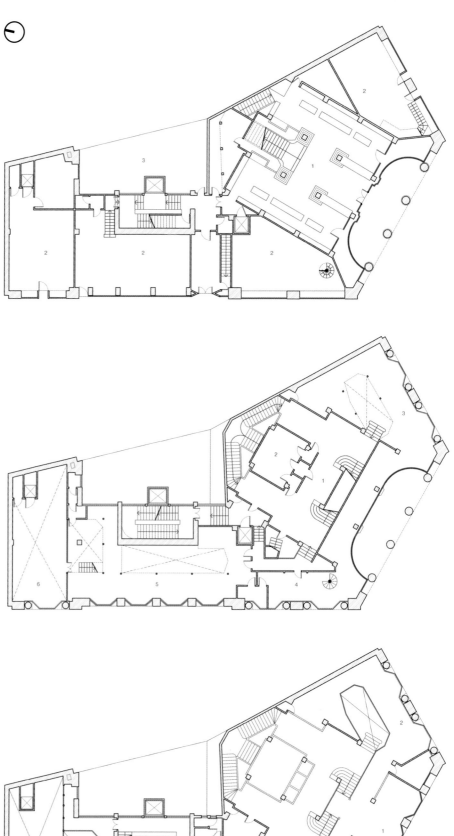

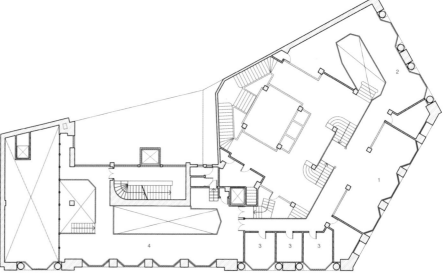

Figure 48 Goldman & Salatsch Building, view of the stair leading to the mezzanine.

opposite **Figure 49** Goldman & Salatsch Building, entry to the mezzanine.

disjunctures—a set of ground plans can convey reasonably well most of what is going on along the entry path. Even if the visual and somatic experience cannot be completely reproduced from looking at a graphic representation, one can mostly imagine it. This is not true of the Looshaus. The paths are too intricate and the views too varied.

It is possible, however, to communicate more fully the nature of this kind of space, if a different sort of rendering is employed—a "continuous path plan," a graphic linking together of the route, which shows the unbroken route on multiple levels (fig. 53).[25] Essentially, this is a series of linked ground plans, the connections between the plans occurring at the place where the path aligns. On the one hand, to render this way is a distortion—a visual contrivance that is more akin to a diagram than a drawn version of reality. Yet by representing the path as a line extending as a thread throughout, the movements and possible vistas become at least more readily manifest.

Yet what a plan—even a continuous one—cannot demonstrate completely is Loos's seeming desire to engage the observer's spatial awareness. Even more, it cannot disclose his intention to provoke the observer's emotional responses because much relies on other factors, such as lighting, materials, and finishes. In the case of the Goldman & Salatsch shop, there is the obvious appearance of luxury and exclusivity—unquestionably the right impression for such an establishment. Loos's manipulations of light, the continual spatial compression and then opening up, were doubtless also part of his desire to develop full architectural awareness—to foster multiple and divergent "moments" along the main path. There are the repeated changes in direction inherent in the spatial sequence, and they prompt a somatic as well as a visual experience. This is reinforced in the many short flights of stairs. Strnad's notion of employing disruptions to enhance the viewer's mindfulness of the built world is very much in evidence here. In the mezzanine space, they come about through the many abrupt shifts in direction along the paths, and, also, by means of the many short flights of stairs.

Despite the lack of any specific commentary on Loos's part about his intentions, a few things do seem clear. The spatial ordering of the Goldman & Salatsch shop is an attempt to enhance its functionality. And it is simultaneously an effort to make a new kind of spatial experience. In the initial planning stages, we know that Loos worked closely with Goldman to ensure that the arrangement of the spaces would make for an efficient flow of work and serve the needs of the gentlemen customers. That Loos's plan was significantly better in this regard than the other submitted designs appears to have been one of the principal reasons he received the commission.[26] And Goldman, from all that we know, was quite pleased with the result.

From our remove, the question of just how functional and economical these spaces were is still open. Moving about the mezzanine during the course of a normal workday would have entailed a considerable amount of going up and down stairs. It would have been physically demanding, and some of the routes are less direct than they could have been. At the same time, Loos's meticulous portioning of spaces by function probably worked well. The obvious divisions between the areas where gentlemen were received and served and the workspaces provided the necessary level of decorum. Yet their adjacency would have made it quick to move back and forth.

Loos from all indications appears to have thought about functionality quite broadly. It was the function of the mezzanine not only to allow for the fitting and making of clothing, but also to please the customers. The mahogany, brass, and glass fittings evoked the look of the best tailor shops on London's Savile Row, the model for the shop in the first place. The main stair from the ground floor and the cutting up of the upper spaces

opposite **Figure 50** Goldman & Salatsch Building,
lower mezzanine.

Figure 51 Goldman & Salatsch Building, view from
the lower mezzanine to the changing areas above.

opposite **Figure 52** Goldman & Salatsch Building, view from the lower mezzanine to the tailors' workspace above and below.

Figure 53 Goldman & Salatsch Building, continuous plan showing the path through the store, 1:200. Drawing by Nicolas Allinder. 1. Main shop floor, men's outfits and accessories; 2. Reception area for the tailor shop; 3. Accounting; 4. Lounge; 5. Fabrics; 6. Tailor workspace.

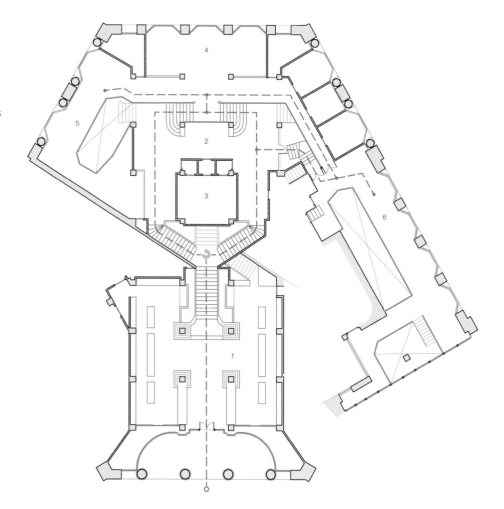

into smaller zones gave the fitting areas a feeling of separation and intimacy—precisely the right mood for those places where the gentlemen were served and where they would change in and out of clothes. If Loos had achieved only this, his design would have been a success. His sequencing of spaces, the precise routing of the paths, however, also promoted a feeling of venture and newness. His work held within it a sense of the familiar, of luxury and privacy, and also of unfamiliarity—a changed mode of spatial recognition that provoked novel sensations and emotions.

The possibilities of manipulating such sensual emotionality would in some part drive Loos's spatial experiments for the next two decades.

CHAPTER FOUR

The Possibilities of Nonorthogonality

In 1913, only a few years after Oskar Strnad and Adolf Loos had first begun to explore the promises of a new spatial ordering, the young Josef Frank added another important and vital concept: the application of nonorthogonal (or non-right-angled) forms to enhance architectural awareness. It would become the most extreme—and the most potentially fertile—of the concepts of the new space, though, as it would happen, its full realization was still many years off.

Frank was born in 1885, the son of a well-to-do Viennese Jewish textile merchant. He too studied with Carl König at the Technische Hochschule, and, like Strnad, he went on to complete a doctorate, in his case writing his dissertation on the churches of the early Florentine Renaissance master Leon Battista Alberti. He completed the work in the summer of 1910; not long thereafter he joined the practice of Strnad and Wlach.[1]

Strnad and Loos both undoubtedly left their impress on Frank's thinking about the new space. As a student, Frank often sat at Loos's table in the Café Museum, taking in what Loos had to say about the reform of architecture and design.[2] Ever after, Frank's theoretical ideas would play out themes and directions that Loos introduced to him. Frank, indeed, became Loos's most important, if wayward, disciple (for he would repeatedly remake Loos's concepts in novel and divergent ways). He would continue to mine Loos's intellectual ground for ideas: for a time in the 1920s it would seem as if they were working in tandem. But at the outset it was Strnad who had the greater impact on his emerging views about space and space-making.

The two men were especially close in the last years before the outbreak of the First World War. Strnad was six years older, more experienced, and he had already commenced his career; Frank, very much the junior associate in the working partnership of Strnad-Wlach-Frank, was still acquiring a knowledge of real practice. By then, Strnad had formed the main tenets of his design philosophy of space and path. Frank would have confronted

them directly in the Wassermann House, which was on the boards at the time he joined his former classmates.[3]

But it must also be stressed that Frank sprang from the same intellectual lineage as Strnad. The years he spent with König left an ineradicable mark on him. Frank took away from his time with König the same allegiance to posing basic questions about the function and meaning of a building, the same inner need to inquire after the sources of the Western tradition in architecture and to ponder their relevance and purpose for modern life. Frank was also notably widely read—more so, it seems, than even Strnad. His approach was always deeply cerebral. As his later assistant Ernst Plischke once remarked, he was "concerned more about what the forms he devised meant than the forms in themselves."[4] It is very possible that Frank read some of the works of Vischer, Hildebrand, Schmarsow, and the other German theorists of the day; even if he did not, he was surely aware at some level of the ongoing art historical discussion about space and movement. Like Strnad, he had also begun very early to contemplate its potential consequences.

Frank initially explored the concept of nonorthogonality in his first commission for a building, a house in Vienna's eighteenth (now nineteenth) district. The commission came from a retired bureaucrat in the naval department, Dr. Emil Scholl. The site was a sloping lot on the Wilbrandtgasse in what was then still a largely undeveloped area on the city's western edge. The house was part of a planned grouping of four houses. In a drawing of the project Frank made at the time all four are shown; only the first from the left (the Scholl House) and the third (the Strauß House) were realized (fig. 54).

The irregular shape of the Scholl House's lot—a trapezoid with the narrower edge facing the street—determined Frank's unconventional design. To squeeze as much buildable area as possible out of the land, he set the outer walls of the house parallel to the property line as the site widened, causing the walls to splay out toward the back (figs. 55–57).

Frank probably worked on the design with Strnad and Wlach; Strnad's hand, in particular, seems to be apparent in another winding entry sequence that extends up from the street (fig. 58). This time one enters at a gate just to the right of the house's center and turns immediately to the right. At the stair, which follows the property line along the right-hand side, the route goes to the left then ascends in two stages before arriving at the front door on the side of the house (necessitating yet another ninety-degree left turn).

Inside, the large central *Halle*—the principal living area—extends the full width of the house, an arrangement that was not at all common in Vienna at the time. The irregular

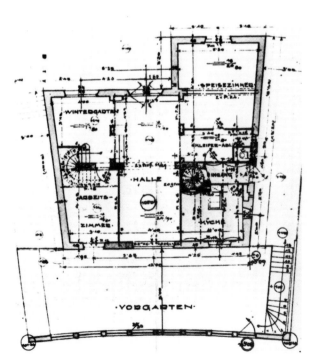

left **Figure 55** Josef Frank, Scholl House, Vienna, 1913–14; plan. Private collection.

above **Figure 56** Scholl House. Bauhaus-Archiv, Berlin.

Figure 57 Scholl House, view from the rear garden.
Bauhaus-Archiv, Berlin.

opposite
Figure 58 Scholl House, main-floor plan showing
the promenade, 1:200. Drawing by Nicolas Allinder.
1. Vestibule; 2. Cloakroom; 3. Dining room; 4. Hall;
5. Conservatory; 6. Study; 7. Kitchen; 8. Front garden.

Figure 59 Scholl House, sections. Private collection.

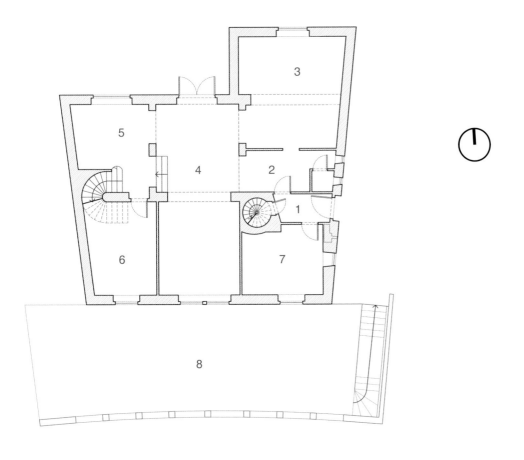

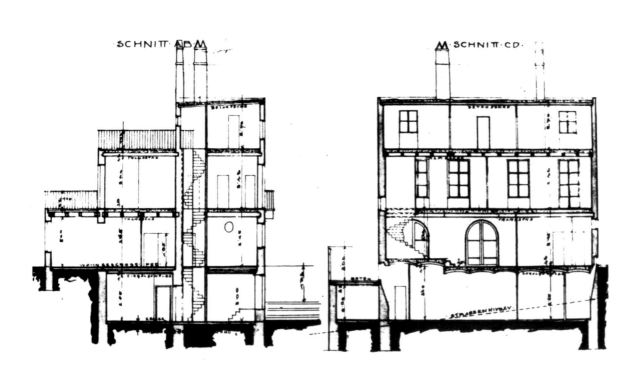

SCHNITT·AB·M   M·SCHNITT·CD·

fenestration pattern, which gives the front façade a peculiar, rather unbalanced appearance (for the windows appear at multiple heights on the walls), hints at an unusual spatial ordering. The sections show, however, that there is no Raumplan in the Loosian sense; instead, the standard horizontal layering of floors is maintained (fig. 59). What is significant is that the spaces are mostly open. Frank's use of a massive reinforced concrete beam that extends the width of the house at its center and carries much of the weight of the upper floors allowed a reduction in the number and size of interior load-bearing walls. This also allowed for the creation of a series of contiguous rooms—including the hall, conservatory, and dining room—so that much of the floor area at the rear of the house merges into a single space. It is not fully open, though, because the rooms are set adjacent to the hall, fanning out along its edges on either side, with partial walls and "corners" in between. The discrete identity of each room, thus, is preserved.

Frank probably modeled the open arrangement after progressive American houses of the time, which he greatly admired.[5] But the novelty of the plan resides in its peculiar footprint. Because of the trapezoidal shape of the house, the rooms resting at the outer edges— on the main floor, these included the conservatory and dining room, as well as the kitchen and study, and on the upper floors, the outer bedrooms—were not standard rectangles but irregular quadrilaterals. Whether this was an afterthought for Frank or whether he had intended it from the outset (as he devised the outer walls), we do not know; he left us nothing that explains his intentions. (And it should be said that this was a common architectural practice when lots were irregular.) In any event, the consequence of his decision to follow the lot lines with the sidewalls of the house changed the impact of the interiors. Frank later noted an important feature of such rooms: precisely because they are not regular, it takes an observer slightly longer to grasp them spatially. And in that "lag" is a means to foster greater architectural engagement.

Almost at the same time, Frank and his new wife Anna (née Sebenius), a Swedish gymnastics teacher who had been living and working in Vienna before their marriage, moved into their new apartment on the Wiedner Hauptstraße in the city's fourth district. Their large unit was on the top floor of a building at Wiedner Hauptstraße 64, designed by Arthur Baron (fig. 60).

Baron, too, had been one of Strnad's classmates in König's studio at the Technische Hochschule (he completed his studies before Frank entered the school), and he had befriended Strnad, Wlach, and Frank. By the early years of the century, he had built a successful practice erecting commercial buildings and apartment houses.[6] Some, including the Residenzpalast (1909–10) in the inner city, borrowed from the stylistic language of Otto Wagner and his students. Most of his subsequent works, however, brought together influences from the neo-Baroque and neo-Biedermeier.

The new building that housed the apartment of Frank and his wife fell into this latter category—a modified and modernized neo-Biedermeier. It had, as a consequence, a high mansard roof, with full, hipped or gabled dormers and a multisided turret, the forms of which were expressed—in negative—in the Franks' new rooms. Since the site the structure occupied was irregular, the plan, too, was complex in shape (fig. 61).[7]

The result was that the apartment that the Franks moved into on the top floor was both partially nonorthogonal in plan and had walls and ceilings with myriad angles and slopes (fig. 62). Some of these features seem deliberately contrived or formed in a way that was unusual for Viennese buildings of the time. Whether these came from Frank or Baron, or whether they collaborated on the design in some fashion is impossible to establish.

But whatever the case, Frank took full advantage of the geometrical and spatial peculiarities, situating the furnishings freely about the rooms, sometimes following the contours of the walls, sometimes setting them into the centers of the spaces.[8] This strategy served both to accentuate but also to normalize what were in fact rather unconventional and "difficult" rooms (figs. 63, 64).

All of the furnishings in the apartment, whether set against the walls or positioned "in space," were movable and free, which is to say that they were not built in and therefore not architectonic; they were neither part of, nor attached to, the architectural frame. They became individual elements, sometimes arranged in functional groupings—set pieces, or as Frank and others referred to them at the time, *Wohninseln* (living islands). And the rooms themselves became places for inhabiting and living, avoiding many bourgeois strictures.[9]

Whether or not Frank took the apartment precisely for its unconventional and eccentric spatial ordering we cannot know. But he would in any event come to see this way of ordering as the most natural and such complex spaces as the most livable. His own apartment became the touchstone of his future design philosophy: many of the buildings and spaces he designed after 1930 would mimic the apartment's spaces in some way. He took

Figure 60 Arthur Baron, apartment house, Wiedner Hauptstraße 64, Vienna, 1912–13. From *Der Bautechniker* 34, no. 1 (2 January 1914): plate 1.

right, top and bottom
Figure 61 Wiedner Hauptstraße 64, typical apartment plan. From *Der Bautechniker* 34, no. 1 (2 January 1914): 1.

Figure 62 Wiedner Hauptstraße 64. Frank's apartment was on the top floor. Private collection.

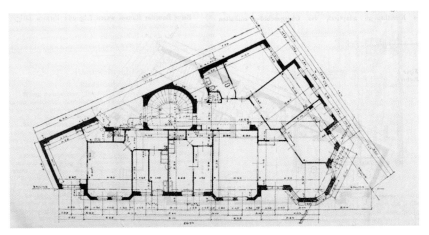

Figure 63 Wiedner Hauptstraße 64, Frank's apartment; view from the living room into the dining area. MAK–Österreichisches Museum für angewandte Kunst / Gegenwartskunst, Vienna, K. I. 14306/15.

Figure 64 Wiedner Hauptstraße 64, Frank's apartment; view of the fireplace and library. MAK–Österreichisches Museum für angewandte Kunst / Gegenwartskunst, Vienna, K. I. 14306/9.

decided pleasure in the idea that the apartment was in some measure an "accident"—what had remained after the outer form of the building had been conceived, exactly as the spaces in the Scholl House had been. Both interiors were the outcome of other architectonic imperatives and requirements. The spaces within were "leftovers," remnants of a process that was, on the surface at least, seemingly "fickle" and inconsistent, and therefore not fully predictable.

The conception of an architecture made up of such "accidents" was by its very nature a radical overturning of the whole premise of the Western classical tradition. In place of regular, considered, and logical space—the belief in harmony and equipoise that had been the guiding rule of classicism—this way of thinking about space posited a building art founded upon what was seemingly random, jumbled, and messy. It privileged happenstance over punctilious planning, apparent disorder over rationality, and disarrayed (or, at a minimum, composite) spaces over those that were regular and readily legible.

Such a vision also seemingly flew in the face of much of architectural modernism itself. The preference on the part of so many early modernists for spaces that were the product of discursive design processes and careful attention to functionality (however they defined it) appeared to pose the very opposite of what Frank was beginning to posit: an architecture of deliberate disorder. But such contradictions, or, at least, divergent viewpoints, were very much part of the new architecture: Frank's evolving spatial ideas, as radical as they might have been, were merely one more answer to the question of how to remake traditional architecture as a spatial medium.[10]

If the central role of space and space-making was already starting to become fixed in the thinking of most modernists by 1914 (the year, it should be recalled, that the Scholl House was completed), the mounting differences of opinion about what the new architecture should be and do spatially were also becoming ever more plain. There were those, such as the young Walter Gropius and Adolf Meyer in their Fagus factory complex of 1913, who were promoting an architecture of spatial openness and pragmatism; for others, such as Bruno Taut (whose Glass Pavilion at the 1914 German Werkbund Exhibition was primarily about space—or more exactly, space lit in multiple colors), it was an artistic gesture. Max Berg's 1913 Jahrhunderthalle in Breslau—its inner diameter of sixty-nine meters (226 feet) and height of forty-two meters (138 feet) making it the largest building of its kind at the time it opened—offered an enormous volume: pure, flowing, unencumbered space of a sort that had not been seen at such a scale in the West since late antiquity.

But such spaces, whether for factory, pavilion, or assembly hall, were spaces to be utilized or, at most, contemplated. Countering this conception, of course, was the belief that space should be "felt"—that it would or should elicit an empathic response. In 1914 the most unalloyed expression of this idea appeared in the book *The Architecture of Humanism*, written by the English poet and architectural historian Geoffrey Scott.

Scott had served as Bernard Berenson's secretary a few years before; he had become part of Berenson's Florence circle of thinkers and writers, and through them, he had come into contact with the theories of Lipps, Schmarsow, Riegl, and others.[11] His book is in some measure an effort to bring together their ideas into a single theoretical construct. He writes, for instance: "To enclose a space is the object of building; when we build we do detach a convenient quantity of space, seclude it and protect it, and all architecture springs from that necessity. But aesthetically space is even more supreme. The architect models in space as a sculptor in clay. He designs his space as a work of art; that is, he attempts through its means to excite a certain mood in those who enter it."[12]

Here one can readily detect the influences of Vischer and Lipps. But Scott, it is quite evident, also appropriated from Hildebrand and Schmarsow: "What is his method? Once again his appeal to Movement. Space, in fact, is liberty of movement. That is its value to us, and as such it enters our physical consciousness. We adapt ourselves instinctively to the spaces in which we stand, project ourselves into them, fill them ideally with our movements."[13]

Experiencing space in this way—through movement—"humanizes" the spaces, according to Scott; they become responsive to us, and a part of us. If one reads on, though, what emerges is that Scott's view of *what* the subject would or should feel is rather narrowly defined: she or he might experience a sense of beauty or ugliness, or equilibrium, or disharmony. But these are all essentially aesthetic judgments. And these judgments for Scott were strictly aligned with issues of style and form and his notion of "humanism." The possibility that they might produce more deeply felt personal emotions he seemingly disregards.

There were other responses at the time to the question of what an empathic reaction to architecture might yield. In that same year, 1914, the Prague-born art historian Paul Frankl sought in his book *Die Entwicklungsphasen der neueren Baukunst* to discern the varied patterns of spatial experience and how they changed over time. It is worth recalling that Frankl was the first to develop into a full historical analysis Schmarsow's ideas of the evolution of architectural space. Frankl had studied with Wölfflin in Munich, but his work, which he submitted as his *Habilitationsschrift*, deviated from Wölfflin's formalist views. Frankl regarded space and spatial perception as only one of four critical categories driving the development of Renaissance and post-Renaissance architecture. The others—"corporeality" (the treatment of mass and surface), "visible form" (the handling of light, color, and other surface effects), and "purposive intention" (the relationship of design to social function)—he deemed of equal import.[14] Frankl's analysis was also greatly indebted to Hildebrand, Fiedler, and Riegl ("whose distinction between 'haptic' and 'optic' experiences," as James Ackerman noted, "must have influenced Frankl's separation of 'corporeal' and 'visible' form").[15] His description of the process of three-dimensional perception, for example, follows very closely that of Hildebrand: "We interpret as three-dimensional every single image of an object that we receive from any viewpoint, but what is essential in viewing architecture is that we accept these isolated images as merely preliminary arrangements, not as ends in themselves. To see architecture means to draw together in a single mental image the series of three-dimensionally interpreted images that are presented to us as we walk through interior spaces and round their exterior shell. When I speak of the *architectural image*, I mean this one *mental image*."[16]

For Frankl, the impact of these mental images on the observer is, again, essentially aesthetic. The meaning of what one "sees" is given in the arrangement of the space, with only a single, conventional interpretation possible. In his short commentary on Frankl's book, Ackerman puts this concisely: "as observers, [we] are servants of the aesthetic forces of architecture." Spatial form, beyond this, can only tell us something about a building's "purposive intention."[17]

But for Frank, as, indeed, for Strnad and Loos, neither such aesthetic issues nor the revealing of space's function was primary. In Frank's conception of nonorthogonal space what is central is that it is capable of arousing particular emotions in the viewer. Irregular rooms, such as those in his Wiedner Hauptstraße apartment or the Scholl House, can—first—compel in us a stronger engagement with architecture: because we have to contemplate them for a moment in order to take in what is actually occurring spatially, we necessarily make more thorough note of the spaces and the spatial progression. Yet, even more meaningful for Frank is the possibility that such spaces will also convey to us two fundamental emotions: a feeling of liberation from the constraints of the ordinary and a sense of *Gemüt*—warmth, sentimentality, and ease. Complexity he saw as a tool for promoting freedom, well-being, and "well-living."

Frank's highly—even naively—positive picture of the intersection of movement and "difficult" space was not universally shared, however. A few years before, in his dissertation and book *Abstraktion und Einfühlung: Ein Beitrag zur Stilpsychologie* (Abstraction and Empathy: A Contribution to the Psychology of Style), the young art historian Wilhelm Worringer had called into question the belief that empathy was necessarily affirmative and "fulfilling."[18]

Worringer had heard Lipps's lectures at the University of Munich in 1904–5, and at the outset in his study he leans heavily on Lipps's thinking, without, however, specifically acknowledging his teacher's claims. His argument is based on a condensed version of Lipps's formula for Einfühlung, empathy: "Aesthetischer Genuss ist objectiver Selbstgenuss" (aesthetic enjoyment is objectified self-enjoyment).[19] At first, he ostensibly accepts this claim, but as his argument unfolds it becomes evident that he is using it as a foil to undermine previous claims for Einfühlung. He contends instead that all aesthetic activity can be reduced to the two concepts in the book's title: a tendency either toward abstraction (a reduced or stylized representation of nature) or empathy (an art that is naturalistic and readily evokes emotion). He argues that the tension between these two directions governs creative pursuit and that they form the opposing poles of a dialectic. Abstraction he identifies with primitive peoples, for whom the "thing in itself" is foremost; Einfühlung he regards as the basis for the naturalistic art of ancient Greece and the Renaissance.[20]

Worringer's reframing of earlier ideas about the inner dynamic of art—whether from Wölfflin, Riegl, or others—was instrumental in shaping the discourse of those last years before the war. His avowal that an abstract or stylized art was not the result of a culture's inability to produce more realistic representations, but rather was born of a need to show objects in a more spiritual manner, would inspire the German Expressionists (who found in it a justification for their approach) and later radical art movements.

For modern architecture, though, his assertions played out differently. Drawing on the distinction between abstraction and empathy, Worringer claimed that in the case of art "aesthetic enjoyment" and "objectified self-enjoyment" were not identical impulses but opposed. The former he associated with abstraction, the latter with empathy. But both, he insisted, led to self-estrangement: in the case of abstraction, because of the unease it fostered by delving into the realm of the spiritual; in the case of empathy, because when a viewer permitted him- or herself to dissolve into the pleasure of a work of art, the process entailed a loss of self. A person experiencing an extreme empathic response would feel not comfort but estrangement. Applied to architecture, this would mean that to enter a building and become trenchantly moved by it would evoke feelings of alienation and anxiety.[21]

For Worringer, this impulse toward estrangement—self-distancing or self-alienation—could also lead to a spiritual fear of space (*geistige Raumscheu*). To have an empathic experience of an architectural work—visually and somatically—would provoke deep inner discomfort. "The instinct of man," he writes in the book's appendix, "is not reverent devotion to the world, but fear of it. Not physical fear, but a fear that is of the spirit. A kind of spiritual agoraphobia in the face of the motley disorder and caprice of the phenomenal world. It is the growing assurance and mobility of the understanding, which links the vague impressions and works them up into facts of experience, that first give man a conception of the world; prior to that he possesses only an eternally changing and uncertain visual image, which does not permit the emergence of a confident, pantheistic relationship to nature. He stands frightened and lost amidst the universe."[22]

Such a glum and pessimistic view allows little place for an affirmative experience of space, though Worringer believed we might overcome the fear of the world around us through the application of reason. For Frank, whose gaze was set firmly on the domestic sphere, such thoughts held little appeal or validity. Whether he had read Worringer's little book and dismissed it, or whether he simply was not interested in such philosophical arguments—or, perhaps, was it that he himself had merely put up insufficient theoretical collateral—is unclear. But this is, in any event, beside the point. Frank assumed at this time, and he remained convinced to his last days, that the architect's role was to make dwellings that were pleasant and habitable, that might offer succor and psychological warmth. What he sought were the means to enrich such emotional responses, and he was convinced that complex and composite spaces, which avoided standard right-angled planning, offered a fertile course toward the making of a new and better way of living.

It would, however, be nearly two decades before he would give himself over fully to making such nonorthogonal spaces. Frank, like Loos, still had to work through many other ideas related to the concept of an affective path; those efforts would drive their architectural experiments of the 1920s.

CHAPTER FIVE

Domesticating the Raumplan

At the time that Adolf Loos was casting the finishing details for the Goldman & Salatsch
Building, he was in the process of designing or had recently completed several houses.
One—his first—was a townhouse for Leopold Goldman on Hardtgasse (1909–11), a work
that to this day is very largely disregarded in the literature on Loos.[1] The other two, the
Steiner House on St. Veitgasse (1910) and the Scheu House on Larochegasse (1912–13), are
far better known and often cited as examples of his prescient modernism. What is surprising and worth commenting on is that none of these designs offers much in the way
of a Raumplan: in all three houses, the regular horizontal layering of floors is preserved.
What Loos had so insistently put at the heart of his design for the Goldman & Salatsch
shop is scarcely discernable in his early domestic works.

Two of these houses, however, the Steiner and Scheu villas, display marks of his
mounting interest in space and movement. The Scheu House, which was designed and
built later, is less ambitious in this regard. There is a faint echo in the house of the Goldman
& Salatsch walkways in the partially open stair leading up to the second-story bedrooms,
which offers a few "soft" visual and bodily effects as it ascends along the edge of the hall
(figs. 65–67). And there is in the same house another imperative, if subtle, expression of
the possibility of affective space and movement. It is found in the inglenook of the living
room, in the placement of the mirror, which allows someone seated in the right place to
see in the reflection anyone coming or leaving (fig. 68).[2] Whether this was intentional or
not (given Loos's frequent use of mirrors to expand sightlines, the former seems likely),
the spatial play here is the inverse of the Goldman & Salatsch shop: it is those inhabitants
who are stationary that have the operative view, not those in motion.

The Steiner House, on the other hand, proffers a first indication of the design idea
that would rest at the core of the great majority of his later houses: the imposition of a
winding and physically exacting entry sequence.[3] This has been mostly overlooked in

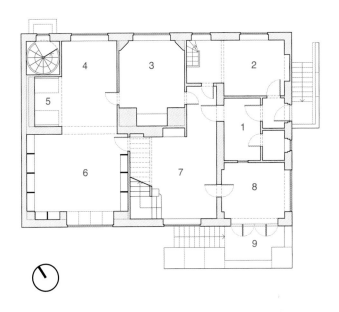

Figure 65 Adolf Loos, Scheu House, Vienna, 1912–13. Photo by Martin Gerlach Jr., ca. 1930. Grafische Sammlung Albertina, Vienna, ALA 3230.

Figure 66 Scheu House, raised ground-floor plan, 1:200. Drawing by Nicolas Allinder. 1. Vestibule; 2. Kitchen; 3. Dining room; 4. Living room; 5. Inglenook; 6. Library and music salon; 7. Hall; 8. Veranda; 9. Terrace.

opposite **Figure 67** Scheu House, stair.

Figure 68 Scheu House, inglenook.

below **Figure 69** Adolf Loos, Steiner House, Vienna, 1910; view from the rear garden. Photo by Bruno Reiffenstein. Grafische Sammlung Albertina, Vienna, ALA 2577.

opposite

Figure 70 Steiner House, salon and dining area. Photo by Martin Gerlach Jr., ca. 1930. Grafische Sammlung Albertina, Vienna, ALA 3238.

Figure 71 Steiner House, raised ground-floor plan 1:200. Drawing by Nicolas Allinder. 1. Kitchen; 2. Pantry; 3. Cloakroom; 4. Hall; 5. Foyer and library; 6. Work desk; 7. Salon; 8. Dining room; 9. Conservatory; 10. Terrace; 11. Water feature.

previous writings about Loos. For decades—nearly since the house was completed—the attention of most observers has instead been fixated on its exterior, especially its spare rear garden façade, which has been held up repeatedly—since the time of the first modernist histories by Walter Curt Behrendt and Nikolaus Pevsner—as a progenitor of the coming "International Style" (fig. 69).[4] Often commented upon, too, is the relative openness of the main living areas on the ground floor (fig. 70). But how one reaches this space is equally significant and foretelling.

The path of entry begins at the house's middle, directly from a street-side gate (fig. 71). After ascending a short flight of stairs, one comes into the house through a double door into a small vestibule. Immediately ahead, where one would expect to find the main hall, is a wall with three small windows. One is forced instead to make a ninety-degree turn, either to the left, into the kitchen, or to the right, along the principal route, into a narrow hallway that extends along the inside front of the house. At the corner, one is again forced to turn ninety degrees, this time to the left, into a small foyer (*Diele*) and library (fig. 72). Two doors in the entry hallway separate the vestibule from the foyer. Within the foyer are two seating areas: the first, along the outer wall, is placed in an inglenook; the second, along the interior wall, is wrapped with a built-in bench around a table. Just at the point where one comes into the space is a stair leading to the second-story bedrooms (fig. 73). But the main path through the house continues on the far side of the foyer, to another narrow hallway. This corridor, which extends nearly the full width of the house at its

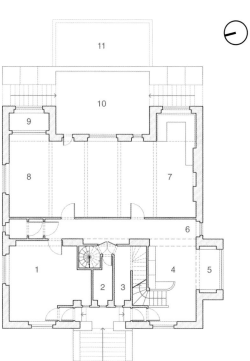

Figure 73 Steiner House, foyer and stair. Photo by Martin Gerlach Jr., ca. 1930. Grafische Sammlung Albertina, Vienna, ALA 3242.

Figure 74 Richard Norman Shaw, Shaw House, Hampstead, London, 1875. Photo by Steve Cadman.

opposite **Figure 72** Steiner House, foyer and library. Photo by Martin Gerlach Jr., ca. 1930. Grafische Sammlung Albertina, Vienna, ALA 3241.

midpoint, provides access to the salon and dining room. Anyone entering the house from the street, therefore, is obliged first to climb a set of stairs, walk a good distance, and make a minimum of four ninety-degree turns before coming into the living spaces.

One possible explanation for this rather cumbrous path rests with Loos's oft-stated desire to draw a well-defined separation between the exterior—the public domain—and the private living spaces. One could also assert that it was associated with the normal functioning of his houses, setting out places in which guests might be received, briefly engaged, or entertained for a longer period. (Each place along the path thus becomes a halting point for different types of visits, ranging from formal to informal.)

Yet it is hard to imagine that Loos did not also have in mind the same sort of affective path that he was creating at the time for the Goldman & Salatsch store. The designs for the two buildings were conceived within months of each other, and they adopt some of the same strategies: somatic involvement, the spectacle of changing light effects (from full light, to modulated light, to semidark, and so on), compression (a narrowing of the space along the route) and expansion, and the spirited concealing and revealing of what lay beyond. These strategies are perhaps more advanced in the Goldman & Salatsch store because it was far larger and more functionally variegated, but they are nonetheless quite apparent in the Steiner House. It became his first full experiment with domesticating his spatial concept.

If the idea of the affective path à la Schmarsow now occupied some place in his design thinking (whether consciously and deliberately or not), Loos almost certainly also drew on another tradition: that of the nineteenth-century English and American house. In an essay written in the mid-1980s, the German architect and historian Julius Posener—for decades one of the most discerning observers of the early modernist scene—argued (correctly, in my view) that the direct antecedents of Loos's Raumplan concept were the works of the English architects Richard Norman Shaw, Philip Webb, Edwin Lutyens, and the American H. H. Richardson. What Posener was after was how Shaw, Webb, and the others had relied on architectural devices such as two-story halls, galleries, and open staircases in the living areas of their houses. Removing walls and other barriers was for them a means to make warm, relaxed, and accommodating spaces. Such planning was also a form of release—from the constraints of what they all viewed as outdated modes of habitation and the tensions of the workaday world.[5] In most instances, the experiments of these architects were limited; only rarely would they approach the radical volumetric play of Loos's later designs. Posener, though, cites one instance of a more ambitious effort: Shaw's own house on Ellerdale Road in Hampstead, London, built in 1875.

It is a striking design even today. Half of the house is two-storied, the other half three, an arrangement that is readily legible on its front façade (fig. 74). And the relationship between the disparate zones bears a close kinship with the Loosian Raumplan. The dining room is one-and-a-half stories high, attached to it is a very low inglenook, and above the inglenook was originally Shaw's study. A narrow stair led up to his "refugium," from which he could look down on the dining space—the central room in the house—through a window.[6]

Loos, as Posener notes, was very much aware of the developments in domestic architecture in England and the United States. He knew of Hermann Muthesius's *Das englishe Haus*, the three-volume compendium of the latest in British domestic design Muthesius had written in response to his time serving as German cultural attaché in England, and he had undoubtedly seen examples of the new American house during his sojourns in New York, Philadelphia, and Chicago in the 1890s.[7] He was slow to apply these lessons to

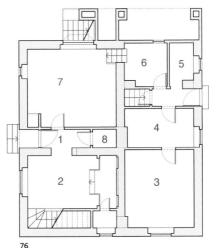

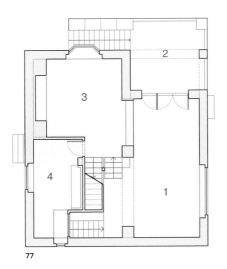

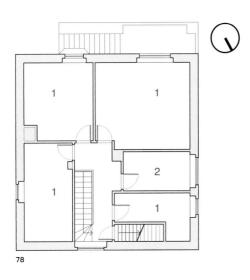

76   77   78

79

opposite **Figure 75** Adolf Loos, Rufer House, Vienna, 1922. Photo by Martin Gerlach Jr., ca. 1930. Grafische Sammlung Albertina, Vienna, ALA 3223.

Figure 76 Rufer House, ground-floor plan, 1:200. Drawing by Nicolas Allinder. 1. Entry; 2. Entrance Hall; 3. Maid's room; 4. Kitchen; 5. WC; 6. Pre-cellar; 7. Kitchen; 8. Coat closet.

Figure 77 Rufer House, first-floor plan, 1:200. Drawing by Nicolas Allinder. 1. Salon; 2. Terrace; 3. Dining room; 4. Library.

Figure 78 Rufer House, second-floor plan, 1:200. Drawing by Nicolas Allinder. 1. Bedroom; 2. Bathroom.

Figure 79 Rufer House, third-floor plan, 1:200. Drawing by Nicolas Allinder. 1. Roof terrace; 2. Bedroom; 3. Maid's room; 4. Laundry; 5. Pantry; 6. Sewing room.

his own designs, however. This was, one can imagine, in some measure because he had no suitable commissions. But it may also be that he was still working out what such lessons might mean for his own design logic. In any event, it was only at the end of the first decade of the new century that he began to pursue them in his houses and a few commercial projects.

Loos would continue to investigate the possibilities for movement and perception in his works over the next several years. They are very much in evidence, for example, in his design for the Kniže Tailor Salon on the Graben (1910–13). Similar design moves are also present in the Stoessl House (1911–13), the Horner House (1912), the Duschnitz Villa (1915–16), the Mandl House (1916), and the Strasser House (1918–19). But it was not until the early 1920s in his design for the Rufer House (1922) that Loos would at last fully ally his notion of an affective path with the Raumplan in a residential project.

The clients for the house were sugar importer Josef Rufer and his wife Maria (fig. 75). The site for the house was a small lot on the Schliessmanngasse in the western suburb of Hietzing. Unlike several of Loos's other house projects of the preceding years, which were renovations of existing structures, the Rufer House was a new construction. This allowed him to determine the structure of the house in a way that could facilitate the making of a Raumplan—something that had not been the case, for example, for the Duschnitz and Mandl houses.[8]

The house has load-bearing masonry walls along its exterior perimeter; a single, concrete pier positioned at the center of the house supports the beams and floor joists. This arrangement aided the creation of a Raumplan since floors could be readily raised or lowered by moving the horizontal supports up or down. The single central pier also to some extent determined the spatial ordering. The interior spaces of the house rise in stages, spiraling around it, until they reach the bedrooms.[9]

The form of the house is roughly that of a tall cube (10 × 10.4 × 11 meters), with the windows at many levels reflecting the complex spatial ordering within (figs. 76–79). Once more, Loos resorted to a winding path leading to the main living areas. The entry is at ground level on the east side of the house, away from the street. One enters on the north (street) side through a gate and proceeds to the middle of the east side façade. There, up a few steps, is a small, rather inconspicuous door, which opens into a vestibule; a cloak closet is positioned opposite the door. To the right—requiring a ninety-degree turn—is the

opposite **Figure 80** Rufer House, entrance hall. Photo by Martin Gerlach Jr., ca. 1930. Grafische Sammlung Albertina, Vienna, ALA 3222.

above **Figure 81** Rufer House, view from the salon toward the stair. The terminus of the stair from the ground floor is visible in the corner. Photo by Martin Gerlach Jr., ca. 1930. Grafische Sammlung Albertina, Vienna, ALA 3218.

right **Figure 82** Rufer House, view from the salon into the dining room. Photo by Martin Gerlach Jr., ca. 1930. Grafische Sammlung Albertina, Vienna, ALA 3219.

entrance hall. It is differentiated in height, with the lower portion containing a sink and separate enclosed toilet (fig. 80). The stair, the main route, is set along the house's far edge, following its outer wall. At the top of the staircase, after an abrupt turn to the left, one reaches the raised ground floor. To the right is the salon and just beyond it is the dining room (fig. 81). Here the house is open: the large pier that carries all of the floors (visible on the left in a period photograph of the view from the salon to the dining room above) is the only interruption within the space (fig. 82). The house at this point is essentially a split-level: one half of the space (containing the salon) is at one height; the remainder (housing the dining room and the library) is positioned approximately a meter and a half higher. The spaces are connected by a short flight of stairs (extending along the edge of the salon), which carries one directly into the dining room (fig. 83). From there, one could enter the library or continue upstairs, by means of a partially open staircase (fig. 84).

It should be remarked that although the path is not at all easy to describe (or imagine from a description), the actual experience of being in and moving through the house is

Figure 83 Rufer House, view from the salon to the dining room. Photo by Martin Gerlach Jr., ca. 1930. Grafische Sammlung Albertina, Vienna, ALA 2523.

opposite
Figure 84 Rufer House, view from the dining room into the salon. Photo by Martin Gerlach Jr., ca. 1930. Grafische Sammlung Albertina, Vienna, ALA 2522.

Figure 85 Rufer House, continuous plan, 1:200. Drawing by Nicolas Allinder. 1. Entry; 2. Entrance hall; 3. Salon; 4. Terrace; 5. Dining room.

natural and unforced. One quickly takes in how the spaces work. And while the house is comparatively small, it feels livable—even cozy.

The experience of being in the house is so pleasant, in fact, that it is easy to miss one of its most unusual features: some of the windows are placed in such a way (usually by raising them up) that it is difficult, if not impossible, to look outside. Loos once explained this by stating that cultured people do not spend time peering out of windows. The effect is subtle but important. Loos's rooms are often illuminated with natural light—even while the inhabitant, the viewer, cannot see directly outside, especially if he or she is seated. For an observer in motion this means that there is often a dynamic play of light in Strnad's sense, but the views, even for someone standing, are blocked or restricted, and only occasionally can he or she capture a glimpse of the world beyond. Loos's houses are in this way "interiorized"; the affective path is thus rigorously controlled and the observer's experience is focused and delimited.

The range of sensual experiences in a later Loosian house, nonetheless, is extensive—and the Rufer House despite its small size is no exception. Every movement, every repositioning of one's head offers a new vista, and the wide array of materials and surfaces presents multiple haptic stimuli. Examining a conventional plan of the Rufer House, one can see the spiraling motion of the path. What is also apparent, though, is that most of the movement is confined to one quadrant of the house. The involvement of the adjoining spaces—the principal rooms—is secondary; they become side branches—terminal points—along the route.

A continuous path plan of the house, however, discloses another feature of the movement sequence (fig. 85). The shifts, as one progresses from place to place, are decidedly sudden. Each individual segment of the path is short; the turns occur in rapid sequence; and the transitions are direct and immediate. The tight composition of the house—its constriction within the outer cubic form—compelled Loos to reduce and contain all of the movements.

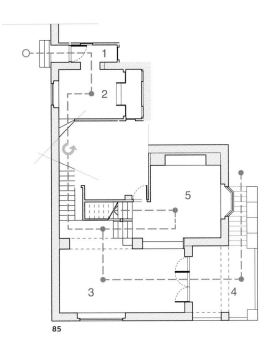

85

84

Something else is also evident in the plans and photographs of the Rufer House—and, in point of fact, in almost all of Loos's later domestic designs: although the spaces flow into each other, they are never fully open. There are always walls, columns, or other interruptions. The much freer and unconstrained spatial ordering of, for example, the later Mies van der Rohe is never in evidence. In Loos's designs, the rooms retain their separate identities, and movement from room to room takes place at their boundaries. These boundaries often assume the form of a short staircase, or they sometimes occur at a threshold. But rarely are the thresholds and the paths axially aligned. They are instead displaced, shifted in one direction or the other off an axis. And where a path might extend straight through a space—as in the foyer of the Steiner House—the connection with the next space occurs only after a complete ninety-degree turn. Every change in direction or level happens within a very tight framework; each is enfolded into a compact volume.

One might make the argument that such reduction was necessary to save space—Loos's only stated goal for the Raumplan. Yet it is nearly effortless to imagine a simpler and more spatially economical way to connect the rooms (an open stair along one edge, for example). The resulting experience, however, would have been perfunctory and uninteresting. What becomes apparent if one studies the plans of the Rufer House is that the routing of the path for Loos is an exercise in finding a compromise between three competing aims: his stated desire to save space; the necessity of making appealing and functional rooms; and his wish to contrive a powerfully affective ordering of movement. Yet these three goals are, in fact, very nearly contradictory. The imperative of saving space, for instance, is a long way from fashioning an affective movement sequence. And functionality, in the purest sense, does not align with making complex pathways. Such objectives are not easily allied.

Loos's houses of the next eight years—his most celebrated Raumplan designs—were all in some measure attempts to find solutions to these problems.

CHAPTER SIX

Experiments in Volume and Movement

In 1921, the year before Loos designed and built the Rufer House, Frank made his next important contribution to the idea of the affective path. It came in the form of an entirely modest building in a place few ever visit—a one-story school in the tiny Lower Austrian village of Ortmann.

It was Frank's first important building of the early years after the First World War. Unlike Loos, who was in his mid forties at the time of the outbreak of the conflict (old enough thus to forgo military service), the younger Frank's experience of the war, as for so many younger modernist architects, formed a decided break in his career and in his thinking. He was called up to his reserve army unit straightaway when the conflict broke out in 1914, and he spent much of the next four years in Bosnia, near what had been the border between Austria-Hungary and Serbia, constructing and repairing bridges and railway lines. He would occasionally make designs for furniture and objects during this period, but he seems to have produced not a single architectural project.

When the war ended, the fragmentation of the old empire left the economy of the new Austrian republic in ruin. Frank, having returned to Vienna, found himself with few prospects for commissions. For a time, building activity in the city nearly ceased altogether. Over the next several years, he devoted himself—as did many other progressive architects—to working to solve the postwar housing crisis. But the budgets for the government- and privately funded housing settlements he designed left no room to continue his prewar spatial experiments.[1]

His first opportunity to work on a project that was more architecturally ambitious came from one of his relatives, Hugo Bunzl. Bunzl was a cousin of his mother's by marriage. (Frank's younger sister Hedwig was also married to one of Bunzl's cousins.) He owned a paper factory in Ortmann, in the Piesting Valley in the foothills of the Alps. Frank had previously worked for Bunzl: he had built him a house near the factory in 1913–14, and

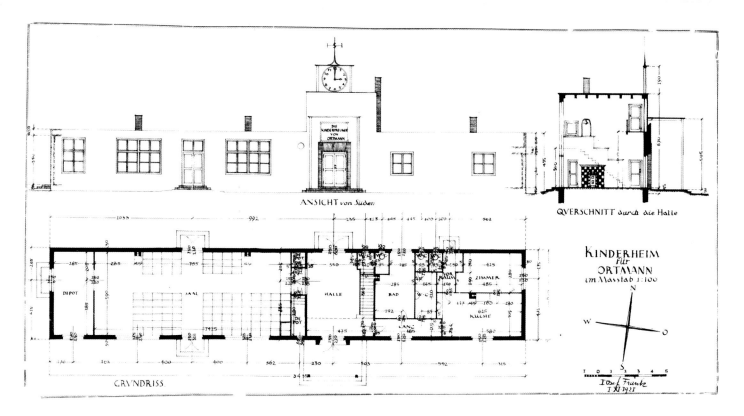

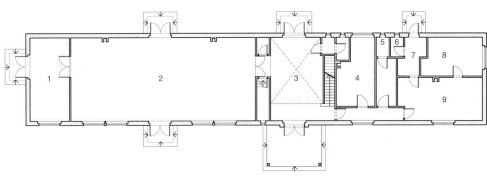

just after the war he erected two groups of row houses for the workers and their families. In late 1920, hoping to improve their lot (he earned the nickname the "industrial Red Baron" for his socially minded undertakings), Bunzl asked Frank to design a preschool for the children.[2]

What Frank created in response was one of the first fully "functionalist" (in terms of its appearance) buildings in postwar Austria, a structure of radically simplified masses and unadorned surfaces (fig. 86). Its most noteworthy feature—still arresting even now—is the centrally positioned entry block, which sports a plain porch, a brick door surround, and, above, a sundial—all set jauntily off to one side (fig. 87). The unusual composition was an expression of Frank's mounting interest in abjuring any form of regimentation.

The plan is straightforward: it consists of nothing more than an entry hall that extends the full depth of the narrow building, with a few rooms to either side (figs. 88, 89). To the left as one enters is a classroom space for the children, and beyond, a storage room; to the right are a bathroom, kitchen, and a small room for the teacher. (The structure was later expanded, altering and in some sense undermining the clarity of the original design.) A plan of such notable simplicity leaves few possibilities for spatial play. Yet Frank would

opposite
Figure 86 Josef Frank, Kinderheim (nursery school), Ortmann, Lower Austria, 1921.

Figure 87 Kinderheim, entry (detail).

above
Figure 88 Kinderheim, ground plan, elevation, and section. Private collection.

Figure 89 Kinderheim, ground-floor plan, 1:200. Drawing by Nicolas Allinder. 1. Storage; 2. Classroom; 3. Entry hall; 4. Bathroom; 5. WC; 6. WC; 7. Vestibule; 8. Teacher's room; 9. Kitchen.

Experiments in Volume and Movement

93

opposite **Figure 90** Kinderheim, entry hall.

Figure 91 Kinderheim, classroom.

Figure 92 Kinderheim, entry hall plan and elevation. Private collection.

Figure 93 Kinderheim, entry hall looking toward the stair.

introduce a number of what were then still novel ideas. Most obvious is the overall openness of the plan (a harbinger of the many modernist school buildings of coming years), the tall, well-lit entry, and the airy classroom space, which has doors directly to the outside and into the adjacent rooms (figs. 90, 91).

But there are also elements of an extended path—and in a different way than in the works of Loos or Strnad. Along one side of the entry hall is a stair (figs. 92, 93). It runs up to a door that opens out on the roof (fig. 94). From there, a second door at the rear of the same side of the entry block opens onto a catwalk inside that extends across the full length of the block to the opposite side of the roof (fig. 95).

91

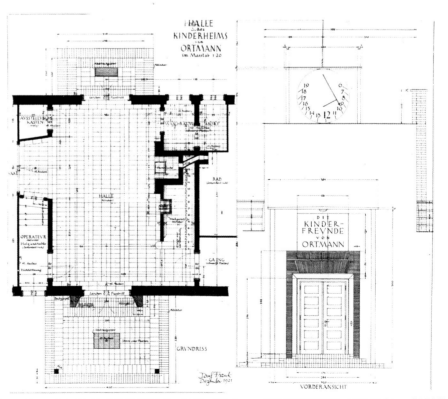

opposite **Figure 94** Kinderheim, entry block
from the side.

Figure 95 Kinderheim, drawing of the
entry hall. Alexander Koch, *Farbige Wohnräume
der Neuzeit* (Darmstadt, 1926), 60.

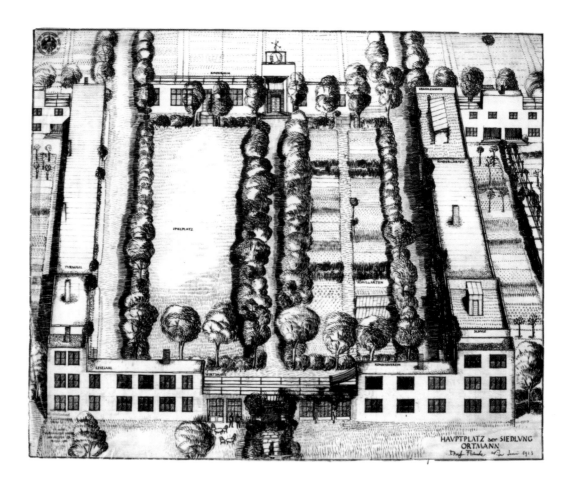

The purpose of such an arrangement is at first unclear. It appears to be discordant and impractical. Frank may have intended the two roof spaces to serve as play areas for the children—a widely promoted concept among the modernists a few years hence. But the parapets are low—far too low to offer a safe place for children to be. A drawing Frank made two years later of the Kinderheim complete with his proposed additions for a town center (which were never realized) offers a partial answer; it shows the left-hand side of the roof with railings (fig. 96). Perhaps he also envisioned railings for the other side of the roof. Whatever the case, they were never added, and the stair is now unused, piled high with boxes. Frank's intention to foster an affective path, though, is unmistakable. It would have been an amusing one: up the stairs, through a door to the outside, then up a few more stairs, back inside, across the top of the entry hall on the catwalk, and, through another door, outside again—a perfect game for children. Why it was never completed is lost to us.

What is worth remarking on is that Frank had begun to reinvestigate the concept of the extended path. His inspiration appears to have come from Strnad, rather than Loos, because the paths are protracted in the way that Strnad's are, and there are few elements of a Raumplan. What Frank made in Ortmann, indeed, is nearly the opposite of Loos's tight, interlocking spaces and the abbreviated connections between them. It is loosened, freer in spatial terms. It is also less forced, albeit no less determined.

Beyond this, what precisely Frank's intentions were for these idiosyncratic paths and spaces is uncertain. He left us no account of his thoughts, no description of his design process. How much the Ortmann school was a rejoinder to what was happening then in architecture beyond Austria—in Germany, or, for example, in Russia and the Netherlands— is impossible now to say. Frank's quirky handling of the building's front façade was surely

Figure 96 Josef Frank, project for the main square
of the workers' settlement in Ortmann, Lower
Austria, 1923; aerial perspective. Kunst-und Design
sammlung, Universität für angewandte Kunst, Vienna.

a reply to the emerging imperatives about uniformity and simplicity; beyond that we can only speculate.

The period during and just after the war was another fertile time for theoretical writing about the new architectural space. Munich architect Herman Sörgel wrote one of the principal texts. Born in 1885 (making him the same age as Frank), Sörgel studied architecture at the Technical University in Munich with Theodor Fischer (who also taught Paul Bonatz, Hugo Häring, Ernst May, Erich Mendelsohn, and Bruno Taut); he wrote not one but two dissertations, both of which were refused. Despite these setbacks, Sörgel salvaged some of the material to produce his book *Einführung in die Architektur-Ästhetik: Prolegomena zu einer Theorie der Baukunst* (Introduction to Architectural Aesthetics: Prolegomena to a Theory of Architecture), which he published in 1918 (though a good deal of the manuscript was already completed in 1914).[3] He intended it as a systematic contribution to aesthetic theory, an attempt to erect an all-embracing scaffold of thought about the subject, complete with a healthy measure of Hegelian metaphysics; it was to be one of the last such efforts in German art history to produce a comprehensive architectural theory.[4]

Sörgel's book is divided into three sections. The first is a summary and critique of previous German aesthetic and architectural theory, starting with Semper, with further, individual chapters on Friedrich Theodor Vischer, Fechner, Lipps, Wölfflin, Schmarsow, and Hildebrand; the second part examines the theory of aesthetics as it applies to architecture; and the third offers Sörgel's "practical" and "applied" recommendations for building. What soon emerges in the work is that Sörgel accepts Schmarsow's basic premise that the essence of architecture is spatial and that all architectural form is an outcome of our conscious ideas of space: "Since architecture is neither the art of masses, which is to say, sculpture, nor that of light and color—in other words painting—but is a three-dimensional, spatial art, it follows that the most fully realized spaces can exist as a self-sufficient art, without recourse to painting or sculpture. . . . Architecture concerns always and everywhere the creation of artistic space, and architecture is generated from a spatial idea (*raumliche Vorstellung*)."[5]

Sörgel also accepts the idea that human feelings and sensitivities (*seelische Gefühlsempfinden*) have a great deal to do with how we perceive and receive spatial experience.[6] But while acknowledging Hildebrand's argument about movement as an essential part of envisioning and comprehending three-dimensionality, he is not particularly concerned with how a prescribed ambulatory or path can contribute to our architectural pleasure. A significant part of the theoretical discussion has to do instead with his belief that true architectural space is the outcome of *addition*—assembling a tectonic frame around a space and thereby producing a volume—rather than subtraction (which, he contends, is how sculptors work).[7]

The question of how architectural paths should be laid out is examined in detail, however, in another book of the period, Hermann Muthesius's *Wie baue ich mein Haus?* (How Should I Build My House?), which first appeared in 1915.[8] Muthesius by that time had settled into an architectural practice in Berlin, mostly designing villas. He ostensibly wrote the book for laypeople, so that they might understand the process of building a house and speak with some knowledge with their architects. Read another way, though, the work functions as a primer for architects on the basics of building and fundamental design principles. Two chapters, "Der Weg zum Haus" (The Path to the House) and "Verkehrswege im Haus" (Traffic Patterns within the House), bear directly on the issue of the path. Muthesius writes, for instance, about the moment a guest arrives: "The door having been opened and the visitor welcomed, he must wait for some minutes before being received: Where is this to happen? Precisely in this matter the rules remain rather unresolved in German houses. . . . For this purpose the vestibule [*Windfang*, literally, "draft guard"] can suffice provided it is well appointed and supplied with a seat. The seat is understood as symbolic, no one would sit down here. But it makes the space appear comfortable and conveys the impression that one can wait there for a time."[9]

In this passage, Muthesius is manifestly concerned with the messages—the psychological impressions—a space, in this case, a vestibule, might convey: it is a place where one may wait in comfort. But in other passages it becomes evident that he is also very much concerned with the social relationships within the house, with the ways in which the servants and owners should relate to each other, and how this should be dictated by the plan of the spaces. Further on, he writes: "Two parties inhabit the house, who are intimately familiar with each other but belong to different strata of society: the gentry and the servants. An essential task of the house is to allow both parties to move freely as they wish but to divide the circulation of the gentry from that of the servants, while retaining all the connections for the maintenance of domestic life."[10]

For Muthesius, the plan of a house consists precisely of the intersection of all such moments and considerations: it is primarily—in truth, nearly exclusively—about solutions to a collection of practical problems that arise out of the patterns of daily living.

Similarly, Frank—and, for that matter, also Strnad and Loos—generated plans with an eye on such quotidian moments; they calculated and provided for nearly every type of encounter. What is missing in Muthesius's prescriptive breviary is any deeper sense of architectural involvement. He considers each separate moment, but not the full range of the experience. Frank, Loos, and Strnad, by contrast, while not neglecting such practical features in their designs (Loos, in particular, as we have seen, was especially attentive to how guests were to be received and servants accorded their own zones of movement and habitation), made their planning decisions with an eye toward the composite effect of the entire movement sequence—how each experience along the path contributes to the whole. They were attentive to everyday practicalities, but far more important for them were rhythm, texture, materiality, scale, and prospect—everything that contributes to a sense of space and place.

They appear, however, to have considered in only a very basic way the fact that in their houses there are architectural "moments" arrayed together in a sequence, that the path concerns a temporal as well as a spatial element. The notion of space-time—which had already moved from Einstein's physics into art and philosophy before the war, and in its wake had become almost a new religious doctrine—never seems to have entered their thinking.

The notion was, however, brought into the architectural mainstream in those years in two ways: through the dynamic Futurist drawings of Antonio Sant'Elia during the war, and, afterward, in the writings of the Berlin architect and theorist Paul Zucker. Born in 1888, Zucker had studied at the Technical University in Berlin and completed a doctorate with a study on pictorial space in the Florentine Renaissance. During the last years of the war, he published two essays on space and experience, "Formempfinden und Raumgefühl" (The Perception of Form and Spatial Feeling) and "Die Unwirklichkeit des Raumes" (The Unreality of Space), in which he dealt with the "artistic design of space."[11] In 1921, however, Zucker took a different tack (picking up, it seems, on Schmarsow's ideas about movement), arguing that "continuity"—essentially uninterrupted movement through space—was a better indication of space than the mere idea of it.[12] In 1924, spurred on by the discussions about the "fourth dimension" in art and philosophy, Zucker added the notion of space-time—that our perception of space happens in a temporal continuum.[13] But Zucker modified the discussion in a rather novel way: he began to discuss the "purposiveness" (*Zweck*) of a building and its relation to space. Thus, he writes about "purposeful motion" (zweckhafte Bewegung), which he insists was the true task of architecture.[14]

Zucker's argument was soon lost, but ideas of space and time, along with perspective, would go on to have a long afterlife in writings about modern architecture, none more prominently than in Sigfried Giedeon's milestone book *Space, Time and Architecture: The Growth of a New Tradition*.[15] Frank, though, was seemingly unaffected by it all. If he took any notice of the writings of either Sörgel or Zucker, he did not record it in his texts. But he would soon find a new means for making an affective path, and in a way that essentially combined what Loos and Strnad had been doing up until then.

The first instance of Frank's new approach came in an unrealized project for a house and dance school in Tel Aviv. We know nothing about the commission aside from the fact, as he notes on some of the drawings, that it was for a Mr. Ornstein, who presumably was a Viennese Jew about to move—or who had already emigrated—from Austria to Palestine. He must have asked Frank to come up with a plan for his new domicile and school there.

Only a few renderings of the project exist, but they disclose that what Frank had in mind was decidedly unlike the school in Ortmann (figs. 97, 98). The building, set into a row of conjoined houses, is nearly cubic in form, with a terraced rear and a large patio partially covered by a pergola. The plans and sections show that it is spatially far more aspiring than any of Frank's previous designs (fig. 99). It is functionally split into three

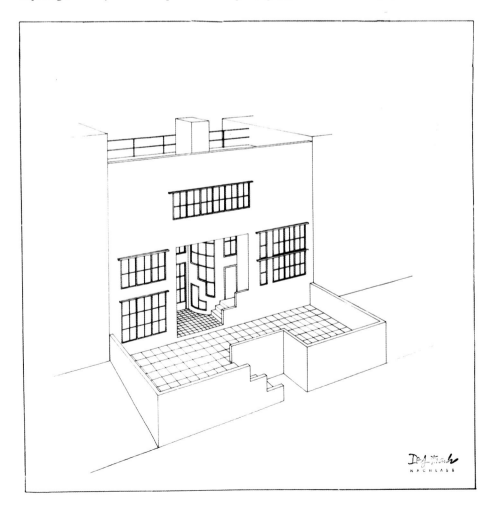

Figure 97 Josef Frank, project for a house and dance studio for Mr. Ornstein, Tel Aviv, ca. 1926; perspective, from the front. Private collection.

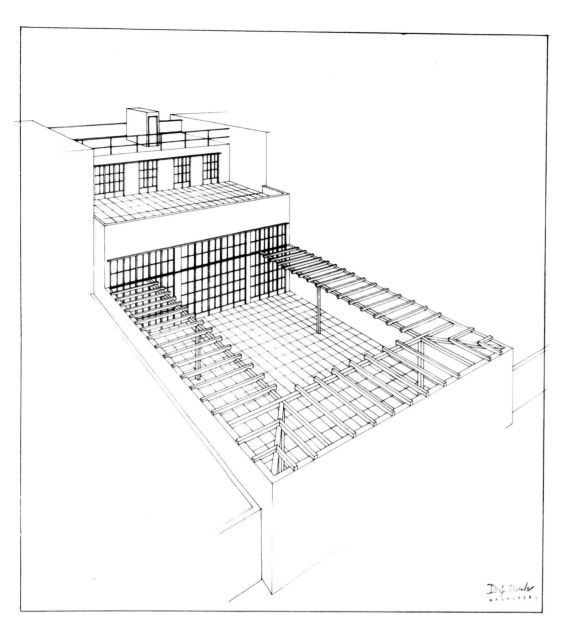

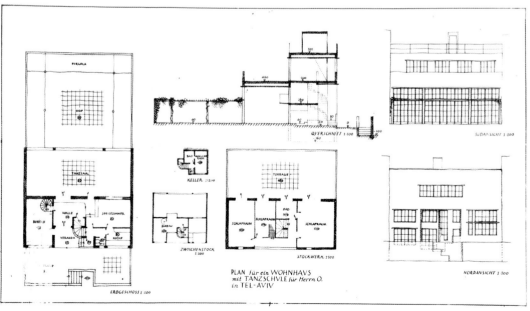

PLAN für ein WOHNHAVS
mit TANZSCHVLE für Herrn O.
in TEL-AVIV

Figure 98 Ornstein project, perspective, from the rear. Private collection.

Figure 99 Ornstein project, plans, elevations, and section. Grafische Sammlung Albertina, Vienna, Josef Frank Archiv (hereafter JFA) 17.

parts: the dance school and an office occupy much of the ground-floor space; some of the living spaces are on the lower portion and there are more living spaces on the upper floors. In accord with the building's multiple uses, there are three separate paths of entry. All begin at the street and lead up, by means of a stair positioned parallel to the house's front, to an elevated terrace. Beyond, set into the center of the front façade, is an open space—Frank labels it a "vestibule" in his drawing—with entrances on either side. The entry to the left leads into the double-height office, the one on the right to the school and house. The latter two paths diverge inside; one continues on into the large dance school in the rear, the other, down a set of stairs, to the living room.

There are several curious features to the program. The living room, dining room, and kitchen are not directly connected to the bedrooms. The access to the bedrooms instead is through the office, which means that to reach them one would have first had to ascend a spiral staircase and then a second stair at the building's center. The ground floor of the house is divided into several levels. Frank notes the height of each space in the plan with numbers (in centimeters) set into a circle. In section, it is also evident that there is a midlevel—Frank labeled it a *Zwischenstock* or entresol—positioned between the ground and upper floors. It forms the upper portion of the office and the connector with the bedrooms above. It also serves as a place of observation (from the rear, the room overlooks the dance studio).

At first view, it might appear as if Frank has merely adopted the principles of Loos's Raumplan concept. We have the interconnected volumes, the differentiated heights of the rooms, and the intricate paths linking them. Frank's approach to forming the paths is quite dissimilar, however. For one, here they are longer and more varied. The climb to what is effectively the third floor housing the bedrooms involves multiple changes of direction, in part because Frank makes use one of Strnad's tactics and repeatedly alters the routing of the stair. The somatic experience of this ascent would have been highly charged, forcing a good bit of physical engagement (perhaps not inappropriately for a dance school!). The visual experiences would have also been greatly varied, more so perhaps even than in Loos's works of the early 1920s because Frank's design presents multiple views to the outside, whereas Loos's houses are, as we have seen, relatively closed, and the vistas are decidedly concentrated on the interior.

Although the plans for the Ornstein House and Dance School are not dated, they were likely completed around 1926, or four years after the Rufer House. There is no evidence that Loos directly influenced Frank's design, though it is certainly possible that he did. The two men were on friendly terms—exceptionally for Loos, who kept a measured distance from most of the other Viennese architects—and it is likely that Frank had seen some of Loos's designs of the period firsthand, including the Rufer House.

Whatever the case, there now came a sudden acceleration in Frank's ambitions to design houses with elaborate spatial plans. Between 1926 and 1928, he produced more than a dozen such houses. All of these designs remained projects; not one of them was realized. Whether he even had prospective clients for any of the houses or whether the drawings were merely conceptual experiments is not known. For nearly half of these designs there are no surviving plans, so it is not possible to reconstruct the interior arrangements of their spaces (although the façades in many cases offer tantalizing hints at what is happening inside). Few of the drawings, moreover, are dated, so that establishing any reliable sequence for the designs is not practicable.

If Frank had indeed drawn inspiration from Loos's early Raumplan houses for the Ornstein project, several of his other designs of this period are very different from Loos's works, employing strategies that seem more advanced. This is evident in another of Frank's projects, a house described only as for "Vienna XIII."

His perspective sketch of the house suggests that it is a three-story structure, with the front portion raised on thin columns (fig. 100). The accompanying plans and section reveal that the rooms are actually arranged—if one does not count the basement—on five levels (fig. 101). Some of the variations were likely due to Frank's attempt to accommodate the house to its gently sloping hillside site by dividing it into two separate zones, with a court-yard at the center. The spaces within the two zones, however, are also differentiated in height so that the open hall at the house's center extends up to the second floor.

Once again, Frank included a winding entry sequence that continues over several different sets of stairs. The main stair is set within the courtyard, on the exterior. It separates into two principal routes: one leads into the rear of the ground floor, which houses the main living spaces; the other, extending up to the second floor, is positioned in the front portion, which contains the bedrooms. In the basement are a kitchen, pantry, and tearoom, and there is a third-floor attic with several additional rooms.

What is new for Frank is that the staircases are tightly gathered, with little space between them. Moving from one level of the house to the next would have involved taking only a few steps. This arrangement is in that sense far more Loosian than anything Frank had attempted until that time, and in his use of multiple levels is also an unmistakable echo of the Raumplan. The main difference lies in Frank's willingness to allow the envelope of the house to spread (in contradistinction to Loos's tight cubic ordering) and his intro-duction of large windows in most of the rooms.

WOHNHAUS für WIEN XIII

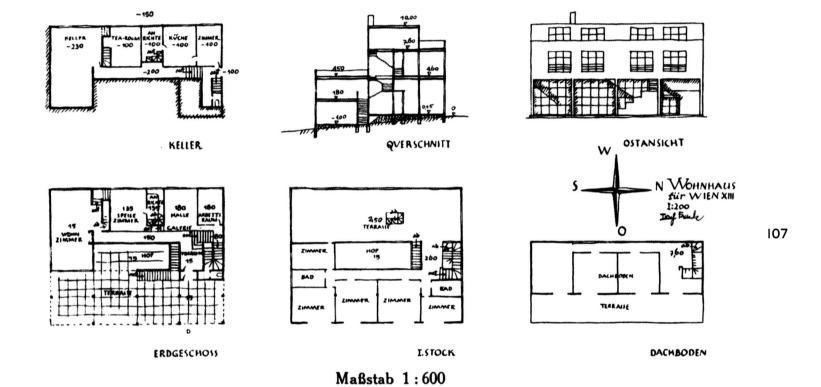

KELLER

QVERSCHNITT

OSTANSICHT

ERDGESCHOSS

I.STOCK

DACHBODEN

Maßstab 1 : 600

opposite **Figure 100** Josef Frank, project for
a house for Vienna XIII, ca. 1926; perspective.
Moderne Bauformen 26 (1927), 183.

Figure 101 Vienna XIII project, plans, section,
elevation. *Moderne Bauformen* 26 (1927), 183.

For reasons that are now unclear, Frank quickly moved away from this sort of dense planning. In two other house projects of this period, he opened up both the massing of the buildings and the connections between them. One of these is a house Frank describes only as "in Salzburg" (fig. 102). It probably dates to the same time as the House for Vienna XIII. The renderings of the two houses are very similar, and both were published together in *Moderne Bauformen* in 1927.[16]

But with even a casual glance their differences are immediately obvious. Although both are "courtyard houses" after a fashion, the courtyard of the Salzburg house is far larger. The body of the house wraps around the courtyard on three sides, and there is a large garden on the fourth. The entry from the street leads directly into the house, along a narrow hallway past the kitchen and other service spaces and into the dining room at the rear. But the main route continues to the right and up a short stair to the hall (which contains the stair to the upstairs bedrooms) and the living room. There is also a second path, up an exterior stair in the courtyard and then along the rooftops and through several terraces to the uppermost terrace atop the house's main block.

What both of these routes share is that they are extended. There are significant distances involved, and lengthy walkways separate the various rooms or stairways. The quick, almost frenetic climbing and changing of direction in Loos's early Raumplan designs has given way here to a leisurely stroll. Frank was also careful to create multiple stopping points along the way—seating areas or specific activity zones—so that what is indicated is a sort of disrupted movement, a continual starting and stopping. It was an idea that would come to be the controlling scheme for many of his later house designs.

The house project for Salzburg and several other designs that he finished in this period, however, are still relatively compact.[17] An important change in Frank's conception came in another unrealized residence, the House for H. R. S. (or in one version, S. H. B.) (fig. 103). Again, we know very little about the commission, or, indeed, if it was an actual commission. The only information we have, beyond the initials of the purported client or clients, is its location: Pasadena, California. Frank did apparently travel to the United States in 1927.[18] It is uncertain, though, whether this and two other house projects from this period, described as being for sites in Los Angeles and Columbus, Ohio, were responses to requests from people Frank met during his stay.

Whether or not Frank had a real client and site, what is significant about the House for H. R. S. is the complexity of its spatial plan as well as the way it spreads along its hillside site. Rather than using a tightly bounded envelope, he fragmented the body of the house into blocks of varied sizes and heights. Each block or segment is then slipped outward and back up the slope, adjoining it in stair-step fashion.

The accompanying plans in the only surviving rendering of the house suggest that it is a three-story affair, and, in accord with European custom, Frank labeled the three levels "ground floor," "first floor," and "upstairs." Yet if one counts the various heights of the rooms (once more shown in circles, in centimeters), there are at least seven different levels. These are connected with staircases of varied lengths; some are short, others are much longer. There are also multiple paths of entry into and through the house, but what they all share in common is a gradual climbing to the uppermost floor. The Raumplan idea is reiterated multiple times, as the rooms are shifted up or down in relation to each other. Yet it is the way in which Frank begins to attenuate the passages between the spaces, essentially by shifting the house rearward in stages up the hillside and interjecting long hallways or passages, that allows his new spatial concept to emerge. The effect is especially visible in the accompanying section, which gives one a sense of the considerable distance

WOHNHAUS in SALZBURG

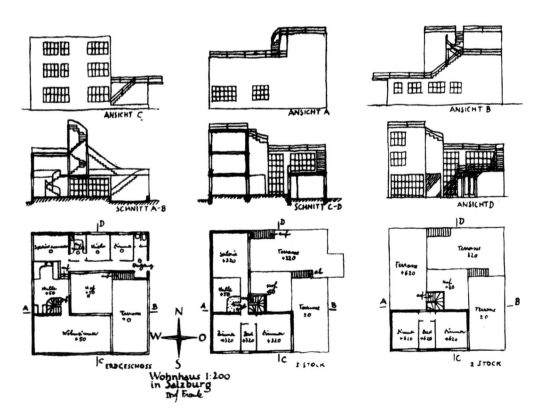

ANSICHT C

ANSICHT A

ANSICHT B

SCHNITT A-B

SCHNITT C-D

ANSICHT D

ERDGESCHOSS

I. STOCK

2 STOCK

Wohnhaus 1:200
in Salzburg

N
W · O
S

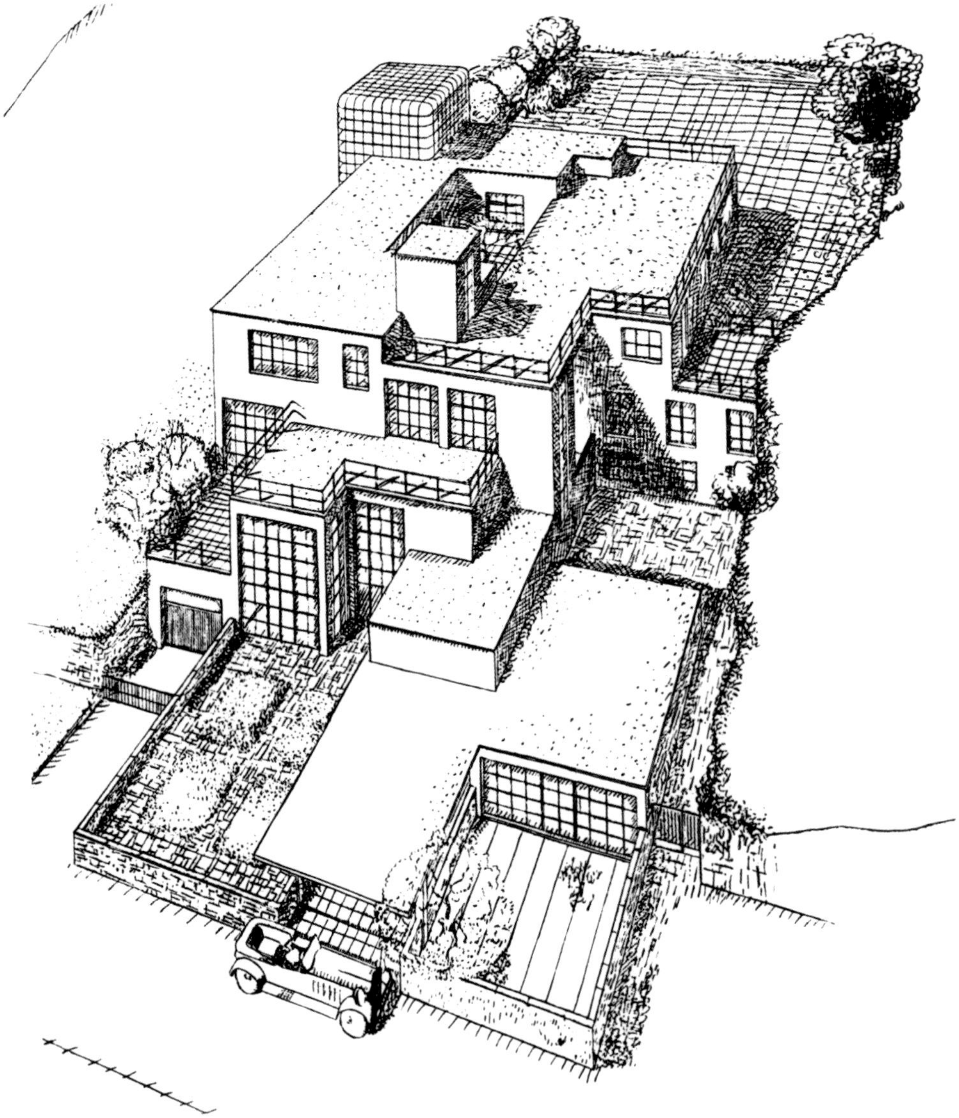

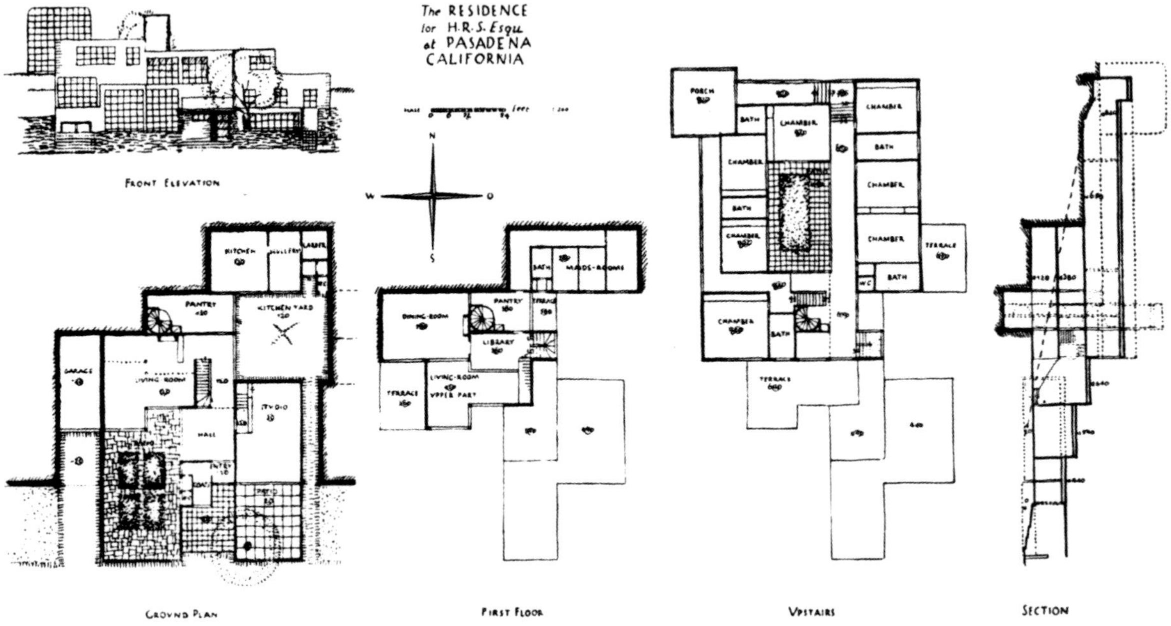
The RESIDENCE
for H.R.S. Esqu
at PASADENA
CALIFORNIA
FRONT ELEVATION
N
S
W
O
KITCHEN
SCULLERY
PANTRY
KITCHEN YARD
GARAGE
LIVING ROOM
HALL
STUDIO
PATIO
DINING ROOM
LIBRARY
TERRACE
LIVING-ROOM UPPER PART
BATH
MAIDS-ROOMS
PORCH
CHAMBER
WC
GROUND PLAN
FIRST FLOOR
VPSTAIRS
SECTION

from the street to the rearmost covered porch on the top level. The path—or more accurately, paths—are consequently extended, which would have made for a protracted architectural and spatial experience as one moved through the house. The multiple openings in the body of the house—the very large windows facing the front and several courtyards—would have also enriched the experience, giving rise to the sort of multifarious lighting effects that Strnad had prescribed a decade before. And the fact that nearly every room on the lower floors was a different size and had a separate height would have further intensified a viewer's sense of the architectonic features.

All of these ideas were still merely lines on the drawing board, however. It would be another full year before Frank would have the opportunity to realize them.

CHAPTER SEVEN

The Punctuated Path

In 1924, a little more than a year after Loos had put the last touches on the Rufer House, he decided to leave Vienna and move to Paris. His reasons had to do in part with his displeasure over the decision of the Socialist municipal authorities in Vienna to shift the emphasis of the city housing program from low-density row house settlements to high-density urban apartment blocks. Loos had headed up the housing office for several years after the war, and he was truly troubled by the idea. He had long advocated an approach that gave more freedom to the "settlers"—the city's legions of homeless or under-housed—to determine the form of their own dwellings. But he had also grown weary of the criticism he faced in Vienna, and he was irritated and resentful that grand public commissions were still not forthcoming. He wanted the chance to build important works.

In Paris, though, he found only modest success. He was lionized for his early writings and hailed for anti-ornament views, yet precious few opportunities to build came his way.[1] He completed only a single Raumplan house there, in 1926, for the Dadaist writer and poet Tristan Tzara.[2] But the next significant advance in his thinking about the affective path appeared in an entirely different project, a villa in Vienna, which he designed while still living in France.

Work on the Villa Moller, on Starkfriedgasse near the northwestern edge of the city, began in 1926 and was completed the following year. Loos made several trips back to Austria to supervise its design and construction. The client was Hans Moller, owner of a cotton mill near Náchod in what is now the Czech Republic, and his wife Anny. They were a progressive, cultured couple: Anny had studied art at the Bauhaus, and among their intimate circle of friends were Karl Kraus and Arnold Schönberg—which is doubtless how they had come to make Loos's acquaintance.

Loos gave them one of his most complete Raumplan houses, an exuberant tour de force of his spatial planning ideas.[3] But far more than that, he was able to reimagine the ways in which a dwelling might compel new perceptive and somatic sensations. For the Moller House marked the beginning of a new chapter for Loos: up to this juncture in his career the affective path had been a mostly contained and discrete portion of his planning strategies. Now he made it a far more integral constituent.

From a distance, the Villa Moller appears at once deceptively simple and strangely discordant (fig. 104). The structure is again in the form of a cube, with a large projecting front oriel. Its street-side façade, like almost all of Loos's urban dwellings, is nearly blank, a mask to shield its inner domain. But the rear side is more open, with broad terraces giving out onto a capacious garden—once more, a typically Loosian gesture, which he thought apposite for what was the private face of the house (fig. 105).

Figure 104 Adolf Loos, Villa Moller, Vienna, 1926–27. Photo by Martin Gerlach Jr. Bildarchiv der Österreichischen Nationalbibliothek, Vienna.

Figure 105 Villa Moller, rear. Photo by Bruno Reiffenstein. Bildarchiv der Österreichischen Nationalbibliothek, Vienna.

right **Figure 106** Villa Moller, entry.

115

The entry sequence resembles in some ways that of the Rufer House, tracing a line from a central opening along the front edge and the sidewall. There are, though, dissimilarities that are telling and of consequence. The main door is at the center of the house's street-side façade, under the oriel (fig. 106). Beyond is a narrow anteroom, lit by a clerestory window and a three-tiered lamp (fig. 107). To the right, the path continues up a short flight of steps; then, where it reaches the sidewall, it turns abruptly ninety degrees to the left (fig. 108). And, just as one reaches the top of this first flight of stairs, one is compelled to turn again, this time a full 180 degrees. Here, for the first time, the upstairs spaces erupt into view (fig. 109). From this vantage, it is possible to see up and through the house because Loos sliced through the walls in several places, devising several thin sight corridors.

107

109

Figure 107 Villa Moller, clerestory window and light fixture in the vestibule.

Figure 108 Villa Moller, view from the vestibule to the first stair.

Figure 109 Villa Moller, stair.

The Punctuated Path

Although the Raumplan in the Moller House is abundantly developed, it is these apertures that form the essential innovation in its design (figs. 110–13). Loos's previous houses had all essentially relied on either open staircases or fully enclosed ones. As one climbed from level to level, one could either take in the spatial spectacle fully, or it was shielded, with the spaces to be revealed only at the end. What Loos achieved with the "partial" walls of the Moller House was something quite apart: a dotted or, better, punctuated, viewing experience. The vistas open and close with each change in the viewer's position, and, because at certain moments or positions for the observer two or more of the apertures align, the prospect might be extended, only to be foreshortened or obstructed altogether again as one moves along (fig. 114). To walk up the stair, thus, is to be confronted with a series of clipped impressions, the views mixing seamlessly with the details of the house itself.

Loos achieved in this way the full dynamic realization of Strnad's idea of serial disruptions and distortions. As the subject moves upward a vista is opened, and where a partial wall intervenes, it is blocked again. The result is a layered sequence. Or, to express it

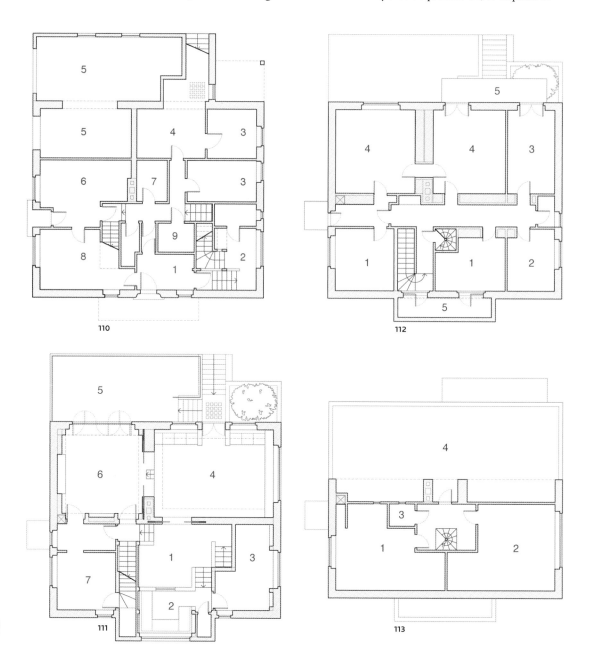

opposite

Figure 110 Villa Moller, ground-floor plan, 1:200. Drawing by Nicolas Allinder. 1. Vestibule; 2. Cloakroom; 3. Maid's room; 4. Laundry; 5. Garage; 6. Kitchen; 7. Storage; 8. Housekeeper's room; 9. Pantry.

Figure 111 Villa Moller, first-floor plan, 1:200. Drawing by Nicolas Allinder. 1. Hall; 2. Upper portion of the hall; 3. Study; 4. Music salon; 5. Terrace; 6. Dining room; 7. Kitchen.

Figure 112 Villa Moller, second-floor plan, 1:200. Drawing by Nicolas Allinder. 1. Room; 2. Bath; 3. Room; 4. Bedroom; 5. Terrace.

Figure 113 Villa Moller, top-floor plan. Drawing by Nicolas Allinder. 1. Guest room; 2. Atelier; 3. WC; 4. Roof terrace.

left **Figure 114** Villa Moller, view of raised seating area and stairs.

The Punctuated Path

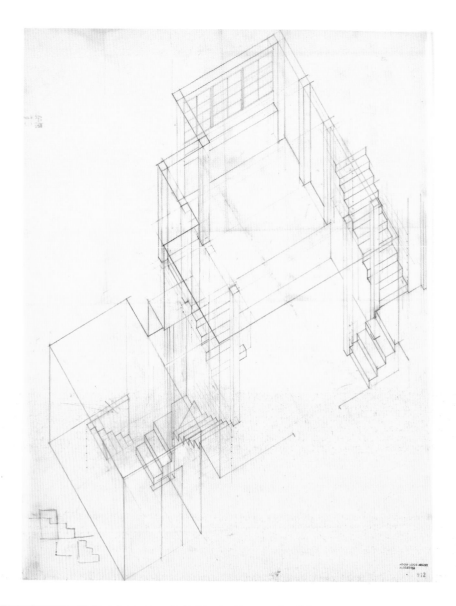

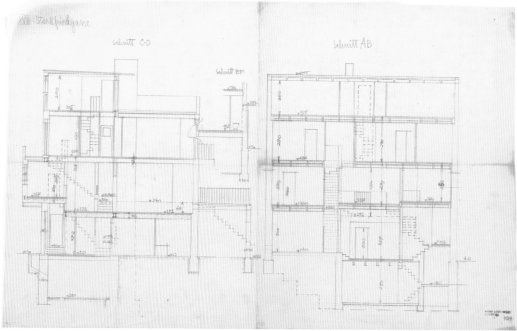

121

another way: at the very moment one begins to take in the spatial ordering there is a fluctuation of the display, and one is made to re-form or recalibrate her or his mental image. The rerouting of the Moller House's stair—the upper portion of the entry stair jogs sharply to the right—serves to reinforce this sense of constant realignment by introducing a somatic element—and, where one might touch the house's surfaces (the railings, walls, and stairs), also a haptic one. The experience of moving, looking, and touching, along with the attendant rapid changes in sensations, fosters a complete and powerful architectural engagement—even before one reaches the hall.

Loos was especially attentive to the routing of this sequence, even going so far as to have it drawn in detail as an isometric projection (fig. 115). His reason for doing this is abundantly apparent if one examines the sections, which reveal little about how the stair functions (fig. 116). It is, indeed, almost impossible to take in completely how the sequence works without the isometric view. Even while one is walking along the route for the first time, it is hard to comprehend fully. It is only after making the final turn at the top of the last flight of stairs and the hall at last becomes wholly visible that the path is completely understandable (fig. 117).

Figure 118 Villa Moller, view from the dining room
to the music salon. Photo by Martin Gerlach Jr.,
ca. 1930. Grafische Sammlung Albertina, Vienna,
ALA 3194.

opposite **Figure 119** Villa Moller, view from the
music salon to the dining room. Photo by Martin
Gerlach Jr., ca. 1930. Grafische Sammlung
Albertina, Vienna, ALA 3191.

On this main floor is a splendid instance of Loos's spatial economy, with each zone
accorded the height it requires. The hall is divided into lower and upper seating areas.
The raised portion has a lower ceiling and is effectively an inglenook, intended for more
intimate social interaction—for close and relaxed conversation—while the front space
(on the main floor level) establishes a stopping point—a brief "eddy" along the path—and
is higher and more open, suggesting only a quick and momentary stop before one
should move on.

Along one side of the main floor, facing the rear terrace, is another important destination: the music salon. Roughly a meter higher, the dining room is also positioned along
the rear wall of the house. Loos had originally drawn a nearly full physical separation
between the rooms (figs. 118, 119). The very narrow stair that he originally placed at the
edges of the two rooms was not easy to climb, a problem that later residents remedied
by converting the entire edge between the rooms into a stair (fig. 120). Loos, so it appears,
was more concerned with the visual interaction between the two rooms than with generating a practicable way of moving back and forth from one to the other. He seems to have
wanted those visiting to stroll back into the hall, and then up the short stair there before
entering the dining room. The path thus functioned one way, the view possibilities another—
a situation that is quite evident in the path plan (fig. 121).

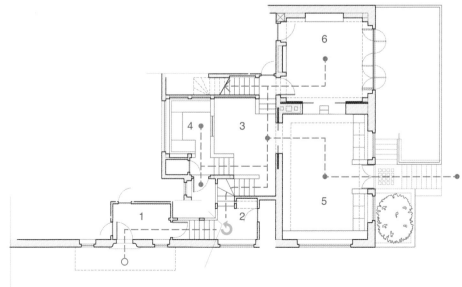

Figure 120 Villa Moller, view of the dining room.

Figure 121 Villa Moller, continuous plan. Drawing by Nicolas Allinder. 1. Entry; 2. Cloakroom; 3. Hall; 4. Upper hall; 5. Music salon; 6. Dining room.

below **Figure 122** Villa Moller, view of the stair from the dining room.

Loos's strategy of opening and closing views (and, also, the physical connections between spaces) is facilitated further through the use of doors in some of the spaces. From the edge of the dining room, for example, it is possible to look up the stair to the upper-floor bedrooms (and to the outside through the window) (fig. 122). Someone seated in the dining room can also glimpse the hall through the stair. Another sliding door in the music room enlarges the view; from several positions in the dining room, it is possible to see both sets of stairs in the hall (fig. 123). Closing one or both of the doors conceals these views. Pocket doors between the dining and music rooms permit the view to be foreshortened even more and thereby make the dining experience more intimate. Here, as ever, Loos also showed particular concern with the haptic qualities of the hardware (fig. 124). If one begins to move, all of the views come into play again. They become manifold and swiftly changing. Along the route that leads upstairs to the bedrooms, for instance, almost the entire spatial field is disclosed, including the entirety of the hall, the end of the stair from the lower story, and the stair to the library (fig. 125). After slowly, progressively laying bare the various segments of the Raumplan along the entry path, Loos provides a nearly full résumé of it.

127

opposite
Figure 123 Villa Moller, view of both stairs from
the dining room.

Figure 124 Villa Moller, detail of the pocket door
between the dining and music rooms.

above **Figure 125** Villa Moller, view of the hall
from the stair.

Figure 126 Adolf Loos, project for a house for Josephine Baker, Paris, 1927; model. Photo by Martin Gerlach Jr., ca. 1930. Grafische Sammlung Albertina, Vienna, ALA 3145. Copyright Kulka Estate, reproduced with permission of Mara Bing and the Kulka Estate, New Zealand.

Figure 127 Project for a house for Josephine Baker, plans 1:100. Drawing by Heinrich Kulka. Grafische Sammlung Albertina, Vienna, ALA 588. Copyright Kulka Estate, reproduced with permission of Mara Bing and the Kulka Estate, New Zealand.

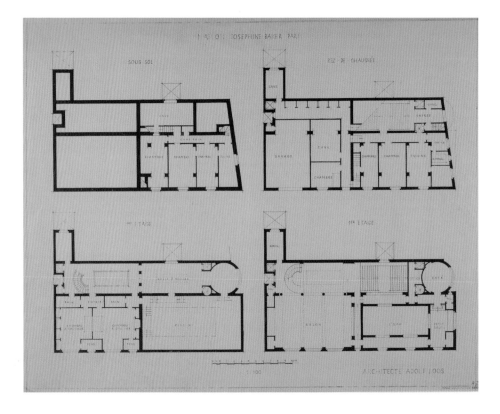

The concept of a punctuated path appears again in another of Loos's designs of this period, his unrealized house for the dancer, singer, and social activist Josephine Baker. Loos worked on the design in 1927.[4] He seems to have met Baker several years before, but quite uncertain is whether she actually commissioned him to design the house or whether he undertook the project on his own volition. (The latter, given the evidence we now have, seems more likely.) The intended site, as it is shown on some of the drawings, was in Paris, on a corner of the Avenue Bugeaud, in the sixteenth arrondissement. All that now survives of the project are a model and a few plans—documents that raise more questions about Loos's intentions than they can answer (figs. 126, 127).

Figure 128 Project for a house for Josephine Baker, ground-floor plan. Drawing by Nicolas Allinder. 1. Entrance; 2. Office; 3. Kitchen; 4. Servant's room; 5. Garage; 6. Changing rooms.

Figure 129 Project for a house for Josephine Baker, first-floor plan. Drawing by Nicolas Allinder. 1. Wardrobe; 2. Hall; 3. Office; 4. Café; 5. Petit salon; 6. Swimming pool (underwater portion); 7. Grand salon.

Figure 130 Project for a house for Josephine Baker, second-floor plan. Drawing by Nicolas Allinder. 1. Void and skylight above; 2. Salle à manger (dining room); 3. Swimming hall and ambulatory; 4. Swimming pool (water level, with skylight above); 5. Bedroom; 6. Bathroom.

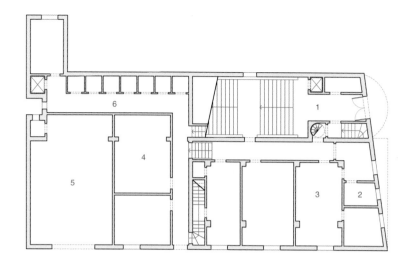

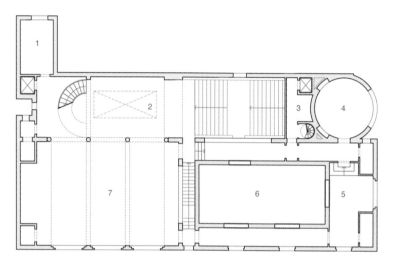

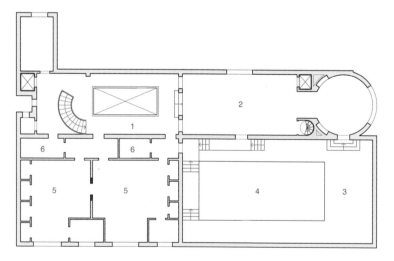

The fragmentary nature of what is left to us in the Loos archive and the dearth of other records has occasioned a great deal of speculation about the house. Largely passed over, however, has been the rather singular nature of the entry sequence (figs. 128–30). Its routing was a one-off for Loos: it was surely an experiment and, as it would turn out, one he would not repeat.

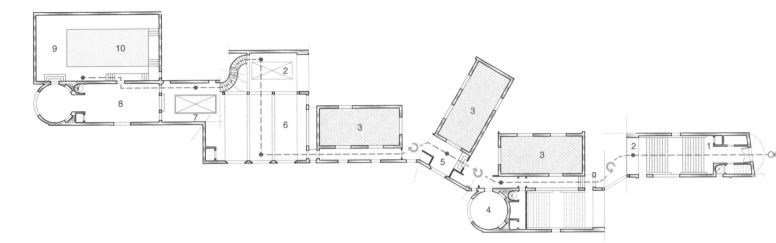

The first anomaly appears at the very outset: the double-door main entry leads to a grand stair that extends straight up to the main floor. It is broad—exceptionally broad for Loos—and absent are the twists and turns so central to his other Raumplan houses. The ceiling is also partially open to the second floor, which would have made this space unusually light and airy for one of Loos's domestic entries.

On the second floor, the stair leads directly into the hall—still along the same axis. Only here is one required to turn, slightly to the right, to reach the stair to the third floor—or ninety degrees to the left, to continue into the grand salon. Almost everything to this point is curiously conventional—hardly Loosian at all—except for the opening in the ceiling, which is illuminated by a skylight above and allows a glimpse into Baker's private sphere and the grand *salle à manger*—the dining space—on the next floor. But it is only when one continues beyond—to the indoor swimming pool adjacent to the salon—that elements of a Raumplan finally come into play. At this point, there is an extended ambulatory that surrounds the pool on all four sides: it is raised along one side; it is at the same height as the salon on two sides; along the fourth is a second stair from the ground floor, extending up from a side entrance. But the pool is not accessible from this part of the house, for its surface is up on the next floor. Instead, placed along this ambulatory are four windows, permitting an observer to peer inside into the water.

There has, in particular, been much speculation about the meaning of these windows. Some years ago, Farès El-Dahdah suggested that Loos had contrived the whole house as a voyeuristic scheme, the windows in the pool especially to gaze upon "an aquatic world in which the naked body of Josephine might dive at any moment. . . . The window becomes a tableau of Loos's own desires."[5] More recently, Anne Anlin Cheng made a similar argument: "[T]he inhabitant of the house (that is, Baker), instead of the subject securely enclosed, is the object of the gaze. Loos's usual emphasis on the primacy of interiority, instead of offering comfort and covering, here translates into theatricality and exposure."[6] Perhaps—although there is far too little evidence for any of this, and it must also be said that it is equally possible that Baker herself could have taken on the role of voyeur!

More to the point, it could be argued that the whole arrangement is both voyeuristic and exhibitionistic. It is about seeing and being seen, about movement and discovery. Because the pool is illuminated by the windows and the skylight above, its depths are visible not only from the ambulatory but also from the stair—which is given a broad proscenium— and also from the outside. Moreover, one must walk past the pool to reach two of the main spaces on this level, the *petit salon*—which is itself a sort of observatory—and the corner café. The whole arrangement is somatic, haptic, visual, and sensual.[7]

Figure 131 Project for a house for Josephine Baker, continuous plan. Drawing by Nicolas Allinder. 1. Entrance; 2. Hall with skylight; 3. Swimming pool (underwater portion); 4. Café; 5. Ambulatory and landing; 6. Bedroom; 7. Vestibule; 8. Salle à manger (dining room); 9. Swimming pool (water level); 10. Swimming hall.

Beatriz Colomina offers a perceptive reading, one that begins to suggest the multifarious nature of the space alongside the pool. In every Loos house, she writes,

there is a point of maximum tension, and it always coincides with a threshold or boundary. In the Moller house it is the raised alcove protruding from the street façade, where the occupant is ensconced in the security of the interior yet detached from it. The subject of Loos's interiors is a stranger, an intruder in his own space. In Josephine Baker's house, the wall of the swimming pool is punctured by windows. It has been pulled apart leaving a narrow passage surrounding the pool, and splitting each of the windows into an internal window and an external window. The visitor literally inhabits this wall, which enables him to look both inside, at the pool, and outside, at the city, but he is neither inside nor outside the house.[8]

Colomina is undeniably correct about how Loos creates places of great tension in his designs. But her imagined observer is fixed in place, motionless, the views static and unchanging. Loos's conception here—and, indeed, elsewhere in his later domestic designs—was assuredly intended to be dynamic. It is not only about a singular viewing experience, but also one that is constantly changing as the subject moves her or his body and head.

The third-floor plan nearly mirrors the floor below, with another ambulatory extending around the pool mostly at water level. There are also two bedrooms, and, along the side of the structure, above the main stair, is the salle à manger. On this floor, too, there are a few shifts in height and the associated short stairs. The movement sequence throughout is otherwise almost ordinary, however. Aside from the imposition of the swimming pool, the spatial play seems understated, even tentative. Compared with the Moller House, it is certainly much less developed.

What is remarkable is the manner in which the views function along the paths, and here comparisons with the Moller House are revealing. At the outset, the path in the Baker House affords little in the way of sensory experience, only what comes with the act of walking and climbing in a straight line, with mostly "ordinary" views (fig. 131). At the beginning of the ambulatory around the pool on the second level this changes abruptly. As one would have moved along the narrow corridor, the interior of the pool would come into view, only to be obscured again as one continued on. This process would have been repeated at each of the other three windows. What one would have experienced was a series of visual "shifts," a cause-and-effect sequence of views set into a temporal chain of openings and closings. On the upper floor, the visual effects continue, as movement and perception elide into a fantastical experience. We have no knowledge at all of what Loos was thinking, but it appears as if the relative simplicity of the path throughout the remainder of the house was a lead-up to this rapid alteration of images and impressions, a means for intensifying these impressions.

One other feature of the house's path is worth commenting on. Exceptionally for Loos, the paths through the house are quite long; the quick, almost frenetic shifts from place to place in his previous Raumplan houses have given way here to an unhurried stroll. This, too, was an experiment he would not repeat—again, for reasons unknown.

But the idea of an extended path does rest at the center of another house of the era, one of the most remarkable of the space-houses of the Viennese modernists: Josef Frank's Beer House.

CHAPTER EIGHT

The House as Path and Place

In the mid-1920s, Josef Frank found only scant success in realizing his many designs. **133** Although he was able to build several sizable apartment blocks for the Socialist city government of Vienna in this period, he constructed only two houses of note, one for a client in Sweden (the Claëson House in Falsterbo in the far south of the country) and a double house at the 1927 Weissenhofsiedlung in Stuttgart.[1] And neither of these houses was particularly aspiring in terms of their spatial planning.

But in 1928, or possibly as early as the autumn of 1927, he at last received the commission he had long awaited—for a large villa.

The clients were Dr. Julius Beer, owner (with his brother Robert) of Berson Kautschuk GmbH, a maker of rubber soles for shoes, and his wife Margarethe, née Blitz. They were acquaintances of Frank and his wife Anna, and close friends of Hugo Bunzl, for whom, it will be recalled, Frank had designed the nursery school in Ortmann.[2]

The site was a large lot in the Viennese suburb of Hietzing—originally three parcels of land, which Beer had purchased between 1923 and 1928.[3] Philipp Ginther, Frank's assistant at the time, remembered that the house was first planned for another site (probably a property Beer owned in the district of Lainz in the south of the city), but that they transferred it to the new site after Beer was able to secure the third of the three lots. Construction of the house began not long thereafter.[4]

The Beers were avid devotees of the city's musical culture; they asked Frank and Wlach to design a house suitable for entertaining guests and business associates and for holding musical soirées. Frank, who was again responsible for the house's design (Wlach, for his part, apparently undertook the task of installing the furniture and finishes), gave them several large, interconnected, and open living areas—splendidly suited for their needs.

From the outside, the villa closely resembles Loos's Moller House, which was being completed around the time that work on Frank's design began (fig. 132). They share the

Figure 132 Josef Frank, Beer House, Vienna, 1928–30.

Figure 133 Beer House, view of the rear.

opposite **Figure 134** Beer House, view from the northeast. Arkitekturmuseet, Stockholm.

134

same basic cubic form: both have a projecting front oriel (though in the case of the Beer House it is supported on two thin pilotis), with the rear façades opening out onto extensive terraces and balconies (fig. 133). The fenestration of the Beer House, however, seems more adamantly random (partly as a result of its complex spatial plan, partly as a result of Frank's penchant for deliberate disorder), and the depth of the house is shallower, a fact that is quite evident when it is viewed from the north side (fig. 134). Spatially, too, the houses are very different, and more importantly for our story, so are the paths (figs. 135–43).

The main entrance into the house—originally a brightly painted red lacquer door—is on the street side, under the oriel (fig. 144). (The door with the rounded-over surround to

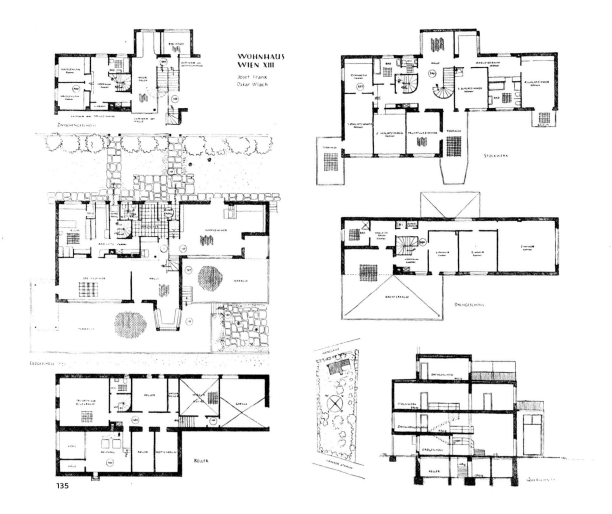

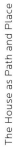

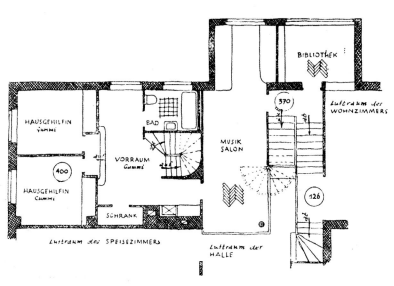

135

136

ZWISCHENGESCHOSS

136

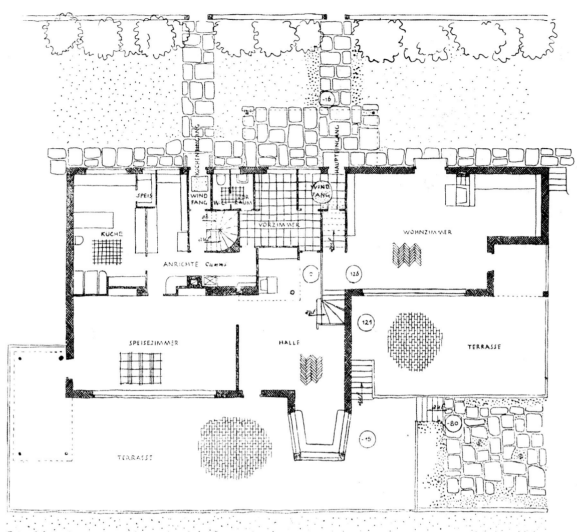

ERDGESCHOSS 1:100

137

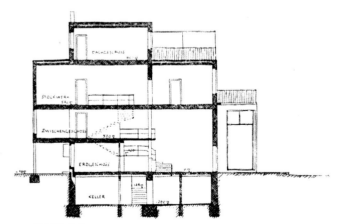

QUERSCHNITT 1:100

138

Figure 135 Beer House, plans, section, site plan. *Moderne Bauformen* 31 (1932).

Figure 136 Beer House, ground-floor plan. *Moderne Bauformen* 31 (1932).

Figure 137 Beer House, entresol. *Moderne Bauformen* 31 (1932).

Figure 138 Beer House, section. *Moderne Bauformen* 31 (1932).

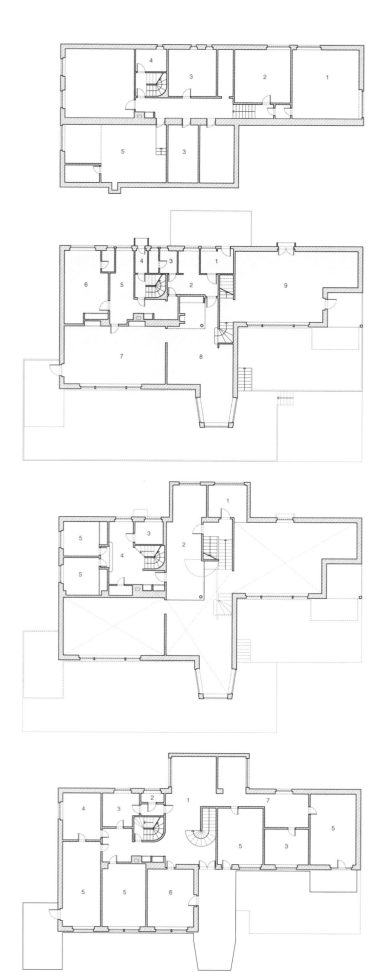

Figure 139 Beer House, basement plan. Drawing by Nicolas Allinder. 1. Garage; 2. Laundry; 3. Storage cellar; 4. WC; 5. Furnace room.

Figure 140 Beer House, ground-floor plan. Drawing by Nicolas Allinder. 1. Vestibule; 2. Cloak room; 3. WC; 4. Service entry; 5. Butler's pantry; 6. Kitchen; 7. Dining room; 8. Hall; 9. Living room.

Figure 141 Beer House, entresol level plan. Drawing by Nicolas Allinder. 1. Library; 2. Music salon; 3. Bathroom; 4. Anteroom; 5. Servant's room.

Figure 142 Beer House, upper-floor plan. Drawing by Nicolas Allinder. 1. Hall; 2. WC; 3. Bathroom; 4. Exercise room; 5. Bedroom; 6. Breakfast room; 7. Dressing room.

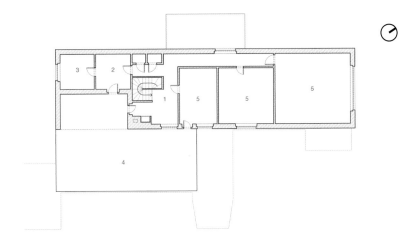

Figure 143 Beer House, attic plan. Drawing by Nicolas Allinder. 1. Anteroom; 2. Dressing room; 3. Bathroom; 4. Terrace; 5. Bedroom.

Figure 144 Beer House, front façade from the side (detail).

Figure 145 Beer House, vestibule and cloakroom. *Innen-Dekoration* 42 (1931).

opposite Figure 146 Beer House, view into the hall.

the right is the service entry and leads into the kitchen.) The route passes through a vestibule and cloakroom and then directly into the two-story hall (figs. 145, 146). To the rear of the hall is a large, glassed-in alcove, and on the left is the main stair.

The impact upon entering this space, as the critic Wolfgang Born wrote at the time, was marked and immediate: "One enters the hall [from the anteroom] through an unobtrusive door and is at once standing, surprised and moved, in the heart of the structure. The first glance instantly offers a clear understanding of the entire arrangement." This impression is enhanced by the impact of the open stair, Born continues, "which simultaneously reveals all of the levels of the house."[5]

Standing in the center of the hall, one can see on the one side into the double-height dining room and on the other to the stairs leading up to the living room (figs. 147, 148). Looking back toward the entry and the front of the house, the continuation of the stair is visible, and just above it is the projecting entresol containing the music salon and other spaces (fig. 149). At this point, as Born noted, the whole lower spatial field can be observed. Frank's concept for the house is also immediately apparent: from the music salon above, which had a Bösendorfer grand piano, music can be heard throughout the living areas, from the dining room up to the living room. It is a perfect arrangement for musical performance and enjoyment.

Figure 147 Beer House, dining room.

opposite **Figure 148** Beer House, view of the lower portion of the stair leading to the living room. MAK—Österreichisches Museum für angewandte Kunst / Gegenwartskunst, Vienna.

Figure 149 Beer House, stair from the hall.

Figure 150 Beer House, view from the living room toward the hall. *Innen-Dekoration* 42 (1931).

opposite
Figure 151 Beer House, music salon. *Innen-Dekoration* 42 (1931).

Figure 152 Beer House, tearoom. *Innen-Dekoration* 42 (1931).

What is also graspable *a prima vista* is Frank's concept for the path. The stairs function as a means for joining the house's spaces, but they also lead to stopping points along the way. The hall is the first of these stopping points; the living room, positioned about a meter and a half higher, is the second (fig. 150). Above is the third, the entresol, which contains the music salon and tearoom, as well as a library (the latter two rooms extend into the lower level of the oriel) (figs. 151, 152). Beyond is the villa's private sphere—two floors housing the bedrooms, an exercise room, and other spaces.

The elaborate progression was the result not only of Frank's "musical program," but it was also, as Born had hastened to point out, an attempt to make a visually and physically affecting experience. "The essence of this design," he writes, "is the complete dissolution of all the usual spatial conventions of boxlike rooms, not only in the horizontal sense, in plan, but also in a vertical sense."[6] Yet, at the same time, Born notes, the complex "interior

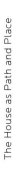

145

spatial configuration . . . arises organically out of the circumstances of 'living'"—as a direct response to the needs of its occupants.[7] The effect, he observed, was subtle but noticeable: movement through the house produced "a wonderful sense of relaxation . . . just as the inglenooks invite one to rest, the stairs induce one to climb. But how easy this upward movement is! New views, new surprises constantly present themselves, until one reaches one of the roof terraces (perfectly adapted for sunbathing), which provide the definitive fusion of interior and open-air spaces. Striding through [the house] provides one with an inexhaustible, resounding experience of space."[8]

In 1931, a year after the house was completed, Frank published an essay he titled "Das Haus als Weg und Platz" (The House as Path and Place), in which he discussed the ideas that guided its design.[9] He had, he explains, conceived of the Beer House as a city in miniature, with traffic patterns and designated areas for specific activities. "A well-ordered house," he wrote, "should be laid out like a city, with streets and alleys that lead inevitably to places that are cut off from traffic, so that one can rest there."[10] Frank emphasized that these paths should follow natural traffic routes, as in the cities of the past, not a simple grid.

> In earlier times—especially in England, to which we owe the modern house form—such arrangements were traditional for cities and houses, but today this tradition has largely died out. The well-laid-out path through the house requires a sensitive understanding, and the architect cannot begin anew, which is why it would be important to revive this tradition. It is of the utmost importance that this path is not marked by some obvious means or decorative scheme, so that the visitor will never have the idea that he is being led around. A well-laid-out house is comparable to one of those beautiful old cities, in which even a stranger immediately knows his way around and can find the city hall and the market square without having to ask.[11]

He insists that every aspect of the plan should contribute to this impression:

> As an example of this, I would like to stress one very important element of the house plan: the staircase. It must be arranged in such a manner that when one approaches and begins to walk up to it one never has the feeling that he has to go back down the same way; one should always go further. If a house has more than two stories it is essential to consider what significance these stories have; if the third story is merely an attic, the flights of stairs should not be placed one above the other because that would awaken the feeling of an apartment block and one would never know when he had arrived. On the other hand, if this second level is a roof terrace, then it should be closely connected with the living areas, and the stairway should be separated as much as possible from the second-story bedrooms. Every twist of the stairway serves to heighten this feeling of continuous movement, not to save space. The largest living space, measured in square meters, is not always the most practicable, the shortest path is not always the most comfortable, and the straight stairway is not always the best—indeed hardly ever.[12]

Frank's language in the essay recalls Viennese urbanist Camillo Sitte's influential text on city planning, *Der Städtebau nach seinen künstlerischen Grundsätzen* (City Planning According to Its Artistic Principles), first published in 1889.[13] In the book's introduction, Sitte writes, for example, of "beautiful vistas" that "all parade before our musing eye, and we savor . . .

the delights of those sublime and graceful things."[14] Like Frank, Sitte must have been influenced by the same earlier theoretical discussions about space and subjective response; he was especially keen to consider how older cities—most of the examples he cites are in Italy—should be studied for the psychological lessons they might offer about our experiences of urban space.[15] He very soon emerged as a leading critic of regularity and uniformity in urban planning, and he became an oft-cited authority by those who rejected "straight streets" and urban regulation.

Sitte's ideas were also very likely a key influence on Frank's thinking. Whether he first read Sitte's book at this time, reread it, or simply recalled it, Sitte's concepts seemingly carry over into his design. Sitte repeatedly stresses the use of "organic" curving streets and irregularly shaped squares; Frank appears to have adapted Sitte's ideas of the ideal cityscape for the domestic sphere, translating his urban ideas to a smaller, more intimate scale.

Yet there is another possible source for Frank's ideas, one also very close to his interests: Leon Battista Alberti. In the fifth book of his *De re aedificatoria* (On the Art of Building), Alberti writes in a similar manner about spatial planning: "The atrium, salon, and so on should relate in the same way to the house as do the forum and public square to the city: they should not be hidden away in some tight and out-of-the way corner, but should be prominent, with easy access to other members. It is here the stairways and passageways begin, and here that visitors are greeted and made welcome."[16]

This could be a nearly faultless description of the paths in the Beer House (here, though, it must be said that Frank, unlike Sitte, for example, always thought of such experiences as *individual*; he was seemingly unconcerned with the notion of collective or public experience, an outlook that Strnad and Loos also shared). But whatever the source for his notion of the relationship of city and house, Frank came increasingly to disregard the call of those architects of the time who wanted to rationalize the built world; he sought instead to create within the house natural, comfortable, and aesthetically pleasing spaces.

It was in the artist's garret instead that Frank found his direct model. He writes:

> The modern house is descended from the old bohemian studio in a mansard roof space. This attic story, condemned by the authorities and by modern architects alike as uninhabitable and unsanitary, which property speculators wrested with great effort from laws enacted to prevent its existence, which is the product of chance, contains that which we seek in vain in the planned and rationally furnished apartments below it: life, large rooms, large windows, multiple corners, angled walls, steps and height differences, columns and beams—in short, all the variety that we search for in the new house in order to counteract the dreary tedium of the regular four-cornered room. The entire struggle for the modern apartment and the modern house has at its core the goal of freeing people from their bourgeois prejudices and providing them with the possibility of a bohemian lifestyle. The prim and orderly home in both its old or new guise will become a nightmare in the future.
>
> The task of the architect is to arrange all of these elements found in the garret into a house.[17]

Frank's own experience in his Wiedner Hauptstraße apartment no doubt had shaped his ideas about the garret and irregular spaces. Yet the plan of the Beer House is more than an assemblage of random or accidental elements. The entire space within is meticulously organized and segmented, with little left to chance. Among the principal divisions is a clear demarcation of the functional and living precincts. The kitchen, pantry, and housekeeper's quarters are confined to a two-story section on the western corner, with their own entrance and stair (fig. 153).[18] They are joined, in turn, with the dining room, music salon, and upper-floor bedrooms by a series of discretely placed doors. The whole constituted thus a continuation and elaboration of the path.

Within the house itself are two further divisions, one between zones of movement and repose, and the other between the public and private spheres. Frank had previously employed walls or stairs to achieve a separation between spaces of transit and those of stasis. But in places in the Beer House this division is merely intimated so that the two merge formlessly. In the main entry sequence, for instance, the cloakroom is positioned to one side and framed by walls, providing an eddy in the circulation flow. As one enters the hall, a variety of possibilities opens up: one path leads to the rear alcove, another continues up the stairs to the living room and beyond. An additional path, subtly indicated, goes to the right, to the inglenook underneath the gallery of the music salon. Yet another route takes one to the dining room or out into the open area of the hall. Although each path is immediately evident, it is only casually "signed."

These paths invariably terminate in casual sitting areas, the "piazzas" of the house—in German, *Plätze*—places or squares. They have a dual character: they are relaxed but they are also the products of precise manipulation. Paradoxically, the sense of comfort

opposite **Figure 153** Beer House, service stair on the entresol level. MAK—Österreichisches Museum für angewandte Kunst / Gegenwartskunst, Vienna.

Figure 154 Beer House, living room.

that pervades the house is the outcome of two seemingly opposite courses of action: a laissez-faire attitude and supreme control.

But control in Frank's Beer House means something different than it does in Loos's domestic Raumplan spaces. In decided contrast to Loos's houses, the Beer House's spaces are more open—both to the outside and to each other. There are large windows on the rear, and the visual field (for example, through the large window of the living room) extends outward—a condition, as we have seen, that is rare in Loosian villas (fig. 154). Frank also exploits windows—and the reflections they make—to foster a sense of spatial complexity and play. (Loos had done this early on in his designs using both windows and mirrors: the Kärntner Bar, the entry to the Looshaus, and the living room of the Scheu House come to mind here, though he mostly abandoned the idea later on.) Even more notable, however, is the relative openness of the Beer House's interior. Standing at the door of the living room, just off the landing, one can look outward and see almost all of the downstairs living spaces; the music salon on the entresol; and, through a small aperture at the top of the stairs, the upper floor, where the stairs terminate (fig. 155). In contrast to Loos's tactic of cloaking and revealing, Frank permits one to see—as Born described very well—nearly the whole of the Raumplan in action. The path extending up the main stair serves to normalize the experience of moving through what are in fact quite convoluted spaces, making the ascent—in actual fact, the entire experience—unhurried, gentle, and restful. In most Loosian villas of the 1920s, walking up and through the spaces is an activated and demanding experience; in Frank's Beer House it is more of a leisurely amble, with many resting places

opposite **Figure 155** Beer House, view of the entresol and hall from the living room.

Figure 156 Beer House, continuous plan. Drawing by Nicolas Allinder. 1. Vestibule; 2. Cloakroom; 3. Hall; 4. Dining room; 5. Living room; 6. Music room.

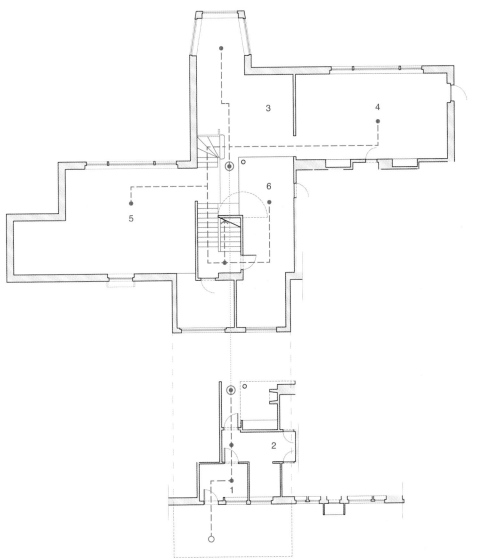

along the way (fig. 156). Most of the paths are fixed and prescribed—hence the control. Frank also sought to determine the inhabitant's pace: here and there he seems to want to invite her or him to slow down, persuading the subject to see, imagine, and feel. But the itinerary in the Beer House is less apparent than in Loos's domestic works; it is not so much written in the architecture as it is sensed.

Here we come to one other principal difference between Loos and Frank in this period. It is articulated in formal terms, in the specific way in which their rooms are ordered. In short, Loos shows far greater rigor in this respect.

The American art historian Debra Schafter—and Czech art historian Lada Hubatová-Vacková after her—suggested that Loos's tight spatial compositions owe something to the lessons in making ornament that he received in his early years while studying in Reichenberg (Liberec) and Brünn (Brno). Schafter writes that Loos, early in his career, had intuited "that the spatial and structural plans of architecture and applied art had gradually begun to absorb the principles worked out in ornament theory and practice."[19] Hubatová-Vacková extends this argument, suggesting that Loos took over the idea that spatial composition (*Raumgestaltung*) and the making of ornament both had at their basis the same themes: "temporality, rhythm, movement, and corporeality." For Loos, she writes, the Raumplan was "not the functional and economically efficient arrangement of accommodation

Figure 157 Beer House, stair viewed from the entresol.

opposite **Figure 158** Beer House, upper-floor landing.

that the modernists were arguing for. Instead, it seems to be a spatial rhythmizing of movement, an abstract transcription of deliberately intricate trajectories of motion. Instead of a 'machine for living,' Loos's Raumplan was more a kind of kinaesthetic and optical play in manipulating space . . . the spatial image of the building's interior is gradually transformed and is composed of the ensuing sequences of images by constantly walking through, descending and ascending and by the psychophysiological use of the space. The architect imposed this rhythmized choreography on the villa's inhabitants. The interior's main theme is virtual movement."[20]

One could expand this line of thinking in another way: the plans of Loos's villas themselves depict a sensibility informed by the logic of making ornament as it was developed in the later nineteenth century. The tight, spiraling forms of many of Loos's houses—or, equally, his reasoned division of the cube into discrete parts—owe something to the sort of pattern-making that every architect of his generation absorbed as a student. If one examines Loos's plans carefully, the "spatial rhythmizing of movement" that Hubatová-Vacková describes becomes apparent not only in the movement sequences, but also in the manner in which the lines of his designs are laid down. Ofttimes, as Hubatová-Vacková notes, they are "picturesque," infused with an older idea of poetry—though, one should add, they are always considered and ordered.[21]

Frank, by contrast, though he demonstrates the same interest in the choreography of movement, usually opts for a much looser ordering. His "dance," while also considered, is mostly liberated from the constraints of traditional patterning—often, it appears, deliberately so. Frank, in keeping with his aversion to systems and systematic planning, wanted to foster a stroll, one that was still largely predetermined but that did not follow the same sorts of strictures and restraints.

What Frank does share with Loos is his insistence on drawing a separation between the public and private domains. For Loos, this usually means shielding the private upper spaces through walls or abrupt turns in the stair. In the Beer House, Frank continues the openness of the space on the upper portion of the main stair. But he uses a subtle shift in its routing to indicate the transition (figs. 157, 158). In "Das Haus als Weg und Platz," he describes the thoughts behind each segment of the stair: "One enters the hall facing the stair. The stair, which turns outward into the room, presents its first step to the person entering. When he begins to climb upward, he can see up to the first landing and through a large opening into the most important room in the house, the living room. From this level, the stair leads straight up to two rooms, the study and salon, which are concealed from the living room but closely connected to it. At this point, the level housing the main living areas comes to an end. To emphasize this fact, the stairs leading up to the next floor containing the bedrooms wind in the other direction, and a clear division of the house is achieved."[22] The partition of the stair resulted from an alteration of the traffic pattern, rather than by means of a physical barrier or an obvious sign. It arose, as Schmarsow had suggested, from experience, one that both informed and directly involved the occupant.

The design of the Beer House departed from Loos's practices in one other important way: the Raumplan and path continue on its exterior. On the villa's rear are stairs and terraces of varying heights that mimic the spatial play within (fig. 159). The process of strolling and resting carries on here; in the summer months, when the doors could be opened, the experience would have been unbroken, as one moved from the inside to the outside and back inside again. The terraces and balconies also represent a continuation of the path on the house's different levels, each a terminus of its own. Although the possibilities for exte-

Figure 159 Beer House, view of the rear.
Der Baumeister 29 (1931).

rior movement are not as developed as they are, for example, in Frank's Salzburg House project, they are still quite varied.

Frank, though, was not fully satisfied with the spatial solutions in the Beer House. By the middle of 1930, if not before, he had begun to rethink some of his basic design assumptions, in particular his allegiance to standard orthogonal planning. The shift is already apparent in "Das Haus als Weg und Platz," which he probably wrote in the spring or early summer of 1931. He had intended his essay as a statement of his design aims for the villa. But partway through the process of writing he had, it seems, a change of heart, for contained within it are references to the idea that would come to define his architectural philosophy: his growing allegiance to nonorthogonality. "The regular four-cornered room," he writes, "is the least suited to living; it is quite useful as a storage space for furniture, but not for anything else. I believe that a polygon drawn by chance, whether with right or acute angles, as a plan for a room is much more appropriate than a regular four-cornered one. Chance also helped in the case of the garret studio, which was always comfortable and impersonal. Practical necessities should never be an inducement to subvert formally a carefully planned layout because the viewer cannot understand its meaning, and, besides that, it is part of the architect's art to bring form and content into a harmonious balance."[23]

After more than a decade and a half, Frank had at last returned to his earlier ideas about complexity and nonorthogonality. At the same time, he was intent that such designs should be natural and unforced. His statement about "practical necessities" not subverting a layout seems to be a swipe at the "functionalists." Yet he also rejects Strnad's ideas about using furniture to enhance the architectonic features of his houses.

155

Time and again, the regular four-cornered room misleads us into making architecture with furniture. One wants to use built-in elements, striking color schemes, and cubic forms to break up and articulate the banal space and to give it some character. The task of the architect, however, consists of creating spaces, not in arranging furniture or painting walls, which is a matter of good taste, something anyone can have. It is a well-known fact that in well-designed rooms it does not really matter what type of furnishings there are, provided that they are not so large that they become architectural elements. The personality of the inhabitant can be freely expressed. The space will emphasize those areas where every place and path should be.[24]

Often forced to work in conventional four-cornered spaces when he and Wlach were called on to install interiors, Frank had been compelled to ameliorate the rigidity of the spaces with a free placement of furnishings. But he began to think at this time about alternatives in spatial planning, and illustrated in the article are three variant plans for a project for a house in Los Angeles.

It is described on the drawings only as the "Residence for Mr. M. S.," without any further information. The only clue to its siting comes from the fact that in all of the designs the rear of the house (or portions of it) are somewhat higher than the front, meaning that it was intended for a gently sloping lot. Some of the drawings are dated—1930—meaning that Frank was probably working on the project while the Beer House was still being completed. The overall outlines of the three schemes are similar. They show a rambling, mostly one-story house arranged around one or more interior patios. In two of the schemes (which according to a note by the editors represent the second and third designs), Frank

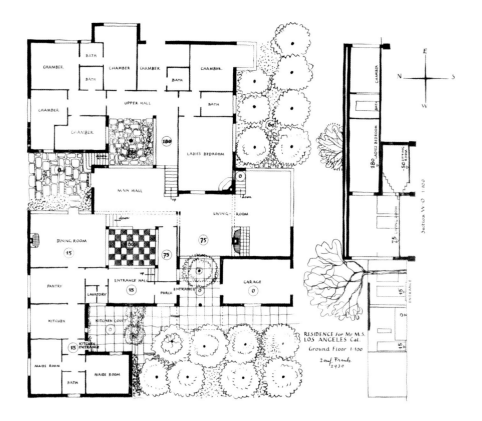

Figure 160 Josef Frank, project for a house for M. S., Los Angeles, 1930; second version; plan and section. *Der Baumeister* 29 (1931): plates 82–83.

opposite **Figure 161** Los Angeles project, third version, plan and elevation. *Der Baumeister* 29 (1931): plates 82–83.

employed conventional orthogonal planning (figs. 160, 161). He staggered and shifted the rooms, however, shaping a complex network of spaces, paths, sitting areas, and terminal points. To enhance the rambling effect of the plans, he also raised or lowered portions of the houses.

Movement in these two house projects would have required repeated abrupt turns because in contrast to the Beer House the paths are often abbreviated. In point of fact, the movement sequences in both cases are highly condensed. The routes also are strictly determined; the relative freedom of movement in the Beer House—especially on the ground floor—is absent. In most cases, the rooms retain their separate identities, and passage from one room to the next occurs at the thresholds, which are sometimes displaced— "slipped" off any apparent axes. It is as if Frank had laid out the individual rooms on a mostly horizontal plane and then slid or shuffled them around, altering their positions relative to each other.

What is also fundamentally new is the way in which he inserted open spaces—small courtyards and patios—into the plans. He had experimented with this idea before—for instance, in the houses for Vienna XIII and H. R. S. in Pasadena—but on a far more limited basis. The two orthogonal versions of the House for M. S. have numerous such insertions, and they form an essential organizing scheme. Groups of rooms—mostly those with the same functions (entry, living, dining, service, bedrooms, and so on)—are arranged around these "openings." This device serves to divide the plans in a logical and practical way. But because there are also large numbers of windows looking into each patio or courtyard, these insertions serve to add complex lighting effects. In places where there are first walls and then openings, the lighting effects are punctuated, as are the views.

The paths in the second and third schemes function in similar ways. They require multiple right-angled turns as one weaves one's way into and through the interiors. Along the paths are numerous stopping points, in inglenooks or other sitting areas. The overall

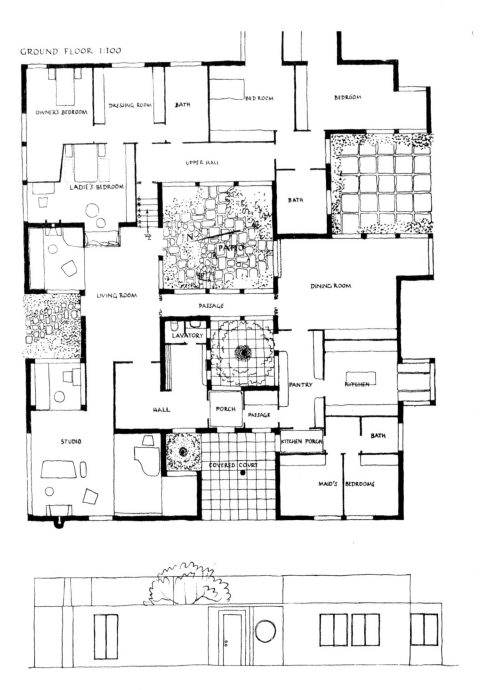

GROUND FLOOR 1:100

OWNER'S BEDROOM | DRESSING ROOM | BATH | BED ROOM | BEDROOM

UPPER HALL

LADIE'S BEDROOM

BATH

LIVING ROOM

PATIO

DINING ROOM

PASSAGE

LAVATORY

HALL

PORCH | PASSAGE

PANTRY | KITCHEN

STUDIO

KITCHEN PORCH | BATH

COVERED COURT

MAID'S BEDROOMS

157

effect, though, is a meandering path through what one might describe as a warren of rooms. The complexity arises in large measure not from the shifts in level or from the differing heights of the rooms but from the circumstance that nearly every axis is quickly interrupted, as are any direct sightlines. Walking through the spaces would have produced a layered sequence of experiences and impressions—richer perhaps even than those of the Beer House. Absent, on the other hand, is the latter's clarity and legibility. The paths in the two projects might have seemed, as Frank hoped, like a stroll through an old city, but one whose plan was not as immediately comprehensible to the visitor.

The first of Frank's three schemes for the House for M. S., however, departed considerably from the other two schemes—and from his previous residential designs (fig. 162). Although the outer footprint is similar to the other two M. S. designs, Frank abandoned right-angled planning, introducing instead curvilinear and oblique lines that produced a series of irregular spaces.

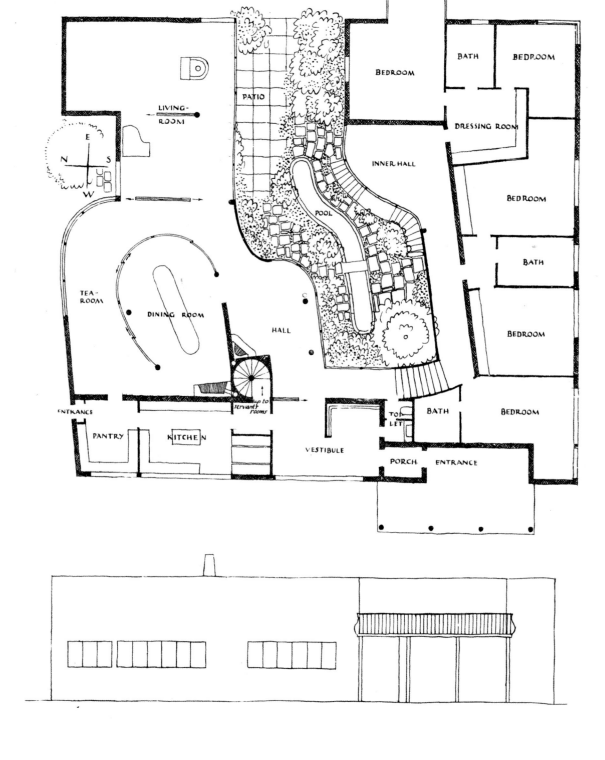

Within the plan:
BEDROOM, BATH, BEDROOM, DRESSING ROOM, BEDROOM, BATH, BEDROOM, BEDROOM

BATH, TOILET

PATIO, INNER HALL

LIVING-ROOM

POOL

N E S W

TEA-ROOM, DINING ROOM, HALL

up to servant's rooms

ENTRANCE

PANTRY, KITCHEN, VESTIBULE, PORCH, ENTRANCE

The mostly one-story house is in the form of a U, with the open side facing the rear. At its center is a serpentine patio arranged around a long "pool." The main body of the house is divided into three functional zones: a service area on the northwest corner (with servants' quarters below); the living spaces—dining room, tearoom, and living room—on the northeast; and a bedroom wing, which takes up the entire south side. The bedroom wing is slightly raised, about a meter and a half, so that it rests slightly above the patio on that side.

The path commences at a four-columned portico, leading first into a small porch, then into a larger vestibule. Upon entering this space, one would have seen an open cloak area to the right. A ninety-degree turn brings one into the elongated hall, the first of the house's nonorthogonal spaces. Directly beyond is the living room; to the left are the dining area and tearoom. Framing the dining space is a long, arcing screen. The screen, whose form is echoed by the outer wall of the tearoom, in turn is divided into separate movable panels, permitting the room to be configured in a number of ways. The dining room, thus, could have been made nearly fully enclosed, almost entirely open, or something in between. By making the panels adjustable, Frank envisioned an active plan, which would have also allowed for variations in the path. He repeated the same idea at the intersection of the dining and living areas, positioning there a straight sliding door of similar construction, which would have also multiplied the spatial and movement possibilities. Long, continuous windows situated along the outer wall of the tearoom / dining room and the inner walls— facing the patio—of the tearoom / dining room and living room would have made for manifold and affective lighting and viewing effects. In combination with the irregular and bending edges of the spaces, Frank sought to weave a highly variegated set of architectonic experiences.

The complexity of this main path is reiterated in the bedroom wing. The path begins in the hall and continues up a short, slightly bending flight of stairs. After another sudden turn—now to the left—one would enter the inner hall. It, too, follows the outline of the serpentine patio along the inside. Along the outer edge, the space is angled. This has the effect of making two of the bedrooms nonorthogonal; the other three are roughly L-shaped polygons. Only two of the bathrooms are conventional rectangular rooms. (The third has one curving wall.)

Frank no doubt intended for the paths in the M. S. House to serve as instruments for accentuating its eccentric spatial ordering. Their routing would have forced an observer into direct confrontation with the unconventional spaces; moving along the succession of features and effects would have underscored each special moment. It is difficult—from the simple lines on paper that we have—to predict precisely how the scheme would have operated in this way, but all of the evidence points to a house that would have been oddly comfortable and nonetheless a little jarring—exactly, it seems, what Frank was aiming for.

He would continue to mine these ideas for the next quarter-century.

CHAPTER NINE

The Apotheosis of Raumplan and Path

The closing years of the 1920s established the high-water mark for the Viennese modernists' efforts to forge the new space of architecture and movement. Between 1928 and 1930, while Frank was at work on the Beer House, Loos made his own signal contributions, designing and building two of his most accomplished Raumplan villas. One, the Khuner Country House, was a summary of everything he had contemplated and all he had devised concerning the affective path. The other, the Müller House, was to be the most complete and potent realization of the merging of Raumplan and path.

Planning for the Khuner House began in 1928. The client, Paul Khuner, was the owner of a factory his grandfather founded that produced a popular cooking oil derived from coconuts called Kunerol (the family had removed the *h* for their brand name).[1] Loos had designed the younger Khuner's apartment on Möllwaldplatz in Vienna's fourth district in 1907, around the time Paul married his wife Hedwig, née Sommer. But afterward, Loos had only sporadic contact with the family until 1927, when Khuner learned from a mutual friend that Loos, by then living in Paris, was in financial difficulties.[2] He wrote Loos a letter:

> In 1907 you designed my apartment. I know many people who had their apartments designed around the same time and who knew as little about furnishings and the rest as I did. Most of these people have had to throw their furniture out in the last twenty years, and those who did not do so have apartments with Seccessionist or "Jugend" style florid excesses that find dread even with those who know nothing about such things. By contrast, I have had to change virtually nothing in my apartment these same twenty years, and the furnishings still give me joy. . . . I thus have the feeling that the fee I paid you back then was much too small and that I owe you something more. If you will allow me to salve my conscience, I would like to send you the enclosed check for 10,000 francs. My wife and I hope to come to Paris in the spring and to see you then.[3]

opposite

Figure 163 Adolf Loos, Khuner Country House, Kreuzberg bei Payerbach, 1928–30. Photo by Martin Gerlach Jr. Grafische Sammlung Albertina, Vienna, ALA 3165.

Figure 164 Khuner Country House.

below **Figure 165** Khuner Country House, longitudinal section. Grafische Sammlung Albertina, Vienna, ALA 68.

Whether Loos met Khuner and his wife in Paris, we do not know; the check and letter were simply an elegant way for Khuner to aid Loos without bearing on his pride. But by the winter of 1928, Loos had begun work on the design for a country house for the couple high in the mountains south of Vienna, in Kreuzberg bei Payerbach. Loos's assistant Heinrich Kulka executed many of the drawings.

The scheme was loosely based on an unrealized project Loos had made in 1918 for Leo Prinz Sapieha, for a two-story house with an asymmetrical pitched roof. At its center was a large hall extending up both stories; ranged around the hall and directly or indirectly connected to it were all of the other rooms.[4] Loos and Kulka adapted the design for the Khuners, introducing into it elements of a Raumplan. Construction began in 1929, and the villa was completed in July 1930.

The exterior was quite unlike any of Loos's previous Raumplan houses. It was in the form of an Alpine chalet, executed in wood and stone (figs. 163, 164). Years before, in his 1913 essay "Regeln für den, der in den Bergen baut" (Rules for Those Building in the Mountains), Loos had described one of its guiding principles: "Respect the forms that the peasant uses because they are the confirmed product of ancient wisdom. But search for the origins of the forms. If new technologies have made it possible to improve the forms, then the new ones should always be employed."[5]

True to his convictions, Loos adapted traditional forms for the house's exterior, but he utilized modern materials for the roof and some other exterior details. For the interior, though, he came up with an arrangement that was decidedly not in accord with the Austrian vernacular tradition, for such houses normally featured two or three conventionally stacked floors (figs. 165–68). The grand two-story hall was out of the norm for Loos as well. Its origins extend back to the Renaissance and to later English models. Loos probably appropriated it directly from late nineteenth-century examples, from the portfolios of architects such as Shaw and Webb, whose works had been extensively illustrated in Muthesius's *Das englische Haus*. The Khuner Country House is Loos's most "English house," in spite of its homespun exterior. The central hall originally featured a cozy inglenook situated around a hearth, beamed ceilings, paneled walls, and, in its original guise, English-inspired furnishings, including Windsor chairs in the dining space (fig. 169).

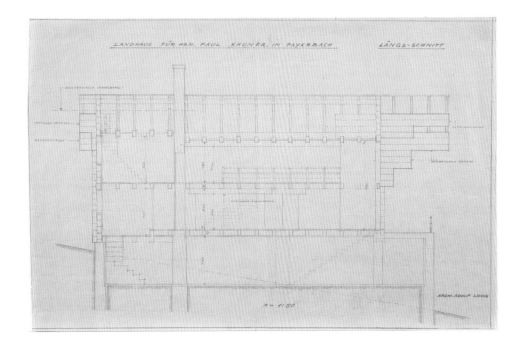

Figure 166 Khuner Country House, ground floor. Drawing by Nicolas Allinder. 1. Anteroom; 2. Vestibule; 3. Guest room; 4. WC; 5. Guest room; 6. Terrace; 7. Hall; 8. Inglenook; 9. Library (gentleman's room); 10. Dining room; 11. Kitchen; 12. Pantry.

Figure 167 Khuner Country House, first floor. Drawing by Nicolas Allinder. 1. Daughter's room; 2. Daughter's room; 3. Son's room; 4. Guest room; 5. Lady's room; 6. Gentleman's room; 7. Maid's room; 8. Maid's room; 9. Guest room; 10. Breakfast nook.

Figure 168 Khuner Country House, second floor. Drawing by Nicolas Allinder.

opposite **Figure 169** Khuner Country House, view of the hall and dining room from the gallery. Photo by Martin Gerlach Jr. Grafische Sammlung Albertina, Vienna, ALA 3174.

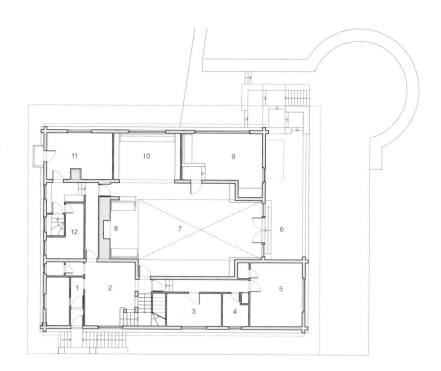

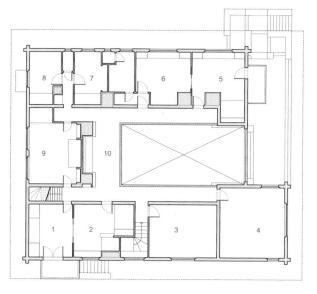

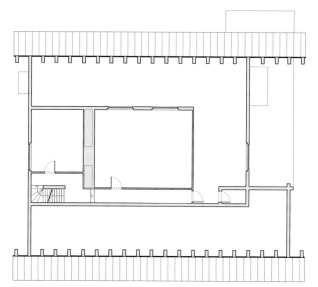

Loos was scarcely alone among Central European architects in turning to the English centralized hall form. Muthesius himself had borrowed it for several of his villas in Germany after the turn of the century, and it was the basis of Slovak architect Dušan Jurkovič's own house in Brno, built a few years afterward. Josef Hoffmann, too, had taken elements of the form for many of his domestic designs. Loos's version came much later, by some two decades, at a time when the idea—especially Loos's more or less literal reading of it— already seemed dated. Today, what remains of the arrangement and fittings comes across as fustian—barely modern at all.

What is certainly striking, then as now, though, is the way in which Loos manipulated the entry sequences and extended paths. One entrance to the building (nowadays an upscale restaurant and inn) is at the southeast corner; the other is on the northwest corner.

The house is perched high up on the mountain, with spectacular views of the valley and surrounding peaks. The road from the town of Payerbach in the valley comes up from the west. A visitor arriving from below might have originally ascended the stair on the front corner and climbed to the front terrace; today this entry is mostly unused (fig. 170). From there, one could enter the hall directly. The form of this exterior stair is usual: one can begin the climb from either of two sides—from the south or north—but in either instance the ascent involves several turns and levels before reaching the terrace (fig. 171). Another short flight of three steps then brings one into the hall.

The routing of the stairs brings to mind once more Strnad's design for the entry sequence of the Hock House. Although shorter and rather less of a climb, it offers, in compacted form, a welter of spatial and sensory moments. Whichever of the two sides one begins on, the paths merge. Yet each route is different: what Loos has achieved in principle is a simple increase of Strnad's basic idea. And the experiential possibilities are further elaborated because one can also exit the stair via another course—which is to say one could enter from the south and exit to the north, or vice versa, and in each case the experience would be different. Such an arrangement is also practical: it allows the occupants or visitors to choose exactly where they want to go. Still, the composite arrangement of the stair for

Figure 172 Khuner Country House, stair from the vestibule.

opposite
Figure 173 Khuner Country House, stair from the vestibule.

Figure 174 Khuner Country House, hall.

168

Loos, one can infer, was as much about what one might sense along the way as it was about meeting any functional requirements.

The second of the two paths of entry, the one from the southeast corner, more closely resembles that of Loos's other Raumplan houses. A stair, again double-sided but simpler in form, leads into a small anteroom (*Windfang*). One side was originally an area to store skis and boots; the other side, after a ninety-degree turn, is a sizable vestibule. The main path continues to another double-sided stair (fig. 172). It is framed with walls on both sides, but the walls are "pierced," as in the lower stair in the Moller House. The openings here, though, permit one to see (or read) the whole arrangement. A mirror on the far wall that is the same size as the openings creates an illusionistic effect of multiple, receding spaces. From one vantage, straight on, it is possible to see the reflections of the mirror and beyond, up the stairs (fig. 173). The space in this way is enlarged, and light from windows to the right (along the outer edge of the house) illuminate the stair and heighten the effect. Indeed, the full sequence, despite its relative complexity, is decidedly brighter than most other Loosian entry arrangements.

It is at this composite node that one begins the climb to the main floor. What follows is far more direct. After a single turn to the left, one comes directly into the hall. Today the space is nearly fully glazed on its north side (fig. 174). Originally, however, the windows were partly screened; in standard Loosian manner, the view and light were more controlled. Above, continuous galleries on three of the four sides of the space provide access to the bedrooms. The stair to the upper story is a continuation of the main stair; upstairs, the whole arrangement is visible from the opposite side (fig. 175).

opposite **Figure 175** Khuner Country House, view of the hall from the gallery.

above **Figure 176** Khuner Country House, bedroom.

right **Figure 177** Khuner Country House, daughter's room.

What is also evident in this view (as it is in section) is that there is little other indication of a Raumplan. There is a decided absence of complex interlocking volumes on sundry levels and few shifts of the axes or thresholds. Yet curious, almost vestigial traces of a Raumplan are found in the upstairs bedrooms. One room has a raised sitting area, another a raised sink space (figs. 176, 177). Some of the furniture in the latter room is also built in: a bed is situated in a sort of inglenook, a desk is set into the window.

What is peculiar about this is that these arrangements in no way save space. There is no taller room below the raised sitting area, only a small storage closet. And the raised sink in the other room confers no spatial dividend at all.

Frank once remarked to his assistant Ernst Plischke that "Loos's contention that the Raumplan saved space was nonsense."[6] Frank did not elaborate, but the examples from the Khuner House bedrooms—at the very least—underscore his point. One suspects, though, that what Frank had in mind was something more far-reaching. Even in Loos's celebrated Raumplan houses, such as the Moller House, only a small amount of space was reclaimed by varying the heights of the rooms and that was mostly expended again in Loos's winding and twisting paths. Frank, who knew Loos well, seems to be hinting at his real agenda: to make the spaces visually and psychologically moving. A low dining room was thus not, as Loos had insisted, an element of a spatial calculus but an effort to make the experience

opposite
Figure 178 Khuner Country House, hallway.

Figure 179 Khuner Country House, stair leading to the roof deck.

above **Figure 180** Khuner Country House, view from the roof deck.

cozy. In the same way, he must have thought that the intricate movement sequences in Loos's houses were not about material or spatial economy but about engaging the psyche of the participant. Frank accepted this for his own works. He knew well that it was spatially "expensive" to build the Beer House as he did; the paths and places gave emotional succor, but not any sort of monetary or spatial recompense. The trajectory of Frank's projects in the 1920s (and, for that matter, also those later in his career) was toward spatial extravagance, not economy. He was certain the same held for Loos.

In the Khuner Country House, Frank's claim seems to bear up throughout. Where there are small changes of level, such as in one of the upper-floor halls, the volume of space redeemed is negligible at best (fig. 178). Loos's true intent here seems to be to render the long narrow hallway more interesting by breaking it into two parts. And where his use of space is more economical, as in the tight stair to the roof deck, Loos employed light (from a window above) and color—a saturated red he often specified—to make the space more alluring (fig. 179). The impressions of the viewer are what count—much more so than any abstract spatial accounting.

The compression of the stair, it seems, also serves a second purpose. An observer is first made to experience a reduction in space (for the stair is narrower than the passageways that lead to it) before he or she is suddenly thrust onto the roof deck, a veritable burst of spatial awareness, as the sky and the prospect of the surrounding peaks explode into view (fig. 180). It is among the most dramatic visual shifts in all of Loos's designs.

A related moment arises in Loos's other key building of this period, the Villa Müller in Prague: from the upper roof deck one can take in a stunning view of the cityscape and Moldau valley below. The Villa Müller, though, is fundamentally about something else: it is a complete and matchless integration of Raumplan and path—the apotheosis of Loos's twenty-year-long exploration of the new space.[7]

Loos received the commission for the large house at a turning point in his life, in late October 1928, while awaiting trial on charges of child molestation.[8] The clients, František Müller and his wife, Milada Müllerová, were acquaintances of Loos's from Pilsen, in western Bohemia, where he had numerous clients. Like many of Loos's supporters, they were convinced of his innocence in the case.

Müller and another Pilsen native, Lumír Kapsa, were partners in a large construction company, Müller and Kapsa, which their fathers had founded in Pilsen before the turn of the century. The Müllers had moved to Prague only a short time before, and in September they purchased a large, hilly lot in the Střešovice district (at Nad Hradním vodojemem 642/14) above Prague Castle and the central city.[9]

The genesis of the commission, however, remains unclear. František Müller evidently first approached Czech architect Karel Lhota, a professor of architecture at the building trades school in Pilsen and Loos's local partner there. Lhota, in turn, asked Loos to participate in the project—an arrangement that Müller seems to have intended from the outset. Both architects signed a contract with him on 30 October 1928.[10]

Lhota, it seems, made the initial drawings for the house, probably with Loos's input, though it is possible that Müller intended for Loos to design only the interiors. In any event, Loos soon became fully involved in the project, apparently modifying the structural system and spatial plan that Lhota had made, which, in turn, necessitated numerous changes to the façade.[11] The first extant drawings probably date from November 1928. Loos and Lhota worked swiftly; by late December, the basic set of plans was complete and submitted to the Prague 6 municipal offices for a building permit.[12]

The work, though, went far from smoothly. Loos, nearly deaf by that time and in ill health, was often absent during the weeks the final decisions were being made about the house's disposition and detailing.[13]

Despite the myriad issues, the house that emerged over the early months of 1930 is one of the extraordinary modernist works of that era. The massive white cubic structure is set near the edge of the upper portion of the steeply sloping lot, immediately adjacent to Nad Hradním vodojemem Street (fig. 181). The north façade, positioned back some distance from Střešovicka Street (the principal thoroughfare in the area) and featuring a large balcony and windows, has the appearance of being the building's main or front façade. But the entry is, in fact, on the south side, largely unarticulated and with much smaller windows. The east and west façades are also differentiated, the west façade only with smaller and unaligned windows, the east sporting a large oriel (fig. 182).

The matter-of-factness of the building's exterior cloaks the richness and complexity of its interior spaces; the path within is perhaps Loos's most complete essay on the idea of movement and perception.

The south entry, which is set into a shallow recess below street level, leads past a travertine door surround and a bench (a late addition to the design) and then continues into a narrow, emerald-green corridor (figs. 183, 184). Just beyond is a vestibule, originally painted white, with a dark blue ceiling and yellow curtains. From there, a right-angled stair leads to the almost double-height salon (fig. 185). This space is unusually large, measuring 11 × 5.6 meters (36 × 18 feet) and 4.3 meters (14 feet) high (fig. 186). On one side of

Figure 181 Adolf Loos, Villa Müller, Prague, 1928–30.

opposite **Figure 182** Villa Müller, view
from the southeast.

above **Figure 183** Villa Müller, entry.

Figure 184 Villa Müller, passage facing toward the vestibule and stair.

opposite
Figure 185 Villa Müller, view from the stair into the salon.

Figure 186 Villa Müller, salon.

the hall are massive windows and a door to the north balcony, on the other is a long green-gray Cippolino marble wall, which conceals two stairways. One of these stairways goes up to the lady's sitting room (or boudoir) and gentleman's study, the other to the dining room and the upper floors (figs. 187–89). Situated just above the hall, the dining room—a more intimate space with a lower ceiling—overlooks the hall (figs. 190, 191).

On the other side of the same intermediate floor are the split-level lady's sitting room, the gentleman's study, and, concealed from public view, the kitchen and pantry. The way to the boudoir and the study on the side opposite the dining room continues the affective path. It leads first to the left, then up a tight stairway (figs. 192, 193). And in the boudoir itself the space is once more differentiated in height, with the highest point occupied by a sitting area (fig. 194). Adjacent to the boudoir is the study; just beyond, the stair continues, this time leading up to the upper-floor bedrooms (fig. 195).

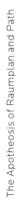

opposite
Figure 187 Villa Müller, stair to the lady's sitting room (boudoir) and gentleman's study.

Figure 188 Villa Müller, stair to the dining room.

above **Figure 189** Villa Müller, view from the salon into the dining room (left) and the lady's sitting room (right).

Figure 190 Villa Müller, dining room.

Figure 191 Villa Müller, view from the dining room into the salon.

opposite **Figure 192** Villa Müller, view from the salon toward the stair to the boudoir and gentleman's study.

below **Figure 193** Villa Müller, stair to the boudoir and gentleman's study.

right **Figure 194** Villa Müller, boudoir.

opposite **Figure 195** Villa Müller, stair from the gentleman's room to the upper floors.

186

At this juncture the stair becomes broader. An open well in the center, voids in the walls, and a large skylight above (similar to the one Loos had projected for the Baker House) generate a wide array of prospects and lighting effects (figs. 196, 197). The stair continues to the topmost floor, which houses a storage space and a summer breakfast room or tearoom, which gives out onto another terrace (offering splendid views of Prague Castle, the inner city, and the river valley below) (fig. 198).

Kulka, in his monograph on Loos published a year after the villa's completion, describes the experience of walking into and through the house: "Through a covered entrance, a wind porch, and a small vestibule, by climbing several winding stairs, we enter the hall, which surprises us by its beauty. . . . The hall, the dining room, and the staircase produce an all-embracing spatial effect of unparalleled harmony. The columns and the stepped banisters of the staircase ascending to the dining room are lined with sublime greenish marble (Cippolino de Salon, Valley of the Rhône), displaying reddish blue and yellow veins. The dining room and study are made from mahogany, the lady's boudoir is from lemonwood."[14]

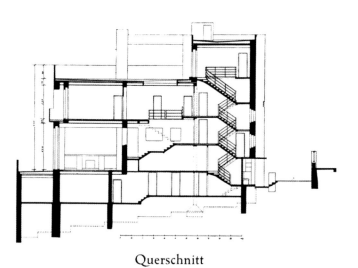

Querschnitt

opposite **Figure 198** Villa Müller, view from the roof terrace.

Figure 199 Villa Müller, plans and section drawn by Heinrich Kulka. From Heinrich Kulka, *Adolf Loos: Das Werk des Architekten* (Vienna: Anton Schroll, 1931): Abb. 258–62. Copyright Kulka Estate, reproduced here with permission of Mara Bing and the Kulka Estate, New Zealand.

Parterre

1. Stock

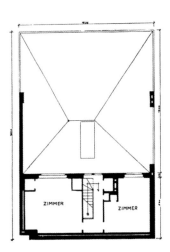

1930

2. Stock

Dachgeschoß

189

The Apotheosis of Raumplan and Path

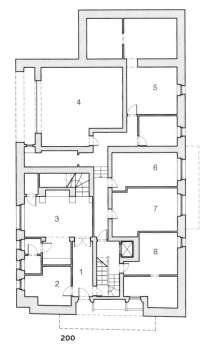

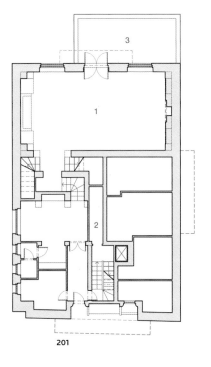

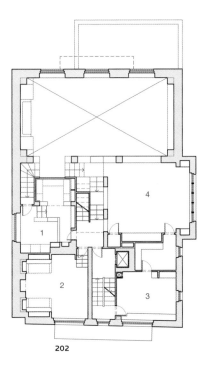

200

201

202

Figure 200 Villa Müller, entrance level. Drawing by Nicolas Allinder. 1. Entrance; 2. Vestibule and cloak storage; 3. Receiving room; 4. Garage; 5. Cellar; 6. Ironing room; 7. Laundry; 8. Furnace.

Figure 201 Villa Müller, ground floor. Drawing by Nicolas Allinder. 1. Salon (hall); 2. Hallway; 3. Terrace.

Figure 202 Villa Müller, raised ground floor. Drawing by Nicolas Allinder. 1. Lady's sitting room (boudoir); 2. Gentleman's study (library); 3. Kitchen; 4. Dining room.

Figure 203 Villa Müller, bedroom level. Drawing by Nicolas Allinder. 1. Master bedroom; 2. Gentleman's dressing room; 3. Bathroom; 4. Guest apartment; 5. Child's bedroom; 6. Child's day room; 7. Lady's dressing room.

Figure 204 Villa Müller, roof level. Drawing by Nicolas Allinder. 1. Summer dining room; 2. Darkroom for photography.

Figure 205 Villa Müller, continuous plan. Drawing by Nicolas Allinder. 1. Entrance; 2. Vestibule; 3. Salon; 4. Terrace; 5. Lady's sitting room (boudoir); 6. Dining room.

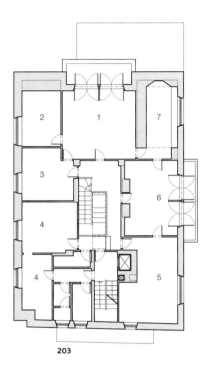

203

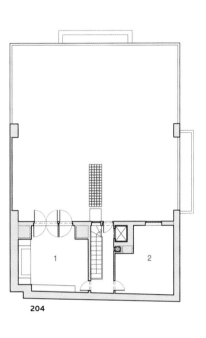

204

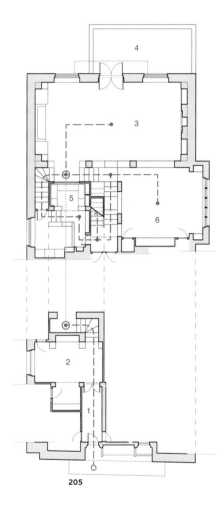

205

Such a description hardly does justice to the sumptuous and complex interiors (figs. 199–205). They are made up of a succession of highly varied spaces, with heterogeneous forms of cladding or surfaces. The house is effectively divided into three zones. One, a service zone, includes the garage and laundry on the lowermost floor, the kitchen and pantry on the main floor, a rear service stair, and a maid's room on the upper level. It has a reduced and practical language of surface. The second zone, made up of the principal living and entertaining spaces on the lower floors, is far more elaborate, with stone and wood projecting a bespoke richness. And the third, which includes the more private bedrooms and children's playroom on what is essentially the third floor and the breakfast room or tearoom on the fourth, is more relaxed and homey, even where Loos opted for more expensive materials.

The house is also subdivided into two spatial spheres: the upper portion, essentially the top two levels, which preserve the conventional horizontal layering of floors; and the lower floors in which the Raumplan idea is fully developed. The functional and spatial partitioning is possible because of the house's unusual structural system. The exterior walls are conventional load-bearing block construction, but the interior supports consist of four reinforced concrete columns that carry the horizontal beams and floors, allowing for the intricate disposition of spaces. The four columns form a rectangle in the building's center and support the upper stairway, which wraps around their edges; the open well, in conjunction with a rooftop skylight, permits light to enter into the interior. The effect, then, in the lower part of the house is a series of stacked and rotating platforms, which resolve in the upper stories into a sort of perimeter plan, with an open stair at the center.

In a discussion with Lhota about the Villa Müller in 1930, Loos remarked that he thought the house was his most accomplished Raumplan design: "It is just this spatial interaction and spatial austerity that thus far I have best been able to realize in Dr. Müller's house."[15] Whether the house, like Loos's other Raumplan designs, was truly "austere" is open to question—as Frank had suggested.

The cost of construction for the house greatly exceeded that of more conventional designs of the same size. In spite of Loos's statements to the contrary, there is not much to his arguments about an economical use of space. But the spatial "action" unquestionably enhances—vitalizes—the rituals of daily life within. To move through the Villa Müller is to engage the architecture both physically and psychologically; everywhere one is confronted with varied architectural effects and architectural realities; living in and moving through it necessitates a high level of mental and physical activity.

Gustav Künstler, who along with Ludwig Münz produced the first complete monograph on Loos's works in 1964, wrote: "The usual scheme of the single-family house—living rooms on the ground floor, bedrooms on the second floor, connected by a stair, which is to say two wholly independent spatial groupings, on different levels and independent of each other—has been rearranged to form a convincing . . . and harmonious sequencing of rooms of different sizes and heights, which through the course of a gradual climb from the entry to the main living floor . . . fuse the house into an extraordinary whole."[16] Giovanni Denti, professor at the Politecnico in Milan, echoed the assessment: "The silence of the exterior protects the interior, which is an ensemble of places offering hospitality to different moments of family life. . . . In the Müller house every place has its own character, its own aspect, determined by materials and Raumplan."[17]

Leslie van Duzer and Kent Kleinman, who wrote one of the best books on the house, *Villa Müller: A Work of Adolf Loos*, have suggested, however, that one's experience of the house can vary greatly, depending on whether one is actively moving—"roving"—through the house or passively seated: The "roving subject . . . is further privileged by the freedom to gaze and peer across boundaries," permitted even "visual access to the landscape beyond the shell of the building," whereas anyone stationary within has a far more limited experience because the rooms are often bounded in ways that reduce or eliminate such visual connectivity.[18]

Beatriz Colomina has drawn a related comparison, emphasizing the tension between elements of theatricality and intimacy in the house.

> In the Müller House . . . the sequence of spaces, articulated around the staircase, follows an increasing sense of privacy from the drawing room to the dining room and study to the "lady's room" (*Zimmer der Dame*) with its raised sitting area, which occupies the center or "heart" of the house. But the window of this space looks onto the living space . . . [T]he most intimate room is like a theater box, placed just over the entrance to the social spaces in this house, so that any intruder could easily be seen. Likewise, the view of the exterior, toward the city, from this "theater box" is contained within a view of the interior. Suspended in the middle of the house, this space assumes the character both of a "sacred" space and a point of control. Comfort is produced by two seemingly opposing conditions, intimacy and control.[19]

We have no way of knowing precisely how much of any of this Loos intended (and it should be said that it is by no means easy to peer out of the window in the boudoir). He left us few clues to his objectives in designing the spaces and even fewer about how he thought his clients should live there. The scant remaining evidence suggests that he thought simply about providing his inhabitants a full and rich environment, one that was intimate, secure, and comfortable, one that allowed a certain degree of flexibility for conducting the rituals of daily life. If the paths through the house describe a distinctive journey and a very specific set of spatial experiences (from closed to open, from darker to lighter, and so on), they are also part of a narrative of dwelling. One enters, one removes one's outer clothing in the cloakroom and then ascends to the salon. There one might relax or entertain. The room is both public and private. The dining room, poised just above, is about a more intimate form of interaction. Whether the Müllers were dining alone or with guests, the space, with its lower ceiling and cozy scale, offered a field for close conversation.

Like almost all grand Central European houses of the time, the villa is also meticulously segmented: there are the servants' spaces, places for them to work and live, always concealed, and spaces for the Müllers and their guests. The divisions between public and private are similarly fully drawn. The public spaces—and the public portion of the path through the house—end at the dining room. The spaces that lie beyond—the boudoir, František Müller's study, and the bedrooms and breakfast room above—are all screened away. To enter this zone is to be admitted to a separate and far more personal realm.

Beyond that, Loos appears to have given his clients the latitude—in both senses, the space—to shape their own lives. The Villa Müller viewed in this way is perhaps less a modernist architectural object than a specific statement about the experience of modernity and relaxed living.

CHAPTER TEN

Accidental Space

Loos died in the late summer of 1933. In his final years, after the completion of the Villa Müller, he worked on several additional significant commissions. But only two of these designs, the Villa Winternitz in Prague, finished in 1932, and the Samler Apartment in Pilsen, completed in 1934, came close to what he had achieved before. By that time he was becoming increasingly frail, unable to sit or concentrate for long periods. Much of the design work for the Winternitz commission fell to Karel Lhota, who fashioned a more modest and restrained version of the Villa Müller.[1] And the Samler Apartment, which Heinrich Kulka completed, repeated in smaller scale some of the same basic ideas.[2]

In the wake of Loos's passing and the death of Oskar Strnad, who expired suddenly of a heart attack in 1935, Frank was left to carry on the investigation into the possibilities of the new space. He, too, would build only one more house of note in Austria, a sprawling U-shaped villa for Hugo and Olga Bunzl in Vienna's eighteenth district.[3] But by then he had mostly abandoned Austria. After the country's brief civil war in 1934 and in response to the rising threat of the Nazis, Frank began spending ever more time in Stockholm. (He would seek permanent exile there after the German takeover of Austria in 1938.) His wife Anna's Swedish connections gave him entrée to the city. They had spent most summers in the later 1920s in the south of the country in the town of Falsterbo, where Frank would build several more houses.

Over the course of the next decade and a half after his departure for Stockholm, Frank—now far removed from Vienna—would realize his most radical contributions to the idea of forging affective movement through space. He would do so in two ways: at first, through a mounting reliance on nonorthogonality, and later, by means of an extreme experiment in what could be achieved through chance ordering—or at least its appearance.

195

Figure 207 Wehtje House, elevations 1:50.Kunst-
und Designsammlung, Universität für angewandte
Kunst, Vienna.

opposite
Figure 206 Josef Frank, house for
Walter and Gundlar Wehtje, Falsterbo, Sweden,
1936; plans 1:50. Kunst- und Designsammlung,
Universität für angewandte Kunst, Vienna.

Figure 208 Josef Frank, project for the Austrian
Pavilion at the 1937 Paris Exposition Internationale;
elevations and section 1:200, 1936. Grafische
Sammlung Albertina, Vienna, JFA 32.

Frank's initial effort came in 1936, in response to a commission from wealthy Stockholm industrialist Walter Wehtje and his wife Gundlar to design a summer house in Falsterbo. Named "Solesand" (Sunny Beach) by the Wehtjes, the house occupies a sandy, pine-studded rise near Frank's other houses (which by this time also included his Låftman and Seth residences) in the small resort community. He devised another U-shaped house, with the main rooms oriented to the south and with views of the sea beyond (fig. 206).

It was completed in 1936. Drawing from Frank's earlier conceptual experiments, especially the House for M. S., the plan features two projecting wings framing a central courtyard. The main entry runs from the south, through the courtyard, into an open, two-story hall. To one's left upon entering is a large dining space; just beyond, filling the entire wing on that side, is the living room. Opposite, in the other wing, are the six bedrooms; above the hall and adjoining kitchen and maid's room are another sitting area and a roof terrace. Along the house's inner and outer walls there is a sequence of generous windows with blank wall surfaces between them.

The plan, with its recurrent shifts in direction and the dotted lighting effects of the windows, offers a train of powerful architectural impressions (fig. 207). Yet what makes the experience of walking through the house so visually forceful and variegated is Frank's recourse to acute and oblique angles, curving walls, and, in some of the rooms—especially the public spaces—a complete departure from conventional right-angled planning. Although movement from place to place is not as complex as it is, for example, in the Beer House, Frank's addition of insistently "amalgamated" rooms—made up ostensibly of miscellaneous geometric parts—has the effect of rendering what one sees along any of the paths diverse and challenging. Every shift in one's position, or merely turning one's head, opens up new and different vistas.

Frank tested this same concept in two other projects in those years—both unrealized—a design for the Austrian pavilion at the 1937 Paris Exposition Internationale and a house for the Wehtje family in the Stockholm suburb of Djursholm.

The Paris pavilion, for which only a single drawing now exists, is made up of a series of assorted and joined volumes arrayed on a hillside (fig. 208). Frank's concept for the path was quite simple: viewers would gradually ascend through the two axes of the T-shaped

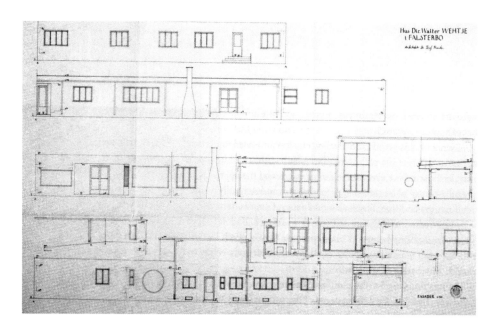

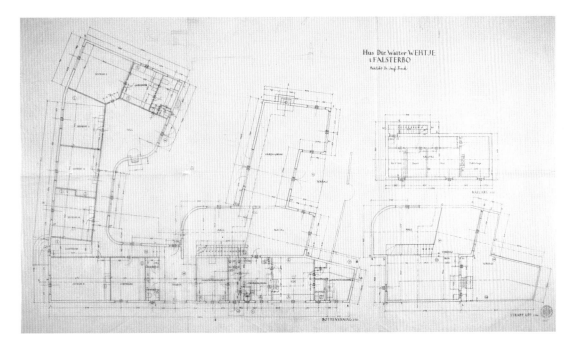

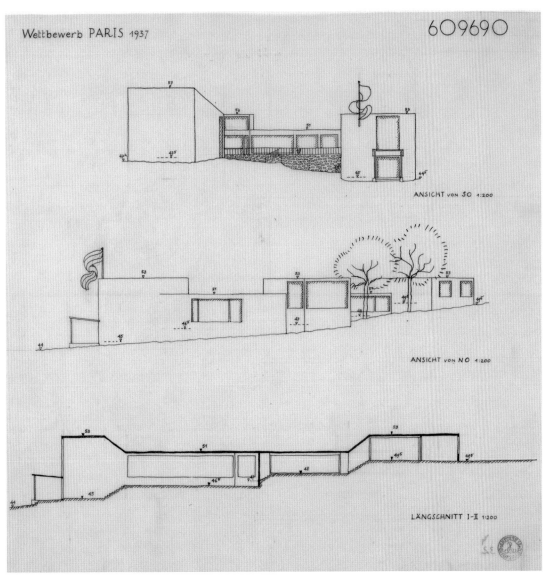

building, strolling through rooms of different dimensions and heights. Stairs of varying lengths and windows of diverse sizes and configurations would have lent additional variety to the experience of visiting the building. But because no plan exists, it is uncertain whether or not the rooms were intended to be orthogonal, though the southeast elevation reveals that at least one of the rooms (on the far left) was canted off the underlying grid.

Frank's project for the Wehtje House in Djursholm, in any event, displays far more variety in the outline and arrangements of the spaces (fig. 209). The two-story house is roughly in the form of an L. The lower floor of the longer side contains a large entry hall and the living and dining rooms; the shorter wing is taken up with the kitchen and other service spaces. Upstairs is another sitting area and the bedrooms. The main path on both floors is an elongated, continuous route through the building's center, but it is inflected or bent, and on the lower story there are subtle changes in height along its length. The path nonetheless is comparatively straightforward by Frank's standards, and he instead employed the irregular shape of the spaces—the living room is a complex polygon with no fewer than ten angles—to enhance and animate the spatial experience. Many of the other rooms on both floors show the same convolution.

Why the Wehtjes decided not to build the house is unknown, but Frank was able to realize a related—if more understated—design several years later. The client was Estrid Ericson, owner of Svenskt Tenn, the modern furniture and accessories store in Stockholm where Frank then served as chief designer.

Ericson owned a small weekend and summer house on the water in the village of Tyresö, southeast of Stockholm. She had rented the house, which she called Tolvekarna, or "Twelve Oaks," since 1932. She purchased it in 1941. A short time later she asked Frank to expand and modify it. He added a bedroom wing to the simple board-and-batten structure and appended a terrace on the rear side facing out to the Stockholm archipelago (fig. 210).[4]

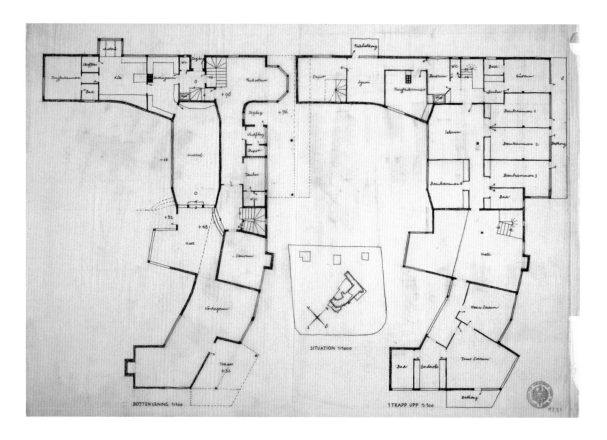

opposite **Figure 209** Josef Frank, project for the Wehtje House in Djursholm, Sweden, 1938; plan 1:100, site plan 1:1000. Kunst- und Designsammlung, Universität für angewandte Kunst, Vienna.

Figure 210 Josef Frank, Tolvekarna, Tyresö, Sweden, 1941. Svenskt Tenn Collection, Josef Frank Archive, Stockholm.

Many of Frank's changes were clear-cut. But he also made a few alterations that rendered what had been a simple rectangular box into a lively field for spatial play. Chief among these was the way in which he set the new rear bedroom wing at an angle to the original house, establishing several oblique junctures at the point where the two volumes meet.

The entry sequence begins outside at the drawn-out stone stair from the garden (fig. 211). It, too, is set at an angle, leading up to the center of what is—because of the sloping terrain on the approach side—essentially the upper floor. To the left upon entering is a large living room, complete with standard "Frankish" furnishings and textiles from Svenskt Tenn, with views out over the water and the surrounding tree-covered hillocks of the framing peninsulas (fig. 212). Beyond the living room, to the right, is one of the bedrooms, its entrance set off axis (fig. 213). The other, added bedroom, however, is on the far side of the house, beyond the angled connector between the two wings (figs. 214, 215).

It is at this junction of the building's two main parts where most of the spatial drama occurs. There are two inflected axes that run more or less parallel to each other (figs. 216–19). At one end of the space, in the house's center, is a vestibule, with a stair leading down to the lower level. The twin paths are illuminated along their length with windows, one in the form of a vitrine set into the wall, with glazing on the outer side (fig. 220). Maps, glued to the walls (a favorite device of Ericson's for her Svenskt Tenn interiors), enliven the passageways (fig. 221). Beyond is the new bedroom Frank designed for Ericson's future husband, Sigfrid Ericson, who was captain of the Swedish passenger liner SS *Gripsholm* (fig. 222). Frank fitted it out to resemble a ship's cabin, complete with a small hatch, which had a ladder to the basement. Along one of the two passageways to the bedroom is a large bathroom (fig. 223).

The fracturing of conventional geometry at the nexus between the house's two wings is mirrored in the large-stone terrazzo floor, which seemingly mimicked the house's angled ordering at smaller scale. It is worth noting that the building as a whole reiterates Frank's

left **Figure 211** Tolvekarna, entry.

above **Figure 212** Tolvekarna, dining area.

opposite **Figure 213** Tolvekarna, view from living room into the bedroom.

203

opposite
Figure 214 Tolvekarna, addition from the front.

Figure 215 Tolvekarna, addition from the end.

above **Figure 216** Tolvekarna, connection between
the old house and the addition on the rear side.

Accidental Space

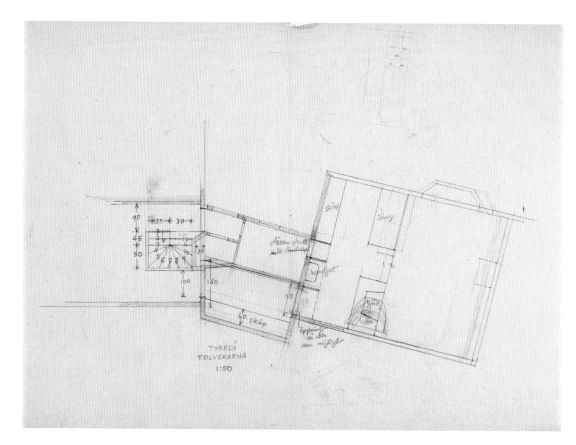

opposite
Figure 217 Tolvekarna, plan 1:50. Collection
Gun Jacobson, Tyresö, Sweden.

Figure 218 Tolvekarna, central hall.

above **Figure 219** Tolvekarna, central hall.

opposite **Figure 220** Tolvekarna, view of the hall.

Figure 221 Tolvekarna, view of the hall.

Figure 222 Tolvekarna, view of the bedroom.

opposite **Figure 223** Tolvekarna, view from the bathroom into the hall.

ideas about domestic planning: the larger rooms form "piazzas," and the "streets" between them are gently bent, so that—as Sitte thought best—one could not discern their full length. But what is so extraordinary in Tolvekarna is how Frank, working with a modest existing building and at a very reduced scale (and, it should also be said, with a meager budget), was able to concoct the many spatial impressions, the many visual options that the paths yield. Any movement would magnify one's sense of what was there, occasioning a flowing stream of sensations.

Work on the house stretched on into 1942. By then, fearing the Nazis might invade Sweden, Frank had fled once more, this time to New York. During the early war years, he taught at the New School for Social Research, and throughout much of 1943 and the first part of 1944 he worked on new textile patterns for Svenskt Tenn. He thought for a time about remaining in New York, but he was unable to establish himself there: his ideas were simply too far outside the mainstream of American modernism at the time. In 1946 he returned to Stockholm.

For a time after the war, he was mostly preoccupied with designing furnishings and objects for Svenskt Tenn. But in the later 1940s he turned his thoughts once more to architecture and to the problem of space. During his years in New York, he had expressed more and more dissatisfaction with standard spatial ordering. In one of his lectures at the New School, "How to Plan a House," he repeated his earlier attack on the right-angled room, asserting that free and irregular planning could overcome the dead hand of history and the "tyranny" of what he termed "Bauhaus functionalism." An architecture founded on "the belief in systematic ordering," he charged, was a product of one's "being reared in an atmosphere lacking in freedom." More than that, he argued, right-angled planning did not yield real comfort, whether at the scale of the house or the city: "The more irregular the streets, the more livable the city." And if straight streets were sometimes necessary "for the purpose of traffic circulation and real estate," this was not true of the house: "modern technology allows every free division of the interior." The yearning for complex and varied spaces, he went on, was universal: "It is no wonder that people have a greater sense of well-being in casually remodeled barns and adapted windmills than in a carefully planned house with scientifically determined divisions into functional areas, and that they seek reprieve from the convenience of the city in the primitive conditions of the countryside."[5]

After his return to Sweden, Frank continued to ponder the problem of space and livability. The issue for him had to do with reconciling the practical needs of a household with the equally important requirements—both physical and psychological—of those who dwelled within, especially their need to find solace. Yet he believed that the spaces that were most comfortable—nonorthogonal spaces that were the result of happy "chance"—had only come about as the product of time and other forces that usually lay beyond the architect's hand. And these did not always suit the necessities of modern life. Near the end of "How to Plan a House," he had put this quite lucidly: "We cannot, of course, assemble a house only from 'accidents' [Zufälligkeiten], we require a conscious plan, one that first and foremost fulfills practical requirements."[6]

By 1947, he began to consider how to resolve this problem. He first explored it in a series of sketches, which he included in a group of seven letters to his wife's cousin, Dagmar Grill, who was thinking about building a house. The drawings depict thirteen house designs, each proposing a different tactic to promote this idea of architectonic "freedom." Later, Frank collected all of the drawings and reproduced them in India ink on three sheets of tracing paper (figs. 224–26). For some of the houses he also prepared larger renderings (fig. 227).[7]

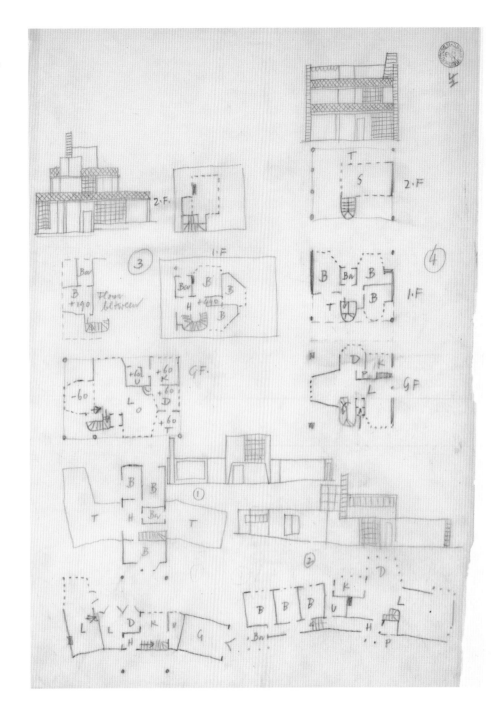

The designs, in and of themselves, are astonishing—a distinctive and entirely eccentric vision, one without direct precedent in the history of Western architecture. What stands out, though, is the manner in which Frank devised the movement sequences. In portions of some of the schemes there is hardly a straight line to be found, and, even in those areas that retain right-angled planning, movement from room to room rarely occurs without some form of turning or bending or twisting. Although Frank here has renounced the Raumplan notion of rooms on multiple levels—the houses more or less preserve the conventional horizontal layering of floors—the "paths and places" are so irregular, so completely unexpected, that walking through them would have generated—at almost every point—sensations of architectural novelty and of a keen awareness. What Frank had achieved at last was the nearly total realization of Schmarsow's conception of architecture as spatial experience.

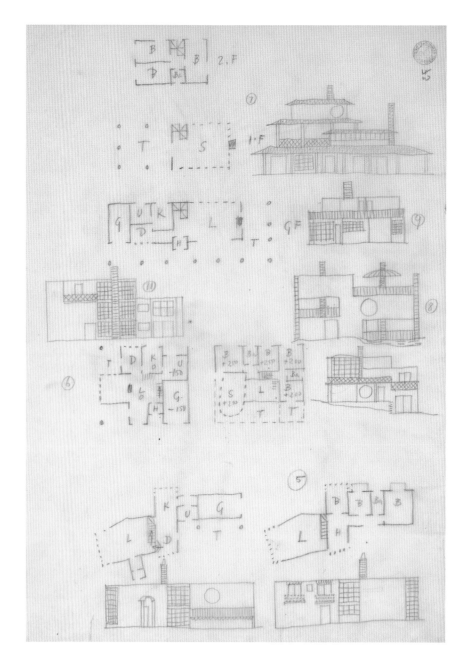

It would be more than a decade before Frank would present a written exposition of his ideas. It came in an essay he titled "Accidentism," which first appeared in the Swedish journal *Form* in 1958.[8] At its heart, the piece is a manifesto against the reductive notions of what—once more—he terms "functionalism." But it is also his last statement about the possibilities of nonorthogonal planning. He writes:

> Every human being needs a certain degree of sentimentality to feel free. This will be taken from him if he is forced to make moral demands of every object, including aesthetic ones. What we need is variety and not stereotyped monumentality. No one feels comfortable in an order that has been forced upon him, even if it has been doused in a sauce of beauty. Therefore, what I am suggesting are not new rules and forms but a radically different attitude toward art. Away with universal styles, away with the idea of equating art and industry, away with the whole system that has become popular under the name functionalism.

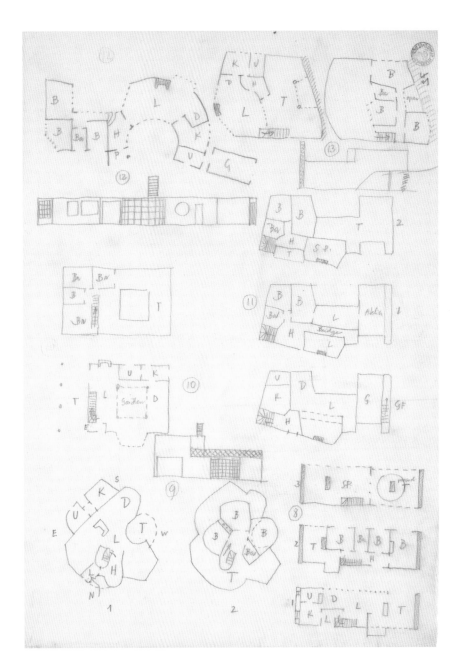

This new architectural system, which is to replace the present one, I would like to give a name in the manner that is currently fashionable, one that explains its basic principles. I will call it *Accidentism* for the time being, and by that I mean that we should design our surroundings as if they originated by chance.

Every place in which one feels comfortable—rooms, streets, and cities—has originated by chance. In cities that have grown up organically over time, buildings of all epochs stand harmoniously next to one another. Something like this, of course, cannot be attained today, but I am convinced that uniformity is not the result of necessity but of an ideology that is not even our own.[9]

Echoing his earlier writings, Frank also specifically addresses the problem of how to overcome the strictures of functional form: "It is not, however, calculated clarity that makes a house comfortable. One yearns once more for spaces that provide greater latitude for fantasy, rather than carefully determined compartments for the various functions of the

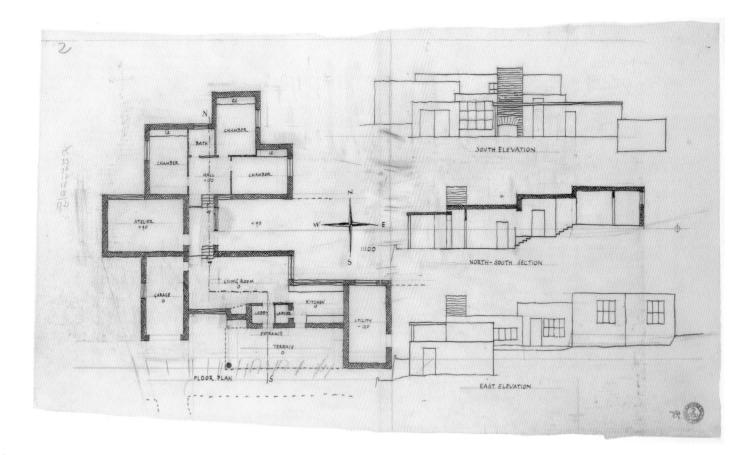

Figure 227 Designs for Dagmar Grill, house 2, elevations and plans. Grafische Sammlung Albertina, Vienna, JFA 80.

opposite
Figure 228 Josef Frank, project for a single-family house on a hillside, n.d.; elevation, plans, and section. Grafische Sammlung Albertina, Vienna, JFA 95.

Figure 229 Josef Frank, project for a round stone house, plans and elevations, mid-1950s. Grafische Sammlung Albertina, Vienna, JFA 98.

dwellings, such as eating, sleeping, and so forth. One yearns for streets that are not merely solutions to traffic problems, no matter how successful they are."[10]

Accordingly, Frank would continue to investigate the idea of how to make "free" and affective spaces. He had stopped building by this time: his last realized architectonic design was Tolvekarna, completed more than a decade and a half before. But throughout the postwar years, until he ceased working around 1964, he churned out new fantasies intended to demonstrate his "cure" for what he saw as the ills of late modernism and to show new ways to evoke a forceful yet livable spatial experience. Some of these last designs still made recourse to standard right-angled planning, all the while employing an amalgam of the strategies he had honed over the course of a long working life: contrasting room heights and volumes, a gradual scaling of a hillside, contrived and repeated alterations in direction (fig. 228). Often in his late years, though, Frank simply employed sinuous lines and rooms that in plan looked almost like indiscriminate splotches (fig. 229).

Such designs flew in the face of the fastidiously ordered works of the great majority of the modernists of those years (and even those, it should be said, who were already questioning modernist orthodoxy). More than that, Frank's last projects were lessons about how to live and move about instinctively and naturally. Or, at the very least, they were suggestions of a new freedom of movement, for Frank's designs were just as methodically plotted as those he criticized. They were about our rehearsed habits, about how we inhabit places and how we find our way in them.

They were, in short, an endeavor to speak eloquently about the experience of space as a fact of daily of life.

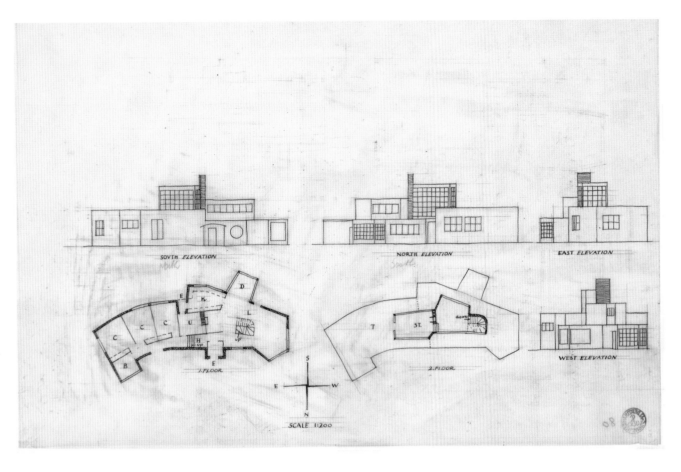

SOUTH ELEVATION   NORTH ELEVATION   EAST ELEVATION

WEST ELEVATION

1.FLOOR   2.FLOOR

SCALE 1:200

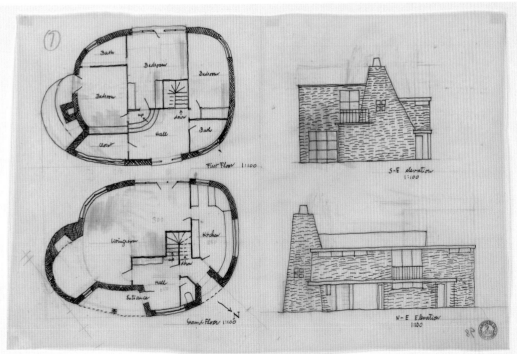

Bath   Bedroom   Bedroom

Bedroom

Hall   Bath

Closet

First Floor 1:100   S-E elevation 1:100

Livingroom   Kitchen

Hall

Entrance

Ground Floor 1:100   N-E Elevation 1:100

CODA

Frank died in 1967. With his passing came the close of the main chapter of the Viennese quest for the new space. But even before his death there were efforts on the part of some of the younger Viennese to pursue related ideas. After Loos died, his former assistant Heinrich Kulka produced several houses employing Raumplan techniques—before he was forced into exile in New Zealand in 1939.[1] Ernst Plischke, after working for Frank in the late 1920s, went on to establish a practice of his own. In the early 1930s he generated a splendidly charged promenade on the stairway of his design for the *Arbeitsamt* (unemployment office) in the Vienna district of Liesing. Later, after he, too, found exile in New Zealand, Plischke would continue his experiments.[2] R. M. Schindler, not long after attending Loos's private *Bauschule*, went off to the United States and in California realized several houses—mostly impressively, perhaps, the Lovell Beach House of 1926—with Raumplan-like elements.[3] And Frederick Kiesler, who likewise would spend much of his career in the United States, in New York, experimented with space and space-making in myriad ways, seeking to find the qualities of "endless" and ineffable space that Strnad had dreamed of.[4] But none of these younger figures quite exactly chased the identical vision of space and path that had driven the experiments of the older generation. With Frank's death, the search effectively ceased.

Frank's last important text had been "Accidentism." For the final nine years of his life, he wrote nothing else of note, no summation of his ideas, no ultimate reckoning with modernism or its meanings, no last word about space or path. His concluding house projects—most not much more than hurried sketches of inner ruminations, for there was little prospect of them ever being built—only underscored his continuing belief in an architecture of experience and joy. Even for his earlier postwar designs, though, there is a quality of cursoriness, as if he had never fully worked out what a new architecture based on "chance ordering" might mean. The full implications of his notion of the house as an "accidental" grouping of paths and places remained unexplored, untried. He seems—frustratingly for us now—content to have offered a portfolio of drawn examples and to have left it at that.

What is conspicuously absent in his writings—and for that matter, also from those of Strnad and Loos—is any sense of how what they were doing in their spatial designs was part of a larger discourse of their time. Vital conversations of the day, such as the dialogues about the fourth dimension or about space-time, which might have had real relevance for their ideas and works, found no resonance in their texts. And when questions about being and living came to the fore in philosophy—in 1927, in Martin Heidegger's *Sein und Zeit* (Being and Time), for instance—they demonstrated no interest at all.

For Frank, at least, his unresponsiveness to such matters was certainly a result of a deep-seated skepticism about anything that smacked of metaphysics. For Strnad, it seems that he merely moved on to other architectural problems. And in the case of Loos, his mission simply did not align with such questions: from his earliest days, he had been focused on achieving a broad cultural understanding and critiquing of the products and ideas of his

217

perceived foes. None of the three architects was by inclination a builder of architectural or philosophical systems.

What Frank, too, had missed in his writings, indeed what Strnad and Loos had also seemingly missed, what they must have considered but never fully explored, was one of the salient features of their discovery of how to make affective spaces: that these spaces constitute a kind of poetry, which in repeated readings would give rise to a succession of meanings. If conscious movement through a complex volume is poetic, then every reading—every trip along a designated path (in either direction!)—is a unique event. Every reading could be different, every stroll infused with unmistakable distinctness. To enter into, to ascend up and through, Loos's Villa Müller, Strnad's Hock House, or Frank's Beer House is to be exposed to ever-shifting kaleidoscopic impressions. The experience for the engaged viewer could be new or renewed. Or it could be, as Frank had thought, a means to revisit memory, a lapse into momentary—or even extended—sentimentality.

The fullest statement of these thoughts came not from the three architects themselves, but in French philosopher Gaston Bachelard's 1957 book *La poétique de l'espace* (The Poetics of Space).[5] Bachelard's approach was strictly phenomenological. He sought not to uncover how we apprehend space either psychologically or rationally but to examine how individual experience builds memories and connotations. His book is a meditation on oneiric space, on how we creatively imagine. The experience of architecture and space he regarded as a kind of daydream, the product of the half-consciousness he called *reverie*. His description of stairs and our involvements with them, for example, evokes at least some of what the Viennese were seeking to make.

> Then there are the stairways, one to three or four of them, all different. We always *go down* the one that leads to the cellar, and it is this going down that we remember. . . . But we both go up and down the stairway that leads to the bed-chamber. It is more commonly used; we are familiar with it. Twelve-year-olds even go up it in ascending scales, in thirds and fourths, trying to do fifths, and liking above all to take it in strides of four steps at a time. What joy for the legs to go up four steps at a time!
>
> Lastly, we always *go up* the attic stairs, which are steeper and more primitive. For they bear the mark of an ascension to a more tranquil solitude.[6]

In a similar way, the buildings of Strnad, Loos, and Frank could function, as the three men had hoped, as adventures in architecture. They were instruments for raising consciousness about the built world, for seeing and "being in" architecture. Bachelard, for his part, was unconcerned with this direct experience of architecture as architects regularly conceive of it. He writes: "We are far removed from any reference to simple geometrical forms. A house that has been experienced is not an inert box. Inhabited space transcends geometrical space."[7] But Strnad, Loos, and Frank had, it seems, wanted to achieve both sets of experiences—a direct confrontation with architecture as a physical fact (through the manipulation of form, space, and light) and as a conduit into personal and poetic knowledge. They thought of architecture as a framework for daily living, a set of places that would enable and enhance human rituals. Space—or a sequence of spaces—was a means to this end, to render domestic life pleasurable and stimulating—or simply meaningful.

But in the architecture they made, the paths through spaces could equally function as plastic palimpsests, with every twist and turn laden with the residue of past impressions. To live in a house was to access memory, for "recorded" on its walls and floors were reminders of everything that had happened there: events of joy, or frustration, or accomplishment, or, even, surpassing sadness. To stroll along a prescribed path was to relive what had happened along the way before.

Such memories, of course, are not fixed because space itself is never precisely fixed or immutable: it has everything to do with our perceptions of it. As a consequence, our experience is not fixed either. Both—perceptions and experiences—are liquid, flowing along in real time, as one moves or stands still, and the thoughts they might arouse flow along in the same temporal torrent. And space could also be viewed in the same way, as time in which one could move backward or forward—perhaps even merging past and present—rather than a one-way linear condition.

Yet a vision of this kind implies a certain kind of viewer. It presupposes a given level of synaptic activity, the possession of a genuine and ready sensitivity. One could equally walk the identical paths without truly seeing or feeling much of anything. It is an old and worn error of artists and architects, the tacit assumption that all people can or want truly to "see." We may all truly navigate the world with more or less the same perceptive apparatus, but not everyone finds meaningful engagement or is willing to pay out the cerebral energy to extract sentiment or develop involvement. If our three protagonists fell short in their ambitions, it stemmed in some part from a misplaced faith in the average observer. Yet for those disposed and willing to participate in the new space, the dividends could be manifold and powerful.

The legacy of the new spatial ideas in Vienna was also mixed. Loos in later years, after his "rediscovery" in the 1960s, would become renowned for his Raumplan idea, his works much studied; they would become the objects—almost fetishized—of admiration and curiosity for generations of historians, practitioners, and architecture students. But too often lost in the discussions of his buildings is a sense of how they functioned as movement sequences, as conveyers of dynamic experience. Frank fared a little better—perhaps because his essay on the "House as Path and Place" made his intentions more explicit. But he and his designs have remained out of the mainstream of modernist studies, more curios of scholarly gaze than a principal subject. For his part, Strnad, despite a few recent publications and an exhibition, continues to be a mostly forgotten figure, except for a small handful of cognoscenti, the great majority of them residing in Vienna. The idea of movement and experience in architecture has instead been very largely accorded to Le Corbusier: the *promenade architecturale* has become the standard modus for thinking about movement through architectural space.

What Loos, Frank, and Strnad were able to bring to reality, however, was a refined and fruitful conception of space, one that still offers broad and long avenues for exploration. And the story recounted here belongs to a significant branch in the genealogy of modernism. It is as much a part of the tale of modernist space-making as the open plan or the interpenetration of inside and outside.

But this history also belongs equally to a separate branch on the modernist tree, one having to do with a new vision of subjectivity and architecture. Loos, Frank, and Strnad sought to weave experiences, to provoke little epiphanies of place and space, of light and substance, of solid and void. What they made beyond that, without perhaps ever quite fully recognizing it, was not architecture at all but sites wholly of, and for, the imagination.

APPENDIX

Essays by Oskar Strnad, Heinrich Kulka, and Josef Frank

OSKAR STRNAD

A FEW THEORETICAL THOUGHTS ON THE ARRANGEMENT OF SPACE (1913)

"Einiges Theoretische zur Raumgestaltung" (1913). Later published as "Einiges Theoretische zur Raumgestaltung," in *Deutsche Kunst und Dekoration* 41 (1 October 1917): 39–68. Reprinted as "Raumgestaltung und Raumgelenke," in *Innen-Dekoration* 30 (July–August 1919): 254–58; 292–93.

I want to speak about things that surround us, whose effect we feel, but that we seldom examine. Everyone knows from experience that an empty room will generally feel uncomfortable and that fully furnished rooms can have varied effects. Everyone will also have seen that a room with a different furniture arrangement will have a completely different spatial impact. That should make us ponder: the dimensions of the room have not changed at all but the spatial effect we sense is entirely new.

An unfurnished room usually looks smaller than a furnished one. A room without curtains seems emptier than a room with them. We know that placing furniture in a room is an art, which not everyone has mastered to the same degree. One tries this or that, puts the cabinet there, the table here, in order to achieve a pleasing effect. Everyone knows that there are things that have a perceptible influence on the way a room works. But seldom can one account precisely for the reasons why the impact of the room has changed.

It would be good at the outset to be clear about what space actually is. The concept for us is in fact not graspable. One cannot think space away. Whether we have our eyes open or shut, whether we listen, see, smell, or feel, space is there; yet we cannot take hold of it with any of our senses. Space has no end and

no beginning. The difficulty of imagining space is actually a result of this. We first achieve a sense of space when we delimit it fully, by enclosing it. The feeling we have for space is the mental image we get of its size; what we feel when it is broad in scope, as in a meadow or at the sea, or when it is reduced, as in a small room, is the ability to comprehend its dimensions. It goes without saying that our eye is the organ that we use to grasp enclosed space in order to develop spatial awareness.

It should be clear, then, that our ability to perceive space is not a simple matter, but consists of two separate components. We first see with the eye; we thus receive a picture and estimate the distance before us, the amount of space, based on our experience. We learn this from childhood on, and we do it so often in life that we are no longer conscious of it and take it for granted.

Think, for example, of a meadow in which some trees stand. The trees offer us the possibility of assessing the space before us. Unconsciously we count one, two, three, four trees, and so on, and develop a solid idea of the space we perceive before us. The more trees there are in the meadow, the more our spatial impression changes. The broad dimensions of the meadow become smaller and smaller until at last we see the trees and not the forest. Which is to say: rather than the original broad spatial impression, we have almost no spatial impression at all. Nothing as far as the space goes has changed, but the spatial effect for us is wholly remade. The forest now offers us no spatial idea, although we still have our spatial awareness. This is a result, however, of our spatial consciousness at that moment, from our ability to move; we know that we can walk forward into the forest, we recognize that our forward motion will alter the relationship of

one tree to the next, in that we move through the space. Our forward motion alters the images that our eyes receive. The spatial impression in this instance remains so weak because from so many, many trees we receive countless images, and this makes it difficult for us to scan the distance from tree to tree. There are so many spatial impressions that we are not in a position to form an overall view and from it to obtain a unified spatial impression.

To make conscious spatial images, which enable a unified understanding of the sort that produces a clear, steady, spatial sense, the elements that allow us to get the measure of a space with our eyes must be grouped in a way—regularly and simply—so that we can take them in at one time. Only when this is possible is our spatial impression convincing and natural. These elements—in our example, trees on a meadow—are once more material bodies, whose characteristics we know from experience. Whether it is a tree or a garden fence, whether these are columns, piers, chairs, tables, or chests, whether they are sculptures or something else, is irrelevant.

Thus, on a wall of a room there should be a clearly delineated line somewhere, which gives us a sure means to estimate the length of that wall. A completely white wall, with absolutely nothing on it, and which has no clearly defined upper edge and no ceiling, gives the eye no pause; the eye is not in a position to sense when it has nothing to take hold of. There must be something on the wall that offers the possibility to read it, to assess it, in order for us to be able to get a feeling for the depth of a room. The means to make a wall readable include all manner of things, such as windows, pilasters, chests, pictures, and so on. The way in which they relate to each other determines the effects that allow us to grasp

The more opportunities for movement a space has, the more discontinuities and displacements there are to see, the richer the spatial creation will be. The unity of this displaced movement will yield the sense of scale.

For the designer, experience with all of these things is the starting point for his work. The designer works unconsciously and instinctively; the knowledge of how these things work is what we call tradition. The layperson sees only what is objective, but concealed within, unconsciously, is the effect.

OSKAR STRNAD
THOUGHTS ON DESIGNING A GROUND PLAN (CA. 1913)

"Gedanken beim Entwurf eines Grundrisses: Notizen für einen Vortrag" (n.d., ca. 1913). Typescript, Österreichische Nationalbibliothek, Vienna, 933804-C; published in Max Eisler, *Oskar Strnad* (Vienna: Gerlach und Wiedling, 1936), 56–57.

The first thought: From disordered and uncontained surroundings, to find the beginning, the beginning of the path (forecourt, the first stage). The first stopping point (door, gate, portal). The continuation of the path and the establishment of barriers in a rhythmical sequence. The establishment of all junctions and all terminal points. The possibilities of such processional planning are endlessly varied.

The second thought: The determination of the floor of this path in its full dimensions and the introduction of barriers, steps, doors, to form the boundaries of its dimensions (width and confinement, area and depth, and so on). These two thoughts arise from our capacity for bodily movement and the sensations we have, and the sensation of the rhythm inherent in our movements (climbing stairs, as well as walking, turning, and the like).

The third thought: the manipulation of light in its variations (slow darkening, brightening, increasing light to the fullest brightness). The manipulation of the way light falls. The placement of openings in the walls that delimited the ground plan (windows). The composition of the harmonies of these light intensities through penetrating and reflected light.

The ceiling can be thought of as the upper limit of the resulting concrete space. It is the logical extension of the dynamic of the path as a movement concept (spatial concept).

Arising at the same time is the thought of the visible as well as the otherwise perceptible substance of a building; architecture is not only seen, but also smelled, heard, and touched. This last sense, our haptic sense, is a particularly complex matter. It consists to a great extent of memories, of experiences, which lie deep within us. All of these sensations must come together to yield a vision of a complex spatial conception. When creating a ground plan all of these sensations must be simultaneously weighed and satisfied. From them, harmonies must be fashioned. The concept of such a composition is similar to that of a musical score and consists of a plethora of notes and handwritten prompts about the lines of the ground plan, about the relationships between the various measurements, about the materials and how they are handled, and sketches concerning colors. The substance of a building, "played" by the craftsman (which is to say translated into material reality), is in its totality what the architect experiences and puts down in his "score" and becomes a fully realized world.

Architecture is by no means a purely visual world, but, on the contrary, is made up of an unlimited number of imponderables. An architectural conception arises from the focused imagination as well as the possibilities we have for movement (as the absolute feeling for space), as well as the effects of light (the color of the material substance), of smell, of hearing, and of touch (of the material substance); not the superficial aspect of the material but also its soul must stand out. The treatment of the surface of the material on no account should be fashioned entirely with regard to aesthetic considerations, but also from the inexplicable spiritual ones. Only the architect is in the position to create from the material a special world in which this dead material can be experienced as a living organism. In this sense, the material is transparent, for it is not its surface that conveys an effect, but its independent existence.

HEINRICH KULKA
DER RAUMPLAN (1931)

From *Adolf Loos: Das Werk des Architekten* (Vienna: Anton Schroll, 1931), 13–15.

In general, up to our time, the principal concern of architects was the design of the façade and the ordering of piers in the interior. The plan was resolved by means of horizontal layers arranged floor by floor. Whatever remained by chance that was not occupied by the piers was what people called space. There was always the desire to connect various rooms to each other, but no one thought of a different way to do it. Thus, what came into being was the house or apartment with contiguous rooms or suites of rooms. Theaters had stacked galleries, each one floor high, or adjacent spaces (loggias) that were visibly linked to the various stories of the main space. Loos recognized that the ceilings of the loggias were uncomfortably low if one was not looking out into the large main space, that by means of a connection with a taller principal space one could save space with a lower adjacent space, and he used this insight in building houses.

Through Adolf Loos an essentially new and superior spatial concept came into being: thinking freely in space; the planning of spaces resting at different heights and that are not joined to any regular system of the horizontal layering of floors; the composing of connected spaces into a harmonic and inseparable whole and a spatially economical entity. Depending on their purpose and importance, the spaces not only had varying sizes but also varying heights. Loos can use the same amount of building material to create more living space, because in this way in the same building envelope, the same foundation, under the same roof, inside the same exterior walls, he can make more spaces. He makes the absolute most of the available building material and the building site. To put it differently: the architect who thinks about space only horizontally in plan needs a larger building envelope to house the same amount of space. And in this way, the pathways become needlessly longer, the running of the house less economical, the livability declines, and such buildings thus require more money to build and are more costly to maintain.

Today, piers and beams can be calculated with great precision. No constructive element should be oversized, and unnecessary expenses for building materials and construction can be avoided. Architectural engineering is the science that is concerned with this issue. But space here is never considered, and it is blissfully wasted.

The basis for spatial economy is the brainchild of one man: Adolf Loos. And as one spoke of up to now about the ground plan, since Loos one must speak about the Raumplan.

From this we get the principle: *only when architectural engineering is allied with spatial frugality may one talk about a modern (economical) building.*

With its wealth of practical tasks and requirements, the execution of the Raumplan requires the fullest concentration of the architect. At the moment of the birth of a spatial construct, he had to think simultaneously about its purpose, its structure, the paths running through it, how one enters it, furnishing, finishes, and the harmony of the rooms. Adolf Loos has this ability to concentrate, this capacity to conceive of space in the most sophisticated way. No one else is able forge the countless and often contradictory requirements into such a perfect solution, in a way that is natural, and that almost makes one forget how difficult the task is.

What is usually described as cubic building came about for quite another reason, as a mere effort toward making a simple plastic composition. It is empty façade-architecture. The Raumplan has nothing to do with such superficial plasticity. For Loos it is the interior that is primary. It determines the exterior form. That is not to say that the spatial arrangement and the exterior appearance are incompatible. Loos is attempting to bring the clearest form, the cube, and the most perfect building in the world, the stepped pyramid, back to life. It is possible for him because of his rigorous spatial discipline and his mastery of space.

JOSEF FRANK
THE HOUSE AS PATH AND PLACE (1931)

"Das Haus als Weg und Platz," in *Der Baumeister* 29 (August 1931): 316–23.

The modern house is descended from the old bohemian studio in a mansard roof space.

This attic story, condemned by the authorities and by modern architects alike as uninhabitable and unsanitary, which property speculators wrested with great effort from laws enacted to prevent its existence, which is the product of chance, contains that which we seek in vain in the planned and rationally furnished apartments below it: life, large rooms, large windows, multiple corners, angled walls, steps and height differences, columns and beams—in short, all the variety that we search for in the new house in order to counteract the dreary tedium of the regular four-cornered room. The entire struggle for the modern apartment and the modern house has at its core the goal of freeing people from their bourgeois prejudices and providing them with the possibility of a bohemian lifestyle. The prim and orderly home in both its old or new guise will become a nightmare in the future.

The task of the architect is to arrange all of these elements found in the garret into a house. A well-ordered house should be laid out like a city, with streets and alleys that lead inevitably to places that are cut off from traffic, so that one can rest there. In earlier times—especially in England, to which we owe the modern house form—such arrangements were traditional for cities and houses, but today this tradition has largely died out. The well-laid-out path through the house requires a sensitive understanding, and the architect cannot begin anew, which is why it would be important to revive this tradition. It is of the utmost importance that this path is not marked by some obvious means or decorative scheme, so that the visitor will never have the idea that he is being led around. A well-laid-out house is comparable to one of those beautiful old cities, in which even a stranger immediately knows his way around and can find the city hall and the market square without having to ask.

As an example of this, I would like to stress one very important element of the house plan: the staircase. It must be arranged in such a manner that when one approaches and begins to walk up to it one never has the feeling that he has to go back down the same way; one should always go further. If a house has more than two stories it is essential to consider

what significance these stories have; if the third story is merely an attic, the flights of stairs should not be placed one above the other because that would awaken the feeling of an apartment block and one would never know when he had arrived. On the other hand, if this second level is a roof terrace, then it should be closely connected with the living areas, and the stairway should be separated as much as possible from the second-story bedrooms. Every twist of the stairway serves to heighten this feeling of continuous movement, not to save space. The largest living space, measured in square meters, is not always the most practicable, the shortest path is not always the most comfortable, and the straight stairway is not always the best—indeed hardly ever. Merely relying on the statistic of the largest "living area" kills architecture because in a well-designed house there is no place that is not living space.

The stair forms the center of the house documented here [Frank is referring here to the Beer House, which is illustrated in the article]. It is arranged in such a way that all of the main living areas are positioned on the various landings. Its underlying concept is the following: One enters the hall facing the stair. The stair, which turns outward into the room, presents its first step to the person entering. When he begins to climb upward, he can see up to the first landing and through a large opening into the most important room in the house, the living room. From this level, the stair leads straight up to two rooms, the study and salon, which are concealed from the living room but closely connected to it. At this point, the level housing the main living areas comes to an end. To emphasize this fact, the stairs leading up to the next floor containing the bedrooms wind in the other direction, and a clear division of the house is achieved.

The regular four-cornered room is the least suited to living; it is quite useful as a storage space for furniture, but not for anything else. I believe that a polygon drawn by chance, whether with right or acute angles, as a plan for a room is much more appropriate than a regular four-cornered one. Chance also helped in the case of the garret studio, which was always comfortable and impersonal. Practical necessities should never be an inducement to subvert formally a carefully planned layout because the viewer cannot understand its meaning, and, besides that, it is part of the architect's art to bring form and content into a harmonious balance.

Time and again, the regular four-cornered room misleads us into making architecture with furniture. One wants to use built-in elements, striking color schemes, and cubic forms to break up and articulate the banal space and to give it some character. The task of the architect, however, consists of creating spaces, not in arranging furniture or painting walls, which is a matter of good taste, something anyone can have. It is a well-known fact that in well-designed rooms it does not really matter what type of furnishings there are, provided that they are not so large that they become architectural elements. The personality of the inhabitant can be freely expressed. The space will emphasize those areas where every place and path should be. The regular four-cornered room bears much of the blame for the excesses of our modern arts and crafts trades, which often have to be called upon, so that, after severe cutbacks, it can still be relatively inexpensively designed and furnished.

The sitting area forms the centerpiece of the house, its piazza. Every living room must have a center, around which it is arranged and which gives the room its character. That was much easier in former times because there was a fireplace or—which is less distinctive—a stove. Today, when such a focal point is often lacking, it is much more difficult to design a plan because this center must be created architectonically. Among the means to do so are windows, niches, columns, and so forth. The absence of this sort of formal center is often what makes the regular four-cornered room so unlivable.

The path that connects these separate zones in the living spaces with each other has to be varied enough so that one never senses its length. Varied lighting effects, steps, and so forth provide important aids. The way a door opens into a room, though often ignored, is of great importance: I would like to mention here that virtually all doors swing the wrong way. They open into the room, toward the

sidewall, in such a way that the person enters suddenly, provoking a sense of unease. If the door swings the other direction, slowly opening into the room, then there is a natural anteroom between the door and the wall, and the space remains undisturbed. In the same way, it is also of great importance whether the door swings toward or away from the person opening it.

None of these considerations is new by any means; on the contrary, they are quite old, but it is important to point them out from time to time. I believe that these are basic issues all too often ignored in schools of architecture. A great deal of emphasis is placed on façades, construction, and economy, and rarely is it borne in mind *that it is not the mission of a school to produce useful objects, but to provide the students with a basic understanding so that they can think for themselves*; instead, all too often, students are crammed with the prejudiced ideas of their teachers with regard to matters of life and form, and too often problems are presented as if they have been solved, as if they are merely matters of construction and cost divorced from experience. I do not want to say that lessons in construction are not of great importance, but it is more a matter of providing students with a general understanding than it is teaching them about specifics. However, it seems to me more important to start with ideal dwellings of every sort, which is to say with attempts to group together rooms—without being concerned about actually realizing them—that are linked to each other in the best possible way, and which have the correct dimensions and relationships to each other. This provides a basic knowledge that is always applicable, and that a practical and independently thinking architect can vary, as he deems necessary with the means available. All of our objects of daily use, to which we must also accord the house, involve compromises of purpose, material, form, quality, price, and everything else. But the rules for a good house do not change in principle and must be constantly considered anew. How does one enter the garden? What should a path to the main entry look like? What form should an anteroom have? How does one proceed from the anteroom past the cloakroom and into the living

room? How should a sitting area be positioned in relation to a door or window? How many such questions there are that have to be answered, and a house is made up of these elements. That is modern architecture.

JOSEF FRANK
HOW TO PLAN A HOUSE (CA. 1942) (EXCERPTS)

"How to Plan a House," ms., ca. 1942; published in Johannes Spalt, ed., *Josef Frank 1885–1967: Möbel & Geräte & Theoretisches* (Vienna: Hochschule für angewandte Kunst, 1981), 156–67.

The modern house should provide its inhabitant with as much freedom as possible—which is to say, enough freedom so that the spaces will not force him into a rigid lifestyle; such a free house will no longer consist of a living room and ancillary spaces, but it will instead be a place of dwelling in which every space fulfills the demands we now often place on living rooms. The house should provide its inhabitant with the possibility to live in the best and freest manner for his circumstances, and in a way he may not even imagine, even when he may have a repressed desire for it. The form of the house, of course, will not create a new society, but it can stimulate people to think more freely. . . . The new way of living did not arise from the good bourgeois domicile of the nineteenth century, but from the artist's atelier in the attic—the bohemian abode. What constitutes the difference? The normal dwelling space was a series of rooms arranged enfilade. The atelier, however, was a high, irregularly shaped space under the roof, and the placement of windows largely a matter of chance; they were not inserted for the purpose of lighting but to fit some silly roof form. And in this space, which was never planned but the product of accidental forces—essentially what was left over—cheap and crude, which the authorities did not even sanction for habitation, the modern dwelling space arose. The inhabitant erected dividers within these spaces, often by means of armoires or curtains, and sometimes he divided the space into two stories; and eventually an irregular living complex came into being, and everything was the result of chance actions.

I do not believe that orthogonal regularity arose because such four-cornered rooms were especially well suited for living, because the corners actually force certain constraints; such orthogonal spaces came to be as a result of necessity, because buildings in cities have to be put in orderly fashion to form streets; but we also know that the desire to make straight streets was greatly over-emphasized in an effort once more to foster representation. The more irregular the streets are, the more livable is the town. But even if there are requirements in the public interest with regard to traffic flow or real estate—and these often call for straight streets in the interest of practicality (even if it is often groundless)—that is not true for the dwelling house; our technology allows for any sort of free ordering within.

It is no wonder that people have a greater sense of well-being in casually remodeled barns and adapted windmills than in a carefully planned house with scientifically determined divisions into functional areas, and that they seek reprieve from the convenience of the city in the primitive conditions of the countryside. The belief in systematic ordering arose from being reared in an atmosphere lacking in freedom. I believe that if the architect takes a pencil and without thinking draws any irregular polygon he chooses, which should then constitute the plan of a living space, it will, as a rule, be better than anything he would make on the basis of various theories. . . .

We cannot, of course, assemble a house only from "accidents," we require a conscious plan, one that first and foremost fulfills practical requirements. . . .

I want to assert that the organization of the modern house is a path; what I mean by that is what is most essential in a good house is the way in which one enters and goes through it. The concept is similar to that of a city that has grown up organically; it consists of main thoroughfares, side streets, and squares that are all so distinctive that one never has the sense that he can lose his way. If a house is well designed, then a visitor who is entering the house for the first time can readily find his way to each space. It is thus necessary that every space for him should be signed, so that

he can recognize through its form and lighting in which direction he should walk, and whether a stop is called for. Here one of the most important rules is that this path is continuous, the straight line is interrupted in significant places, and that every turn appears to have a reason; above all, it is of greatest importance that one does not go backward to repeat part of the path a second time, or that he has to go up stairs and then down again, which is merely confusing. If I add here again that the greatest impact, namely livability, should be made with the least means, I do not mean that in a material sense it should be just enough to make it possible to live in the house or that the space should be reduced to the absolute possible minimum; I mean instead that any path that has to be duplicated symbolizes a waste and provokes a sense of unease. It is not a matter of making all of the rooms as small as possible, but to avoid dead zones, which are neither practical nor aesthetically justified; a room may have places where one can't go, but they should give one a sense of expanse, and in this way they are necessary and useful . . .

When we enter [into the house], we are now separated from nature, and here begins the planned route to the living room. If there are passageways in which one should not pause, then one should move through them longwise, and they should be uniformly illuminated on the long side, so that there is no midpoint. If, however, there is a space that is only intended for a brief stay, which is only intended to make a turn of some sort, then it should be more or less square in form, because this gives it an inviting shape. The entrance into the living room should be clearly visible; it should be on the opposite side of the entry vestibule, and not on one of the sides. If there is a door here, it should be clearly marked as the entry door, which is to say, it should be placed in a niche, though the thickness of the walls here is often sufficient. The living room is the center of the house, in the same way that the main square was the center of a city, but with the difference that it does not have to be in the center because it is not there for a public not residing within. And this center also has a center, which gives the living room its charac-

ter. Only here decorations in any form are unnecessary, which are in essence an effort to give the room some character. In earlier times, the hearth formed the center, creating a natural gathering place; but today it is no longer a necessity [and] for that reason the room should be given a shape that has within it a recognizable resting place; it can be lighter than the rest of the room, or darker, but in any event it should be differentiated so that there is no doubt about where this place is; it has to be such that it can be sensed.

The path we have to walk through the house can also sometimes be given stairs, so that the rooms can lie at different levels and have different heights, which then can become more distinctive and give one the sense of three-dimensional living. Stairs should be so arranged that one can access them directly from any place in the house where one might come from, without having to walk around them; we must have the impression that regardless of the direction we want to go we do not have to retrace our path but always move forward. By breaking the stairs into more than one run, we can eliminate any real possibility of having to repeat the path, or the loss of orientation, which comes from a spiral stair. All of these components of a building, which symbolically hint at the movement through the house, have to be carefully considered, because they make up its actual architecture, which should be more than a sequence of spaces; it is especially important here to note that all of this has to be done is such a manner that it is natural and not overpowering, so that the intention is not immediately obvious—otherwise the house can easily become theatrical.

NOTES

INTRODUCTION

1 Kirk Varnedoe, "Architecture," in Kirk Varnedoe, *Vienna 1900: Art, Architecture & Design*, exh. cat. (New York: Museum of Modern Art / Boston: Little, Brown, 1986), 25.

2 See, for example, Burkhardt Rukschcio, "Studien zu Entwürfen, Projekten und ausgeführten Bauten von Adolf Loos (1870–1933)" (Ph.D. diss., Universität Wien, 1973); Dietrich Worbs, ed., *Adolf Loos 1870–1933: Raumplan–Wohnungsbau*, exh. cat. (Berlin: Akademie der Künste, 1983); Johannes Spalt, "Josef Frank und die räumliche Konzeption seiner Hausentwürfe," *Um Bau* 10 (August 1986): 59–74; Beatriz Colomina, "Intimacy and Spectacle: The Interiors of Adolf Loos," *AA Files* 20 (Autumn 1990): 5–15; Cynthia Jara, "Adolf Loos's Raumplan Theory," *Journal of Architectural Education* 48, no. 3 (February 1995): 185–201; Christopher Long, "The House as Path and Place: Spatial Planning in Josef Frank's Villa Beer, 1928–1930," *Journal of the Society of Architectural Historians* 59 (December 2000): 478–501; Kurt Lustenberger, "Der Schnitt durch den Plan," *Werk, Bauen + Wohnen* 12 (December 1995): 45–52; Werner Oechslin, "Raumplan versus plan libre," *Daidalos* (15 December 1991): 76–83; Max Risselada, ed., *Raumplan versus Plan Libre: Adolf Loos and Le Corbusier, 1919–1930* (New York: Rizzoli, 1988).

3 The literature on Le Corbusier and the *promenade architecturale* is quite extensive. Nearly every text that considers Le Corbusier's work in any detail touches on the issue. The best recent discussion can be found in Armando Manuel de Castilho Rabaça Correia Cordeiro, "Ordering Code and Mediating Machine: Le Corbusier and the Roots of the Architectural Promenade" (Ph.D. diss., Universidade de Coimbra, 2014). See also, e.g., Tim Benton, *The Villas of Le Corbusier and Pierre Jeanneret 1920–1930*

(Basel: Birkhäuser, 2007); Paul Emmons, "Intimate Circulations: Representing Flow in House and City," *AA Files* 51 (2005): 48–57; Flora Samuel, *Le Corbusier and the Architectural Promenade* (Basel: Birkhäuser, 2010); and Francesco Passanti, "Architecture, Proportion, Classicism, and Other Issues," in Stanislaus von Moos and Arthur Rüegg, eds., *Le Corbusier before Le Corbusier* (New Haven: Yale University Press, 2002).

4 Samuel, *Le Corbusier and the Architectural Promenade*, 9.

5 Le Corbusier and Pierre Jenneret, *Oeuvre complète*, vol. 2, 1929–1934 (Zurich: Les Éditions d'Architecture, 1995), 24.

6 Samuel, *Le Corbusier and the Architectural Promenade*, 9.

7 Le Corbusier and Pierre Jenneret, *Oeuvre complète*, vol. 1, 1910–1929 (Zurich: Les Éditions d'Architecture, 1995), 60.

8 Rabaça, "Ordering Code and Mediating Machine: Le Corbusier and the Roots of the Architectural Promenade," i.

9 Ibid., 4. Here Rabaça is drawing on an idea put forward by Richard Etlin. See Etlin, *Symbolic Space: French Enlightenment Architecture and Its Legacy* (Chicago: University of Chicago Press, 1994), xx.

CHAPTER ONE

1 Johannes Jahn, ed., *Die Kunstwissenschaft der Gegenwart in Selbstdarstellungen* (Leipzig: Felix Meiner, 1924). See also Oskar Wulff, "August Schmarsow zum 80. Geburtstag," *Zeitschrift für Kunstgeschichte* 2, no. 3 (1933): 207–9; Ernst Ullmann, "Der Beitrag August Schmarsows zur Architekturtheorie," Habilitationsschrift, Karl-Marx-Universität Leipzig, 1967; Harry Francis Mallgrave and Eleftherios Ikonomou, eds., *Empathy, Form, and Space: Problems in German Aesthetics, 1873–1934* (Santa Monica,

Calif.: Getty Center for the History of Art and the Humanities, 1994): 57–58; and Peter H. Feist, "Schmarsow, August Hannibal," in *Neue Deutsche Biographie* 23 (2007): 121.

2 Ernst Ullmann, *100 Jahre Kunstwissenschaft in Leipzig* (Leipzig: Karl-Marx-Universität Leipzig, 1975), 18.

3 Heinrich Wölfflin, *Renaissance und Barock: Eine Untersuchung über Wesen und Entstehung des Barockstils in Italien* (Munich: Theodor Ackermann, 1888).

4 Quoted in Stephen Games, *Pevsner—The Early Life: Germany and Art* (London: Continuum, 2010), 92.

5 Ibid.

6 Mallgrave and Ikonomou, eds., *Empathy, Form, and Space*, 57–58.

7 Ibid., 58.

8 Schmarsow's lecture was published as a small booklet. The quotations I use throughout come from the published text, August Schmarsow, *Das Wesen der architektonischen Schöpfung: Antrittsvorlesung gehalten in der Aula der k. Universität Leipzig am 8. November 1893* (Leipzig: Karl W. Hiersemann, 1894), 2–3. Unless otherwise noted, all translations here and throughout this book are my own. On the background and meaning of Schmarsow's address, see Rostislav Švácha, "Ke spisu August Schmarsowa o podstatě architektury z roku," *Umění* 49, no. 6 (2001): 561–68. For other discussions of Schmarsow, his ideas, and import, see Eleftherios Ikonomou, "The Transformation of Space in the Architectural Thinking of the Late 19th and Early 20th Century, with Special Reference to Germany" (Ph.D. diss., University of Cambridge, 1985), 126–47; Roy Malcolm Porter, "The Essence of Architecture: August Schmarsow's Theory of Space" (Ph.D. diss., University of Pennsylvania,

2005); Mitchell W. Schwarzer, "The Emergence of Architectural Space: August Schmarsow's Theory of *Raumgestaltung*," *Assemblage* 15 (August 1991): 48–61; Tat'iana Vladova, "La pensée de l'art d'August Schmarsow entre corps et configuration spatiale," *Passagen—Deutsches Forum für Kunstgeschichte/Passages—Centre allemande d'histoire de l'art* 41 (2012): 137–51; Beatrix Zug, *Die Anthropologie des Raumes in der Architekturtheorie des frühen 20. Jahrhunderts* (Tübingen: Ernst Wasmuth, 2006), 11–37; and Beatrix Zug, "Architecture as Enclosure of Man: August Schmarsow's Attempt at a Scientific Grounding of the Hegelian Principle," in Kirsten Wagner and Jasper Cepl, eds., *Images of the Body in Architecture: Anthropology and Built Space* (Tübingen: Ernst Wasmuth, 2014), 189–206.

9 Schmarsow, *Das Wesen der architektonischen Schöpfung*, 2–3.

10 Ibid., 8.

11 Nicolas Le Camus de Mézières, *Le génie de l'architecture, ou L'analogie de cet art avec nos sensations* (1780). English ed.: *The Genius of Architecture; or, The Analogy of That Art with Our Sensations*, introduction by Robin Middleton; trans. David Britt (Santa Monica, Calif.: Getty Center for the History of Art and the Humanities, 1992).

12 Johann Wolfgang von Goethe, *Zur Farbenlehre*, 2 vols. (Tübingen: Cotta, 1810).

13 See, e.g., Hermann von Helmholtz, *Handbuch der physiologischen Optik* (Leipzig: L. Voss, 1867); Gustav Fechner, *Elemente der Psychophysik* (Leipzig: Breitkopf und Hartel, 1860); Carl Stumpf, *Über den psychologischen Ursprung der Raumvorstellung* (Leipzig: Hirzel, 1873); and Wilhelm Wundt, *Beiträge zur Theorie der Sinneswahrnehmung* (Leipzig: Winter, 1862) and *Grundzüge der physiologischen Psychologie*, 2 vols. (Leipzig: Engelmann, 1873–74).

14 Robert Vischer, *Über das optische Formgefühl: Ein Beitrag zur Aesthetik* (Leipzig: Herm. Credner, 1873).

15 Juliet Koss, "On the Limits of Empathy," *Art Bulletin* 88, no. 1 (March 2006): 139–40.

16 Friedrich Theodor Vischer, *Aesthetik oder Wissenschaft des Schönen*, 8 vols. (Reutlingen and Stuttgart: Carl Mäcken, 1846–1857); and Mallgrave and Ikonomou, eds., *Empathy, Form, and Space*, 18–20.

17 Vischer, *Über das optische Formgefühl*, 10; trans.

in Mallgrave and Ikonomou, *Empathy, Form, and Space*, 98; and Koss, "On the Limits of Empathy," 140.

18 Vischer, *Über das optische Formgefühl*, 10; trans. in Mallgrave and Ikonomou, *Empathy, Form, and Space*, 99.

19 Koss, "On the Limits of Empathy," 141.

20 Vischer, *Über das optische Formgefühl*, trans. in Mallgrave and Ikonomou, *Empathy, Form, and Space*, 97.

21 Ibid., 99.

22 Ibid., 99–100.

23 Heinrich Wölfflin, *Prolegomena zu einer Psychologie der Architektur* (Munich: Dr. C. Wolf & Sohn, 1886).

24 Wölfflin, *Prolegomena zu einer Psychologie der Architektur*, trans. in Mallgrave and Ikonomou, *Empathy, Form, and Space*, 151. On Wölfflin's spatial ideas, see Ikonomou, "The Transformation of Space in the Architectural Thinking of the Late 19th and Early 20th Century, with Special Reference to Germany," 108–20.

25 Conrad Fiedler, "Bemerkungen über Wesen und Geschichte der Baukunst," *Deutsche Rundschau* 15 (1878): 361–83; and Mallgrave and Ikonomou, eds., *Empathy, Form, and Space*, 33–34. See also Fiedler's book, *Über die Beurtheilung von Werken der bildenden Kunst* (Leipzig: S. Hirzel, 1876).

26 Adolf von Hildebrand, *Das Problem der Form in der bildenden Kunst* (Strasbourg: Heitz & Mündel, 1893), trans. in Mallgrave and Ikonomou, *Empathy, Form, and Space*, 239.

27 Ibid.

28 Ibid., 260.

29 See Harry Francis Mallgrave, *Architecture and Embodiment: The Implications of the New Sciences and Humanities for Design* (London: Routledge, 2013), 122–26; and the introduction by Mallgrave and Ikonomou in *Empathy, Form, and Space*, esp. 17–29; Schwarzer, "The Emergence of Architectural Space," 53–54; and Bettina Köhler, "Architekturgeschichte als Geschichte der Raumwahrnehmung," *Daidalos* 67 (March 1998): 36–43.

30 Schmarsow, *Das Wesen der architektonischen Schöpfung*, 9–10.

31 Richard Lucae, "Über die Macht des Raumes in der Baukunst," *Zeitschrift für Bauwesen* 19 (1869): 294–306.

32 See the introduction by Mallgrave and Ikonomou in *Empathy, Form, and Space*, 59.

33 Hans Wilhelm Auer, "Die Entwicklung des Raumes in der Baukunst," *Allgemeine Bauzeitung* 48 (1883): 65–68, 73–74; and J. Duncan Berry, "Hans Auer and the Morality of Architectural Space," in Deborah J. Johnson and David Ogawa, eds., *Seeing and Beyond: Essays on Eighteenth- to Twenty-First-Century Art in Honor of Kermit S. Champa* (New York: Peter Lang), 149–84.

34 On the broader discourse about space before Schmarsow, see Mitchell W. Schwarzer, *German Architectural Theory and the Search for Modern Identity* (Cambridge: Cambridge University Press, 1995); and Jindřich Vybíral, "The Architects Have Overslept? On the Concept of Space in 19th-Century Architectural Theory." *Umění* 52 (2004): 110–22.

35 Vybíral, "The Architects Have Overslept?," 116–17.

36 Schmarsow, *Das Wesen der architektonischen Schöpfung*, 11.

37 Ibid.

38 Vybíral, "The Architects Have Overslept?," 117.

39 Schmarsow, *Das Wesen der architektonischen Schöpfung*, 29.

40 Paul Frankl, *Die Entwicklungsphasen der neueren Baukunst* (Leipzig: B. G. Teubner, 1914). A similar but not yet fully developed argument about the relationship between space and the evolution of architecture can be found already in Gustav Ebe, *Architektonische Raumlehre: Entwicklung der Typus des Innenbaues* (Dresden: Gerhard Kühtmann, 1900). For a more recent account, see Köhler, "Architekturgeschichte als Geschichte der Raumwahrnehmung."

41 August Schmarsow, "Über den Werth der Dimensionen im menschlichen Raumgebilde," *Berichte über die Verhandlungen der Königlich Sächsischen Gesellschaft der Wissenschaften zu Leipzig, Philologisch-Historische Klasse* 48 (1896): 44–61; August Schmarsow, *Grundbegriffe der Kunstwissenschaft am Übergang vom Altertum zum Mittelalter, kritisch erörtert und in systematischem Zusammenhange dargestellt* (Leipzig: B. G. Teubner, 1905); and August Schmarsow, "Raumgestaltung als Wesen der architektonischen Schöpfung," *Zeitschrift für Ästhetik und allgemeine Kunstwissenschaft* 9 (1914): 66–95.

42 Schmarsow, *Grundbegriffe der Kunstwissenschaft*, 38–41. See also Zug, *Die Anthropologie des Raumes in der Architekturtheorie des frühen 20. Jahrhunderts*, 33–35.

43 Zug, *Die Anthropologie des Raumes in der*

Architekturtheorie des frühen 20. Jahrhunderts, 182–86.

44 Ibid., 187.

45 Ibid., 184, 190.

46 Bruno Specht, "Raumkunst," *Deutsche Bauzeitung* 29, no. 81 (1895): 502.

47 See, e.g., Heinrich Wölfflin's review of August Schmarsow, *Das Wesen der architektonischen Schöpfung*, in "Theorie und Technik der Kunst," *Repertorium für Kunstwissenschaft* 17 (1894): 141–42; and Karl Illert, "Das Wesen der architektonischen Schöpfung," *Centralblatt der Bauverwaltung*, part 1, 15 August 1896: 369–70; part 2, 22 August 1896: 377–79, and the responses by Richard Streiter, "Architektur und Kunstphilosphie," *Centralblatt der Bauverwaltung*, 12 December 1896: 550–53; and 27 February 1897: 100–1.

48 Richard Streiter, *Ausgewählte Schriften* (Munich: Delphin, 1913), 117, quoted in Schwarzer, "The Emergence of Architectural Space," 61, n. 76.

49 Alois Riegl, *Historische Grammatik der bildenden Künste*, ed. Karl M. Swoboda and Otto Pächt (Graz: privately printed, 1966); translated as *Historical Grammar of the Visual Arts*, trans. Jacqueline E. Jung, foreword by Benjamin Binstock (New York: Zone, 2004), 414.

50 Alois Riegl, *Stilfragen: Grundlegungen zu einer Geschichte der Ornametik* (Berlin: Georg Siemens, 1893), and *Die spätrömische Kunstindustrie nach den Funden in Österreich-Ungarn* (Vienna: Druck und Verlag der kaiserlich-königlichen Hof- und Staatsdruckerei, 1901). See Schwarzer, "The Emergence of Architectural Space," 55; Ulya Vogt-Göknil, *Architektonische Grundbegriffe und Umraumerlebnis* (Zurich: Origo, 1951), esp. 1–36; and Ikonomou, "The Transformation of Space in the Architectural Thinking of the Late 19th and Early 20th Century, with Special Reference to Germany," 120–25.

51 Feist, "Schmarsow, August Hannibal," 122–23.

52 See Oskar Wulff, "Zu August Schmarsows Rücktritt," *Zeitschrift für bildende Kunst* 55 (1919/1920): 318–20. At the university archive in Leipzig, many of the surviving papers related to Schmarsow's tenure have to do with this plagiarism case. Universität Leipzig, Universitätsarchiv, PA 0933.

53 Schmarsow, *Grundbegriffe der Kunstwissenschaft*, 192.

CHAPTER TWO

1 Otto Niedermoser, *Oskar Strnad 1879–1935* (Vienna: Bergland, 1965), 12–13. On Strnad's life and work, see also Juliane Stoklaska, "Oskar Strnad" (Ph.D. diss., Universität Wien), 1959.

2 Niedermoser, *Oskar Strnad*, 13–14.

3 Carl König, "Die Wissenschaft von der Architektur und Ihre praktische Bedeutung," *Wiener Bauindustrie Zeitung* 19, no. 6 (7 November 1901): 42–46.

4 Iris Meder, "Oskar Strnad—Immer bestimmend ist nur der Mensch," in Iris Meder and Evi Fuchs, eds., *Oskar Strnad 1879–1935*, exh. cat. (Vienna: Anton Pustet, 2007), 10–11.

5 Max Eisler, *Oskar Strnad* (Vienna: Gerlach und Wiedling, 1936), 9.

6 For a general discussion and images of the house and its design, see "Landhaus in Wien XIX. Kobenzlgasse," *Der Architekt* 19 (1913): 131–33; Max Eisler, "Wiener Stadtvillen und Landhäuser," in *Wasmuths Monatshefte für Baukunst* 2 (1915–16): 514–15; Eisler, *Oskar Strnad*, 21–22; Niedermoser, *Oskar Strnad*, 18; Friedrich Achleitner, "Ein positives Beispiel: Vorbildliche Renovierung der Strnad-Villa in der Cobenzlgasse," *Die Presse*, 14–15 August 1971; Christopher Long, "'Gedanken beim Entwurf eines Grundrisses': Space and Promenade in Oskar Strnad's Hock and Wassermann Houses, 1912–14," *Umění: Journal of the Institute of Art History, Czech Academy of Sciences* 49, no. 6 (2001): 520–30; Iris Meder, "Offene Welten: Die Wiener Schule in Einfamilienhausbau 1910–1938" (Ph.D. diss., Universität Stuttgart, 2001), 58–63; and Meder, "Oskar Strnad—Immer bestimmend ist nur der Mensch," 11–15.

7 The precise wording was "wegen gröblicher Verunstaltung des Stadtbildes." Niedermoser, *Oskar Strnad*, 18.

8 Ibid.

9 One of the essays, "Einiges Theoretische zur Raumgestaltung" (typescript, Österreichische Nationalbibliothek, Vienna), was first presented as a lecture, titled simply "Raum" (Space) on 17 January 1913, at the Ingenieur- und Architektenverein in Vienna (see appendix). It was first published as "Einiges Theoretische zur Raumgestaltung" in *Deutsche Kunst und Dekoration* 41 (1 October 1917): 39–68. It was reprinted under the title "Raumgestaltung und Raumgelenke" in *Innen-Dekoration* 30 (July–August 1919):

254–58; 292–93. The other essay, "Gedanken beim Entwurf eines Grundrisses," likely was written around the same time. It survives in the form of a typescript now in the Österreichische Nationalbibliothek, Vienna. It was first published in Eisler, *Oskar Strnad*, 56–57. For a wider discussion of Strnad's theoretical ideas, see Ulla Weich, "Die theoretische Ansichten des Architekten und Lehrers Oskar Strnad," Diplomarbeit, Universität Wien, 1995.

10 Strnad, "Einiges Theoretische zur Raumgestaltung," 40, 48.

11 The Czech architectural historian Rostislav Švácha has argued that until the early years of the twentieth century these ideas were widely disseminated and understood among the art historians but architects were only dimly aware of them. See Rostislav Švácha, "The Architects Have Overslept: Space as a Construct of Art Historians, 1888–1914," *Umění* 49, no. 6 (2001): 487–500. Švácha, though essentially correct, overstates his case a little. Even before Schmarsow's time, as we have seen, there were lively discussions about space and its role in forging a new architecture. By the time Strnad was attending the Technische Hochscule in Vienna just after the turn of the century, the issue had increasingly taken a significant place in theoretical discussions about architectural reform. These discussions about space were also felt outside the German speaking universities, at the Czech Technical University in Prague, for example, and in the Netherlands. Still, Schmarsow's ideas found only limited resonance in architectural circles. Harry Mallgrave, for example, has contended that neither Sigfried Gidieon nor Bruno Zevi, who "also come to define architecture in identical terms . . . seem to have been unaware of Schmarsow's earlier effort." Harry Francis Mallgrave and Christina Contandriopoulos, eds., *Architectural Theory: Volume II, An Anthology from 1871 to 2005* (Malden, Mass.: Blackwell, 2008): 82. See also Alina A. Payne, "Architectural History and the History of Art: A Suspended Dialogue," *Journal of the Society of Architectural Historians* 58, no. 3 (September 1999): 292–99.

12 Strnad, "Einiges Theoretische zur Raumgestaltung," 40.

13 Hildebrand, *Das Problem der Form in der bildenden Kunst*, translated in Mallgrave and Ikonomou, *Empathy, Form, and Space*, 261.

14 Strnad, "Einiges Theoretische zur Raumgestaltung," 49.

15 Ibid., 39.

16 Ibid., 67–68.

17 Ibid., 40.

18 Ibid., 50.

19 Ibid., 68.

20 Ibid.

21 See Mallgrave, *Architecture and Embodiment*, 125.

22 Theodor Lipps, *Raumästhetik und geometrisch-optische Täuschungen* (Leipzig: J. A. Barth, 1893–97); *Ästhetik: Psychologie des Schönen und der Kunst* (Hamburg: Leopold Voss, 1903–06); "Einfühlung und ästhetischer Genuss," *Die Zukunft* 54 (1906): 100–14.

23 Mallgrave and Ikonomou, introduction, *Empathy, Form, and Space,* 29.

24 See, for example, Zeynep Çelik, "Kinaesthetic Impulses: Aesthetic Experience, Bodily Knowledge, and Pedagogical Practices in Germany, 1871–1918" (Ph.D. diss., Massachusetts Institute of Technology, 2007); and Stacy Hand, "Embodied Abstraction: Biomorphic Fantasy and Empathy Aesthetics in the Work of Hermann Obrist, August Endell, and Their Followers" (Ph.D. diss., University of Chicago, 2008).

25 Hendrik Petrus Berlage, *Gedanken über Stil in der Baukunst* (Leipzig: Julius Zeitler, 1905), 23. See also Berlage's essay "Raumkunst und Architektur." *Schweizerische Bauzeitung* 49, no. 24 (1907): 293–97; no. 25, 303–6; no. 26, 317–18. Another possible, though much less likely, source for Strnad was Frank Lloyd Wright. Wright's 1909 Robie House offered a complex and elegant plan, with its own circuitous route of entry. But Wright's designs were difficult for Europeans to access until 1911, when the newly released Wasmuth publications became available. Strnad's younger contemporaries, R. M. Schindler and Richard Neutra, took notice of Wright's work, but there is nothing in Strnad's work to suggest that he borrowed in any way from Wright, and the fact that Strnad's design for the Hock House preceded the appearance of the Wasmuth portfolio and *Sonderheft* is a strong argument against any influence. On Wright's use of processional routes, see John Sergeant, "Frank Lloyd Wright's Use of Movement," in Peter Blundell Jones and

Mark Meagher, eds., *Architecture and Movement: The Dynamic Experience of Buildings and Landscapes* (London: Routledge, 2015): 55–64.

26 See Denis Bablet and Marie-Louise Bablet, *Adolphe Appia, 1862–1928: Darsteller–Raum–Licht* (Zurich: Atlantis, 1982); and R. C. Beacham, *Adolphe Appia: Theatre Artist* (Cambridge: Cambridge University Press, 1987).

27 Harry Francis Mallgrave, "New Hellerau: Design in the Biological Age," in Kirsten Wagner and Jasper Cepl, eds. *Images of the Body in Architecture: Anthropology and Built Space* (Tübingen: Ernst Wasmuth, 2014): 207–8.

28 Ibid., 209.

29 In addition to Schmarsow's other writings mentioned in chapter 1, see August Schmarsow, *Zur Frage nach dem Malerischen: Sein Grundbegriff und seine Entwicklung* (Leipzig: S. Hirzel, 1896); *Barock und Rokoko: Eine kritische Auseinandersetzung über das Malerische in der Architektur* (Leipzig: S. Hirzel, 1897); and *Plastik, Malerei und Reliefkunst in ihrem gegenseitigen Verhältnis* (Leipzig: S. Hirzel, 1899).

30 Oskar Strnad, "Der Palast Diokletians," *Neue Freie Presse,* 24 August 1912: 19–20. The book in question was George Niemann, *Der Palast Diokletians in Spalato: Im Auftrag des k.k. Ministeriums für Kultus und Unterricht aufgenommen und beschrieben von George Niemann* (Vienna: Hölder, 1910). I am grateful to Ruth Hanisch for alerting me to the existence of Strnad's review.

31 Strnad, "Der Palast Diokletians," 19–20.

32 Strnad, "Gedanken beim Entwurf eines Grundrisses," in Eisler, *Oskar Strnad,* 56.

33 Ibid.

34 Ibid.

35 Ibid., 56–57.

36 Ibid., 57.

37 See Eisler, "Wiener Stadtvillen und Landhäuser," 518–19; *Österreichische Werkkultur* (Vienna: Anton Schroll, 1916), 82, 85–86, 90, 92; Arthur Roessler, "Professor Dr. Oskar Strnad—Wien," in *Innen-Dekoration* 29 (January–February 1918): 18–21; Eisler, *Oskar Strnad,* 22–23; Niedermoser, *Oskar Strnad,* 18; Long, "'Gedanken beim Entwurf eines Grundrisses': Space and Promenade in Oskar Strnad's Hock and Wassermann Houses, 1912–14"; Meder, "Offene Welten," 63–74; and Meder, "Oskar Strnad—Immer bestimmend ist nur der Mensch," in Meder and Fuchs, eds., *Oskar Strnad 1879–1935*, 15–23.

38 Margarete Schütte-Lihotzky, quoted in Sylvia Mattl-Wurm, *Interieurs: Wiener Künstlerwohnungen 1830–1930* (Vienna: Historisches Museum der Stadt Wien, 1990), 175.

39 Strnad's allusions to color and coloristic effects here probably derive in some measure from the writings of Jakob von Falke, curator and cultural historian at the Österreichisches Museum für Kunst und Industrie. In his book, *Die Kunst im Hause* from 1871, a popular work of the period that Strnad, Frank, and Loos probably all read, Falke wrote, for example: "Color produces the first and most conspicuous impression [and] it produces the general mood. With color, we can make the room appear narrower or wider, lower or higher. If we want to give the room a serious or cheerful mood, spare or opulent, simple or magnificent, if we want to seem cozy and homey, poetic or cold, if we want to create a dreamy nook, a place for solitude and quiet contemplation, or a place of pleasure and conviviality—our first and last means will be color." (Die Farbe macht den ersten und auffallendsten Eindruck, sie giebt die allgemeine Stimmung. Mit der Farbe können wir das Zimmer enger oder weiter, niedriger oder höher erscheinen lassen. Wollen wir das Zimmer ernst oder heiter, nackt oder reich, einfach oder prächtig gestalten, wollen wir ihm eine gemültlich-anheimelnde, eine poetische, eine kalte oder warme Stimmung verleihen, wollen wir uns einen träumerischen Ruhewinkel schaffen, eine Stätte der Einsamkeit und des beschaulichen Nachdenkens oder eine Stätte des Vergnügens und der Geselligkeit—unser erstes und letztes Mittel wird die Farbe sein.) Jakob von Falke, *Die Kunst im Hause: geschichtliche und kritisch-ästhetische Studien über die Decoration und Ausstattung der Wohnung* (Vienna: Gerold, 1871), 180; *Art in the House: Historical, Critical, and Aesthetical Studies on the Decoration and Furnishing of the Dwelling,* authorized American edition, translated from the 3rd German edition (Boston: L. Prang, 1879). My thanks to Eric Anderson for directing me to this quotation.

On Falke and his ideas, see, e.g., Eric Anderson, "Beyond Historicism: Jakob von Falke and the Reform of the Viennese Interior" (Ph.D. diss., Columbia University, 2009); and Eva B. Ottillinger, "Jakob von Falke

(1825–1897) und die Theorie des Kunstgewerbes," *Wiener Jahrbuch für Kunstgeschichte* 42 (1989): 205–23. Another likely influence on Strnad and the others may have been Johann Wolfgang von Goethe's *Farbenlehre* and Ernst von Brücke's color theories. On the latter, see Ernst Wilhelm von Brücke, *Die Physiologie der Farben für die Zwecke der Kunstgewerbe* (Leipzig: Hirzel, 1866).

40 Quoted in Mattl-Wurm, *Interieurs: Wiener Künstlerwohnungen 1830–1930*, 176.

41 "Raum ist Schicksal. Sich von Schicksal befreien ist 'Weg bauen, Raum begrenzen.' Also nicht Wand sondern Weg, Fußboden erleben." Oskar Strnad, "Neue Wege in der Wohnraum-Einrichtung," *Innen-Dekoration* 33 (October 1922): 323.

42 Oskar Strnad, "Projekt für ein Schauspiel-haus," *Wasmuths Monatshefte* 6, no. 6 (1921): 181; Sylvester Bory, "Annäherungen an eine Raum-bühne, die nie so bespielt wurde / Approaches to a Space-Stage on Which No One Ever Played," *Daidalos* 14 (15 December 1984): 85. See also Friedrich Kurrent, "Oskar Strnad und der Theaterbau," in Meder and Fuchs, eds., *Oskar Strnad 1879–1935*, 52–54.

43 Bory, "Annäherungen an eine Raumbühne," 85.

44 Strnad, "Projekt für ein Schauspielhaus," 181, quoted in Bory, "Annäherungen an eine Raumbühne," 85.

45 Strnad, "Projekt für ein Schauspielhaus," 181.

46 Ibid., 182.

47 Ibid.

48 Strnad, "Projekt für ein Schauspielhaus," 181, quoted in Bory, "Annäherungen an eine Raumbühne," 88.

CHAPTER THREE

1 See R. M. Schindler, "Space Architecture," *Dune Forum* (Oceano, California) (February 1934): 44–46; and "Points of View: Contra." *Southwestern Review* 17 (Spring 1932): 353–54. Schindler later claimed that his original manifesto, "Modern Architecture: A Program," was written in 1912. There is, however, a two-page handwritten version dated June 1913, in the R. M. Schindler Archive, Architecture and Design Collection, Art, Design and Architecture Museum, University of California, Santa

Barbara. See Judith Sheine, *R. M. Schindler* (London: Phaidon, 2001), 15, 83, 278 n. 7; and Harry Francis Mallgrave, "Schindler's Program of 1913," in Lionel March and Judith Sheine, eds., *R. M. Schindler: Composition and Construction* (London: Academy, 1995), 15–19. Mallgrave's translation of the 1913 manifesto appears in the same volume, pgs. 10–12.

2 R. M. Schindler, "Modern Architecture: A Program," in March and Sheine, *R. M. Schindler: Composition and Construction,* 10.

3 On the circumstances of the commission and the competition see Karlheinz Gruber, Sabine Höller-Alber, and Markus Kristan, *Ernst Epstein, 1881–1938: Der Bauleiter des Looshauses als Architekt,* exh. cat. (Vienna: Jüdisches Museum der Stadt Wien / Holzhausen, 2002); and Christopher Long, *The Looshaus* (New Haven: Yale University Press, 2011), 4–16.

4 See Adolf Loos, "Mein Haus am Michaeler-platz," lecture delivered 11 December 1911, reprinted in *Parnass,* special issue: "Der Künstlerkreis um Adolf Loos: Aufbruch zur Jahrhundertwende" (1985): ii–xv.

5 Long, *The Looshaus,* 42–52.

6 See, e.g., Ludwig Münz and Gustav Künstler, *Der Architekt Adolf Loos: Darstellung seines Schaffens nach Werkgruppen / Chronolo-gisches Werkverzeichnis* (Vienna: Anton Schroll, 1964), 93–103; Hermann Czech and Wolfgang Mistelbauer, *Das Looshaus,* 3rd ed. (Vienna: Löcker, 1984); Burkhardt Rukschcio and Roland Schachel, *Adolf Loos, Leben und Werk,* 2nd ed. (Salzburg: Residenz, 1987), 460–69; Ralf Bock, *Adolf Loos: Works and Projects* (Milan: Skira, 2007), 126–35; Long, *The Looshaus,* 157–71.

7 For general discussion of the bases of Loos's Raumplan idea, see Dietrich Worbs, "Der Raumplan im Wohnungsbau von Adolf Loos," in Worbs, ed., *Adolf Loos 1870–1933: Raumplan–Wohnungsbau,* 64–77.

8 Adolf Loos, "Josef Veillich," first published in the *Frankfurter Zeitung,* 21 March 1929, reprinted in *Adolf Loos, Trotzdem 1900–1930* (Innsbruck: Brenner, 1931), 248–49.

9 Adolf Loos, "Mein Haus am Michaelerplatz," iii.

10 Heinrich Kulka, *Adolf Loos: Das Werk des Architekten* (Vienna: Anton Schroll, 1931), 13–15.

11 Ibid., 14.

12 Ibid.

13 Ibid., 13. Loos continued to think about theaters and theater spaces. See, e.g., the unsigned essay (very likely the work of Gustav Künstler) "Bauplannung vom Raum aus (ein Theater-Projekt als Beispiel)," in Münz and Künstler, *Der Architekt Adolf Loos,* 16–20.

14 Karel Lhota, "Architekt Adolf Loos," *Architekt SIA* (Prague) 32 (1933): 143.

15 Ibid.

16 Ibid.

17 Ibid.

18 Rukschcio and Schachel, *Adolf Loos: Leben und Werk,* 454.

19 Adolf Loos, "Architektur," *Trotzdem 1900–1930,* 111.

20 Ibid.

21 Adolf Loos, "Das Prinzip der Bekleidung," *Neue Freie Presse,* 4 September 1898, 6. On the development of Loos's Raumplan idea and its connection to Semper, see Worbs, "Der Raumplan im Wohnungsbau von Adolf Loos," 64–65.

22 Loos, "Das Prinzip der Bekleidung," 6.

23 See, e.g., Gottfried Semper, *Der Stil in den technischen und tektonischen Künsten oder Praktische Ästhetik,* vol. 1 (Frankfurt am Main: Verlag für Kunst und Wissenschaft, 1860), 217–31.

24 On the history of the Luxfer prisms and their import for architecture at the time, see Dietrich Neumann, "'The Century's Triumph in Lighting': The Luxfer Prism Companies and Their Contribution to Early Modern Architec-ture," *Journal of the Society of Architectural Historians* 54, no. 1 (March 1995): 24–53.

25 The idea for drawing a Loosian interior in this way comes from my former student, Nicolas Allinder. For a presentation in my seminar on Loos and Mies van der Rohe, he drew a continuous plan of Loos's Josephine Baker House, which made the multipart plan readable and understandable.

26 Long, *The Looshaus,* 46–49.

CHAPTER FOUR

1 On Frank's education and early career, see Christopher Long, *Josef Frank: Life and Work* (Chicago: University of Chicago Press, 2001), chs. 1 and 2.

2 Ibid., 11–12.

3 Ibid., 31–32.

4 Ernst A. Plischke, interview by author, Vienna, 25 August 1986.

5 In addition to their appearance in many architectural journals of the day, Frank probably knew about American houses from F. Rudolf Vogel, *Das amerikanische Haus: Entwicklung, Bedingungen, Anlage, Aufbau, Einrichtung, Innenraum und Umgebung* (Berlin: Wasmuth, 1910).

6 See Ursula Prokop, *Wien: Aufbruch zur Metropole: Geschäfts- und Wohnhäuser der Innenstadt 1910 bis 1914* (Vienna: Böhlau, 1994), 68–88.

7 On the building, see "Wohn- und Geschäfts- haus in Wien, IV, Wiedner Hauptstraße Nr. 64, Dipl. Architekt Arthur Baron in Wien," *Der Bautechniker* 34, no. 1 (2 January 1914): 1–3; and Prokop, *Wien: Aufbruch zur Metropole*, 68–88.

8 See Mattl-Wurm, *Interieurs: Wiener Künstler- wohnungen 1830–1930*, 122; and Marlene Ott- Wodni, *Josef Frank 1885–1967: Raumgestaltung und Möbeldesign* (Vienna: Böhlau, 2015), 30–31, 187–88.

9 On Frank's ideas in this period about how to place furnishings, see, for example, Christopher Long, "Wiener Wohnkultur: Interior Design in Vienna, 1910–1938," *Studies in the Decorative Arts* 5 (Fall–Winter 1997–98): 29–51; Long, *Josef Frank: Life and Work*, 95–97; and Ott-Wodni, *Josef Frank 1885–1967: Raumgestaltung und Möbeldesign*, 27–50.

10 Anthony Vidler, *Warped Space: Art, Architec- ture, and Anxiety in Modern Culture* (Cambridge, Mass.: MIT Press, 2000), 6.

11 Richard M. Dunn, *Geoffrey Scott and the Berenson Circle: Literary and Aesthetic Life in the Early 20th Century* (Lewiston, NY: Edward Mellen, 1998).

12 Geoffrey Scott, *The Architecture of Humanism: A Study in the History of Taste* (Boston: Houghton Mifflin, 1914), 227. On the relationship between aesthetics and the spatial sense of self, see Richard A. Etlin, "Aesthetics and the Spatial Sense of Self," *The Journal of Aesthetics and Art Criticism* 56, no. 1 (Winter 1998): 1–19.

13 Scott, *The Architecture of Humanism*, 227.

14 See James S. Ackerman's introduction to his translation of Frankl's work, in Paul Frankl, *Principles of Architectural History: The Four Phases of Architectural Style, 1420–1900* [1914], trans. and ed. by James F. O'Gorman, foreword by James S. Ackerman (Cambridge, Mass.: MIT Press, 1968, 1973), esp. vii–xi.

15 Ibid., vii.

16 Frankl, *Die Entwicklungsphasen der neueren Baukunst*, 125–26; translated in Frankl, *Principles of Architectural History*, 142.

17 Ackerman, introduction to Frankl, *Principles of Architectural History*, x.

18 Wilhelm Worringer, *Abstraktion und Einfühlung: Ein Beitrag zur Stilpsychologie* (published dissertation, Neuwied, 1907; book, Munich: R. Piper, 1908).

19 For an excellent summary of Worringer's argument, see Juliet Koss, *Modernism after Wagner* (Minneapolis: University of Minnesota Press, 2010), 83–89.

20 Koss, *Modernism after Wagner*, 85–88.

21 Ibid., 88.

22 Worringer, *Abstraktion und Einfühlung*, English ed., *Abstraction and Empathy: A Contribution to the Psychology of Style*, trans. Michael Bullock (Mansfield Center, CT: Martino, 2014), 129.

CHAPTER FIVE

1 See Rukschcio and Schachel, *Adolf Loos: Leben und Werk*, 471; and Long, *The Looshaus*, 147–49.

2 The house's current owner, Johannes Holländer, pointed this out to me during a visit in 2012.

3 For a general discussion of the house, see Münz and Künstler, *Der Architekt Adolf Loos*, 72–79; Rukschcio and Schachel, *Adolf Loos: Leben und Werk*, 476–80; Bock, *Adolf Loos: Works and Projects*, 136–45.

4 Walter Curt Behrendt, *Der Sieg des neuen Baustils* (Stuttgart: Akademischer Verlag Dr. Fr. Wedekind, 1927), translated as *The Victory of the New Building Style*, trans. Harry Francis Mallgrave (Los Angeles: Getty Research Institute, 2000), 139; Nikolaus Pevsner, *Pioneers of the Modern Movement from William Morris to Walter Gropius* (London: Faber & Faber, 1936; rpt. New York: Museum of Modern Art, 1949), 12.

5 Julius Posener, "Der Raumplan: Vorläufer und Zeitgenossen von Adolf Loos," in Worbs, ed., *Adolf Loos 1870–1933 Raumplan—Wohnungs- bau*, 52–63. See also David Leatherbarrow, *The Roots of Architectural Invention: Site, Enclosure, Materials* (Cambridge: Cambridge University Press, 1993), 133.

6 Posener, "Der Raumplan: Vorläufer und Zeitgenossen von Adolf Loos," 54.

7 Hermann Muthesius, *Das englische Haus: Entwicklung, Bedingungen, Anlage, Aufbau, Einrichtung und Innenraum*, 3 vols. (Berlin: Ernst Wasmuth, 1904–5).

8 See Münz and Künstler, *Der Architekt Adolf Loos*, 125–28; and Bock, *Adolf Loos: Works and Projects*, 218–23.

9 Bock, *Adolf Loos: Works and Projects*, 218.

CHAPTER SIX

1 See Long, *Josef Frank: Life and Work*, 47–61.

2 Ibid., 32–35, 53–57, 61–65.

3 Herman Sörgel, *Einführung in die Architektur- Ästhetik: Prolegomena zu einer Theorie der Baukunst* (Munich: Piloty & Loehle, 1918).

4 See the forthcoming dissertation on Sörgel by Rainer Schützeichel, "Die Architekturtheorie von Herman Sörgel," at the ETH in Zurich.

5 Ibid., 159.

6 Ibid., 105.

7 Ibid., 160ff.

8 Hermann Muthesius, *Wie baue ich mein Haus?* (Munich: F. Bruckmann, 1915; 2nd ed. 1917).

9 Ibid., 110–11.

10 Ibid., 115.

11 Paul Zucker, "Formempfinden und Raumgefühl," *Innen-Dekoration* 28, no. 11 (1917): 374–84; and "Die Unwirklichkeit des Raumes," *Das junge Deutschland* 1 (1918): 233–35.

12 Paul Zucker, "Kontinuität und Diskontinu- ität: Grenzprobleme der Architektur und Plastik," *Zeitschrift für Ästhetik und Allgemeine Kunstwissenschaft* 15 (1921): 304–17.

13 Paul Zucker, "Der Begriff der Zeit in der Architektur," *Repertorium für Kunstwissenschaft* 44 (1924): 237–45.

14 Ibid., 239ff. See also Zug, *Die Anthropologie des Raumes in der Architekturtheorie des frühen 20. Jahrhunderts*, 64–88.

15 Sigfried Giedion, *Space, Time and Architecture: The Growth of a New Tradition* (Cambridge, Mass.: Harvard University Press, 1941).

16 "Josef Frank," *Moderne Bauformen* 26 (1927): 170–85. See also "Einiges von Land- und Sommer- häuser," *Der Baumeister* 26 (March 1928): 94–102.

17 The designs included the "House for Dagmar Grill," the "Country House with Two Terraces," the "Country House with Three Terraces," the "House for Columbus, Ohio," and the "House for Mr. and Mrs. A. R. G., Los Angeles" (in one version labeled the "House for Vienna XIX"). For descriptions and analyses of these houses, see Long, *Josef Frank: Life and Work*, 137–40.

18 Frank apparently went to New York in the spring of 1927 to oversee the installation of the Austrian section at the Machine-Age Exhibition, held between May 16 and 28. It is unknown how long he stayed or if he traveled to other parts of the country. In an interview in 1991 with Maria Welzig, Philip Ginther, who was working in Frank's office at the time, told her that he recalled that Frank had traveled to the United States for the exhibition. Maria Welzig, *Josef Frank, 1885–1967: Das architektonische Werk* (Vienna: Böhlau, 1998), 198.

CHAPTER SEVEN

1 On Loos's years in Paris, see Rukschcio and Schachel, *Adolf Loos: Leben und Werk*, 295–337.

2 Ibid., 309–12, 590–93.

3 See Münz and Künstler, *Der Architekt Adolf Loos*, 128–33; Rukschcio and Schachel, *Adolf Loos: Leben und Werk*, 600–03; Bock, *Adolf Loos: Works and Projects*, 236–47.

4 For a general discussion of the project, see Paul Groenendijk and Piet Vollaard, *Adolf Loos, huis voor / house for / maison pour / haus für Josephine Baker* (Rotterdam: Uitgeverij 010, 1985); Rukschcio and Schachel, *Adolf Loos: Leben und Werk*, 323–24, 606–7; and Bock, *Adolf Loos: Works and Projects*, 248–51.

5 Farès El-Dahdah, "The Josephine Baker House: For Loos's Pleasure," *Assemblage* 26 (1996): 79. For different readings, see, e.g., Kim Tanzer, "Baker's Loos and Loos's Loss: Architecting the Body," *Center: A Journal for Architecture in America* 9 (1995): 76–89; Susan R. Henderson, "Bachelor Culture in the Work of Adolf Loos," *Journal of Architectural Education* 55 (2002): 131; and Elana Shapira, "Dressing a Celebrity: Adolf Loos's House for Josephine Baker," *Studies in the Decorative Arts* 11, no. 2 (Spring–Summer 2004): 2–24.

6 Anne Anlin Cheng, *Second Skin: Josephine Baker and the Modern Surface* (Oxford: Oxford University Press, 2011), 52.

7 My argument here is very much indebted to R. Scott Gill, who read and brilliantly commented on a draft of the manuscript.

8 Beatriz Colomina, *Privacy and Publicity: Modern Architecture as Mass Media* (Cambridge, Mass.: MIT Press, 1994), 276.

CHAPTER EIGHT

1 On the Claëson House, see, for example, Long, *Josef Frank: Life and Work*, 88–91. On the Weissenhofsiedlung design, see Karin Kirsch, "Franks Doppelhaus in der Weißenhofsiedlung," *Bauwelt* 26 (12 July 1985): 1054–56; and Long, *Josef Frank: Life and Work*, 104–10.

2 Frank and his partner Wlach had also previously designed an apartment interior for Robert Beer. Tano Bojankin, "Das Haus Beer und seine Bewohner," in Iris Meder, ed., *Josef Frank: Eine Moderne der Unordnung* (Salzburg: Anton Pustet, 2008), 101–3.

3 Ibid., 101.

4 Welzig, *Josef Frank, 1885–1967: Das architektonische Werk*, 135.

5 Wolfgang Born, "Ein Haus in Wien-Hietzing," *Innen-Dekoration* 42 (September 1931): 364, 366. See also Carmela Haerdtl, "Una nuova casa di Josef Frank," *Domus* 4 (August 1931): 48–51; and "Una casa privata a Vienna degli architetti Josef Frank e Oscar [sic] Wlach," *Domus* 4 (August 1931): 28–30, 77; Max Eisler, "Ein Wohnhaus von Josef Frank und Oskar Wlach, Wien," *Moderne Bauformen* 31 (1932): 88–95; and "Una casa en las proximidades de Viena," *Viviendas* 4 (June 1935): 6–15. For later discussions of the Beer House's spatial plan, see Guido Beltramini, "La casa sensibile," in Giovanni Fraziano, ed., *La casa isolata: dalla tautologia alla banalità: Letture, trascrizioni, variazioni su testi di Wittgenstein, Loos, Frank* (Venice: Cluva, 1989), 83–85; Posener, "Der Raumplan: Vorläufer und Zeitgenossen von Adolf Loos," 52; Arthur Rüegg and Adolph Stiller, *Sechs Häuser: Nach Aufnahmen korrigierte Grundrisse der Wohngeschosse sechs bedeutender Häuser der Moderne im Dreieck Prag-Leipzig-Wien* (Zurich: ETH, 1992); and Welzig, *Josef Frank, 1885–1967: Das architektonische Werk*, 129–35.

6 Born, "Ein Haus in Wien-Hietzing," 364–65.

7 Ibid., 363.

8 Ibid., 373.

9 Josef Frank, "Das Haus als Weg und Platz," *Der Baumeister* 29 (August 1931): 316–23 (see appendix).

10 Ibid., 316–17.

11 Ibid., 317, 319.

12 Ibid., 319.

13 Camillo Sitte, *Der Städtebau nach seinen künstlerischen Grundsätzen: Ein Beitrag zur Lösung moderner Fragen der Architektur und monumentalen Plastik unter besonderer Beziehung auf Wien* (Vienna: Karl Graeser, 1889). The fifth edition of the book, published in 1921, has been translated by George Rosenborough Collins and Christiane Collins as *The Birth of Modern City Planning* (New York: Rizzoli, 1986). On Sitte's influence, see Sonja Hnilica, "Stadtmetaphern: Camillo Sittes Bild der Stadt im Architekturdiskurs" (Ph.D. diss., Technische Universität Wien, 2006).

14 Sitte, *Der Städtebau nach seinen künstlerischen Grundsätzen*, introduction.

15 See, e.g., the excellent essays by Heleni Porfyriou, "Camillo Sitte: Optically Constructed Space and Artistic City Building," in Kirsten Wagner and Jasper Cepl, eds., *Images of the Body in Architecture: Anthropology and Built Space* (Tübingen and Berlin: Ernst Wasmuth, 2014), 166–88; and Jean-François Lejeune, "Schinkel, Sitte, and Loos: The 'Body in the Invisible,'" in Charles C. Bohl and Jean-François Lejeune, eds., *Sitte, Hegemann and the Metropolis: Modern Civic Art and International Exchanges* (London and New York: Routledge, 2009), 69–97.

16 Leon Battista Alberti, *De re aedificatoria* (ca. 1450), book 5, ch. 2; English ed., *On the Art of Building in Ten Books*, trans. Joseph Rykwert, Neil Leach, and Robert Tavernor (Cambridge, Mass.: MIT Press, 1988), 119.

17 Frank, "Das Haus als Weg und Platz," 316.

18 A surviving set of plans in the archives of the Baupolizei for the city's thirteenth district shows an unrealized rectangular wing on the house's southwest corner that would have contained several additional servants' rooms. The plans are dated October 1929, when the house was already under construction, but there is no evidence that any work on the wing was undertaken. Plan- und Schriftenkammer der Magistratsamt (MA 37), Vienna.

19 Debra Schafter, *The Order of Ornament, the Structure of Style: Theoretical Foundations of Modern Art and Architecture* (Cambridge: Cambridge University Press, 2003), 186.

20 Lada Hubatová-Vacková, *Silent Revolutions in Ornament: Studies in Applied Arts and Crafts from 1880–1930* (Prague: Academy of Arts, Architecture and Design, 2011), 225.

21 Hubatová-Vacková, *Silent Revolutions in Ornament*, 225–26.

22 Frank, "Das Haus als Weg und Platz," 319.

23 Ibid., 319–20.

24 Ibid., 320–21.

CHAPTER NINE

1 Markus Kristan, *Landhaus Khuner am Kreuzberg* (Vienna: Höhere Graphische Bundes-, Lehr- und Versuchsanstalt, 2004), 16. For a general discussion of the house, see Münz and Künstler, *Der Architekt Adolf Loos*, 57–64; Rukschcio and Schachel, *Adolf Loos, Leben und Werk*, 617–22; and Bock, *Adolf Loos: Works and Projects*, 274–83.

2 Bock, *Adolf Loos: Works and Projects*, 274–83. On the 1907 Khuner apartment, see Rukschcio and Schachel, *Adolf Loos: Leben und Werk*, 452.

3 Kristan, *Landhaus Khuner am Kreuzberg*, 17.

4 Rukschcio and Schachel, *Adolf Loos: Leben und Werk*, 526, 617.

5 Adolf Loos, "Regeln für den, der in den Bergen baut," in *Trotzdem*, 133.

6 Ernst Plischke, interview by author, Vienna, 28 November 1986.

7 For a general discussion of the Müller House, see Münz and Künstler, *Der Architekt Adolf Loos*, 133–43; Rukschcio and Schachel, *Adolf Loos, Leben und Werk*, 610–16; Giovanni Denti, *Adolf Loos: Villa Müller / Casa Müller a Praga* (Florence: Alinea, 1999); Leslie Van Duzer and Kent Kleinman, *Villa Müller: A Work of Adolf Loos* (New York: Princeton Architectural Press, 1994); Karel Ksandr, ed., *Villa Müller* (Prague: Argo, 2000); Bock, *Adolf Loos: Works and Projects*, 258–73; Maria Szadkowska, Leslie van Duzer, and Dagmar Černoušková, *Adolf Loos: Dílo v českých zemích / Adolf Loos: Works in the Czech Lands*, exh. cat. (Prague: Muzeum hlavní města Prahy / Kant, 2009), 226–51.

8 Loos was arrested in September 1928 on charges that he had molested three young girls, ages eight to ten, who had come to his apartment to model. The trial was held in late November and early December of the same year. Loos was acquitted on most of the charges (in large measure because the testimony of the girls was deemed unreliable), but he was convicted of making obscene drawings of them and of having them pose nude in "inappropriate" positions. Most of Loos's friends and clients supported him throughout the affair, convinced that the charges had been trumped up by conservatives within the government and the police force. Only recently has the court file come to light. It reveals that the charges against Loos were serious, and that there was evidence that Loos was guilty of more than what he was convicted of. He was sentenced to time served—the several days he spent in custody before being bailed out and placed on probation. See Christopher Long, *Der Fall Loos* (Vienna: Amalthea, 2015).

9 Petr Domanický and Petr Jindra, *Loos-Plzeň-Souvislosti / Loos-Pilsen-Connections* (Pilsen: Západočeská galerie v Plzni, 2001), 162–67.

10 Lhota had first worked with Loos on the renovation of the Brummel House in Pilsen. Domanický and Jindra, *Loos-Plzeň-Souvislosti / Loos-Pilsen-Connections*, 165–66.

11 Ibid.

12 The city authorities rejected the design because both its footprint and its height exceeded what was permitted for the area. Many of the neighbors also complained that the large, flat-roofed house was decidedly out of character for the area, which was made up of mostly smaller, conventional pitched-roof structures. Müller was forced to resubmit the project twice more, each time with slightly altered plans. The final design was not approved until late June, after the provincial president had issued an override of the authorities' decision. By then, construction on the house was well underway, carried out by the Kapsa & Müller Company. Although Müller had not received permission from the municipal building office to begin work, he fast-tracked the construction process. The walls and roof were completed by mid-July 1929, and the electricity and the exterior stuccowork were finished by the end of September. Work on the interiors began in October, and the Müllers and their four-year-old daughter Eva moved into the house in the spring of 1930, although the final occupancy permit was not issued until July of that year. The most authoritative account of the house's genesis and construction is Karel Ksandr, ed., *Villa Müller*. See especially the essay by Pavel Zahradník, "History of the Villa until the End of 1994," 26–101. See also Rukschcio and Schachel, *Adolf Loos: Leben und Werk*, 610–11; and Van Duzer and Kleinman, *Villa Müller: A Work of Adolf Loos*, 24–32.

13 At one point, flush with money from the Müller commission, Loos went off to Paris for a month, without informing his coworkers. Müller also intervened in the design process, altering some of the details, especially on the façades. Loos refined the plans a number of times during the course of construction or, in a few instances, changed them entirely. See Zahradník, "History of the Villa until the End of 1994," 56–67.

14 Kulka, *Adolf Loos: Das Werk des Architekten*, 43.

15 Stenograph of a conversation between Karel Lhota and Adolf Loos in Pilsen, 1930. Lhota later published his memories of the conversation, in Lhota, "Architekt Adolf Loos," *Architekt SIA* 32: 143. Loos made another similar statement on the occasion of his sixtieth birthday party, held at the house on 10 December 1930. He wrote in the Müller's guestbook that it was his "most beautiful house!" He added that František Müller was "the most intelligent client I have ever had," and "This is the entire secret of architecture." Photostatic copy of the visitor book from the Villa Müller, 1931–1968, Estate of Milada Müllerová, Museum of Arts and Crafts, Prague. Kulka, too, though hardly an objective observer, also described the villa as the most complete expression of Loos's conception of architecture. Kulka, *Adolf Loos: Das Werk des Architekten*, 43.

16 Münz and Künstler, *Der Architekt Adolf Loos*, 135.

17 Denti, *Adolf Loos—Villa Müller / Casa Müller a Praga*, 6–10.

18 Van Duzer and Kleinman, *Villa Müller: A Work of Adolf Loos*, 41–42.

19 Colomina, *Privacy and Publicity*, 244. See also Colomina's essay, "The Split Wall: Domestic Voyeurism," in Beatriz Colomina, *Sexuality and Space* (New York: Princeton Architectural Press, 1992), 73–130.

CHAPTER TEN

1 See Rukschcio and Schachel, *Adolf Loos: Leben und Werk*, 644–45.

2 See Domanický and Jindra, *Loos-Plzeň-Souvislosti / Loos-Pilsen-Connections*, 156–59; and Szadkowska, Van Duzer, and Černoušková, *Adolf Loos: Dílo v českých zemích / Adolf Loos: Works in the Czech Lands*, 354–67.

3 Long, *Josef Frank: Life and Work*, 200–202.

234

4 Ibid., 217–19.

5 Josef Frank, "How to Plan a House," ms., ca. 1942, published in Johannes Spalt, ed., *Josef Frank 1885–1967: Möbel & Geräte & Theoretisches* (Vienna: Hochschule für angewandte Kunst, 1981), 163 (see appendix).

6 Ibid.

7 Hermann Czech, "Josef Frank, The Accidental House: The Thirteen Designs in Letters to Dagmar Grill, *Lotus International* 29 (1981): 108–10, 114–15.

8 Josef Frank, "Accidentism," *Form* 54 (1958): 160–65. Frank later republished the essay in German. See "Akzidentismus," *Baukunst und Werkform* 14 (1961): 216–18.

9 Frank, "Accidentism." The translation here is taken from Tano Bojankin, Christopher Long, and Iris Meder, eds., *Josef Frank: Schriften / Josef Frank: Writings,* vol. 2 (Vienna: Metro, 2012), 385.

10 Ibid., 383.

CODA

1 Tanja Poppelreuter, "Raumplan after Loos: The European Work of Heinrich Kulka, 1930–1939." *Fabrications* 25, no. 1 (2015): 84–103.

2 See August Sarnitz and Eva Ottillinger, *Ernst Plischke: Modern Architecture for the New World* (Munich: Prestel, 2004), esp. 62–70.

3 See, e.g., Elizabeth A. T. Smith, "R. M. Schindler: An Architecture of Invention and Intuition," in Elizabeth A. T. Smith and Michael Darling, eds., *The Architecture of R. M. Schindler,* exh. cat. (Los Angeles: Museum of Contemporary Art / New York: Harry N. Abrams, 2001), 13–85; and Judith Sheine, *R. M. Schindler.*

4 See, e.g., Frederick Kiesler, *Inside the Endless House—Art, People and Architecture: A Journal* (New York: Simon and Schuster, 1966). It is worth noting that Kiesler's last great work, the Shrine of the Book in Jerusalem, does have some of the same qualities of path and experience.

5 Gaston Bachelard, *La poétique de l'espace* (Paris: Presses Universitaires de France, 1957); English ed., *The Poetics of Space,* trans. Maria Jolas (Boston: Beacon, 1969).

6 Ibid., 25–26.

7 Ibid., 47.

BIBLIOGRAPHY

ARCHIVAL SOURCES

Architecture and Design Collection, Art, Design and Architecture Museum. University of California, Santa Barbara, R. M. Schindler Archive

Grafische Sammlung Albertina, Vienna, Adolf Loos Archive and Josef Frank Archive

MAK — Österreichisches Museum für angewandte Kunst/Gegenwartskunst, Vienna

Museum für Gestaltung, Berlin, Bauhaus-Archiv

Österreichische Nationalbibliothek, Bildarchiv, Vienna

Plan- und Schriftenkammer der Magistratsamt (MA 37), Vienna

Svenskt Tenn Collection, Stockholm, Josef Frank Archive

Uměleckoprůmyslové muzeum v Praze (Museum of Decorative Arts, Prague)

Universität für angewandte Kunst Wien, Kunstsammlung und Archiv

Universität Leipzig, Universitätsarchiv, August Schmarsow Nachlass

Various private collections

Wien Museum

Wienbibliothek im Rathaus—Handschriften-sammlung

PRIMARY SOURCES

Alberti, Leon Battista. *De re aedificatoria* (ca. 1450). English ed. *On the Art of Building in Ten Books.* Translated by Joseph Rykwert, Neil Leach, and Robert Tavernor. Cambridge, Mass.: MIT Press, 1988.

Auer, Hans Wilhelm. "Die Entwicklung des Raumes in der Baukunst." *Allgemeine Bauzeitung* 48 (1883): 65–68, 73–74.

Berlage, Hendrik Petrus. *Gedanken über Stil in der Baukunst.* Leipzig: Julius Zeitler, 1905.

——. "Raumkunst und Architektur." *Schweizerische Bauzeitung* 49, no. 24 (1907): 293–97; no. 25, 303–6; no. 26, 317–18.

Bojankin, Tano, Christopher Long, and Iris Meder, eds. *Josef Frank: Schriften / Josef Frank: Writings.* 2 vols. Vienna: Metro, 2012.

Born, Wolfgang. "Ein Haus in Wien-Hietzing." *Innen-Dekoration* 42 (September 1931): 362–98.

Brücke, Ernst Wilhelm von. *Die Physiologie der Farben für die Zwecke der Kunstgewerbe.* Leipzig: Hirzel, 1866.

Ebe, Gustav. *Architektonische Raumlehre: Entwicklung der Typus des Innenbaues.* Dresden: Gerhard Kühtmann, 1900.

"Einiges von Land- und Sommerhäuser." *Der Baumeister* 26 (March 1928): 94–102.

Eisler, Max. "Oskar Strnad." *Dekorative Kunst* 21, no. 5 (February 1918): 145–54.

——. *Oskar Strnad.* Vienna: Gerlach und Wiedling, 1936.

——. "Oskar Strnad zum 50. Geburtstag." *Deutsche Kunst und Dekoration* 33 (January 1930): 253–68.

——. *Österreichische Werkkultur.* Vienna: Anton Schroll, 1916.

——. "Wiener Stadtvillen und Landhäuser." *Wasmuths Monatshefte für Baukunst* 2 (1915–16): 491–524.

——. "Ein Wohnhaus von Josef Frank und Oskar Wlach, Wien." *Moderne Bauformen* 31 (1932): 88–95.

Falke, Jakob von. *Die Kunst im Hause: geschichtliche und kritisch-ästhetische Studien über die Decoration und Ausstattung der Wohnung.* Vienna: Gerold, 1871; English ed. *Art in the House: Historical, Critical, and Aesthetical Studies on the Decoration and Furnishing of the Dwelling.* Boston: L. Prang, 1879.

Fechner, Gustav. *Elemente der Psychophysik.* Leipzig: Breitkopf und Hartel, 1860.

Fiedler, Conrad. "Bemerkungen über Wesen und Geschichte der Baukunst." *Deutsche Rundschau* 15 (1878): 361–83.

——. *Über die Beurtheilung von Werken der bildenden Kunst.* Leipzig: S. Hirzel, 1876.

Frank, Josef. "Accidentism." *Form* 54 (1958): 160–65; German version, "Akzidentismus." *Baukunst und Werkform* 14 (1961): 216–18.

——. "Das Haus als Weg und Platz." *Der Baumeister* 29 (August 1931): 316–23.

——. "How to Plan a House," ca. 1942; published in *Josef Frank 1885–1967: Möbel & Geräte & Theoretisches.* Edited by Johannes Spalt. Vienna: Hochschule für angewandte Kunst, 1981.

——. "Rum och inredning." *Form* 30, no. 10 (1934): 217–25.

——. "Wiens Moderne Architektur bis 1914." *Der Aufbau* 1, no. 8/9 (September 1926), 162–68.

Frankl, Paul. *Die Entwicklungsphasen der neueren Baukunst.* Leipzig: B. G. Teubner, 1914.

——. *Principles of Architectural History: The Four Phases of Architectural Style, 1420–1900.* Translated and edited by James F. O'Gorman. Foreword by James S. Ackerman. Cambridge, Mass.: MIT Press, 1968, 1973.

——. "Raumkunst und Zweck," *Die Raumkunst* 1, no. 11 (1908): 171–74.

Giedion, Sigfried. *Space, Time and Architecture: The Growth of a New Tradition.* Cambridge, Mass.: Harvard University Press, 1941.

Glück, Franz. *Adolf Loos.* Paris: Éditions G. Crès et Cie, 1931.

Goethe, Johann Wolfgang von. *Zur Farbenlehre.* 2 vols. Tübingen: Cotta, 1810.

Gregor, Joseph. *Rede auf Oskar Strnad.* Vienna: Reichner, 1936.

Haerdtl, Carmela. "Una casa privata a Vienna degli architetti Josef Frank e Oscar [*sic*] Wlach." *Domus* 4 (August 1931): 28–30, 77.

——. "Una nuova casa di Josef Frank." *Domus* 4 (July 1931): 48–51.

Helmholtz, Hermann von. *Handbuch der physiologischen Optik.* Leipzig: L. Voss, 1867.

Hildebrand, Adolf von. *Das Problem der Form in der bildenden Kunst.* Strasbourg: Heitz & Mündel, 1893; translated in *Empathy, Form, and Space: Problems in German Aesthetics, 1873-1934.* Edited by Harry Francis Mallgrave and Eleftherios Ikonomou. Santa Monica, Calif.: Getty Center for the History of Art and the Humanities, 1994.

Illert, Karl. "Architektur und Kunstphilosophie." *Centralblatt der Bauverwaltung,* 30 January 1897: 50–52.

———. "Das Wesen der architektonischen Schöpfung." *Centralblatt der Bauverwaltung,* part 1: 15 August 1896: 369–70; part 2: 22 August 1896: 377–79.

Jahn, Johannes, ed. *Die Kunstwissenschaft der Gegenwart in Selbstdarstellungen.* Leipzig: Felix Meiner, 1924.

"Josef Frank." *Moderne Bauformen* 26 (1927): 170–85.

Kiesler, Frederick. *Inside the Endless House—Art, People and Architecture: A Journal.* New York: Simon and Schuster, 1966.

König, Carl. "Die Wissenschaft von der Architektur ind Ihre praktische Bedeutung." *Wiener Bauindustrie Zeitung* 19, no. 6 (7 November 1901): 42–46.

Kulka, Heinrich. *Adolf Loos. Das Werk des Architekten.* Vienna: Anton Schroll, 1931.

"Landhaus in Wien XIX. Kobenzlgasse." *Der Architekt* 19 (1913): 131–33.

Le Camus de Mézières, Nicolas. *Le génie de l'architecture, ou L'analogie de cet art avec nos sensations* (1780). English ed.: *The Genius of Architecture; or, The Analogy of That Art with Our Sensations.* Introduction by Robin Middleton. Translated by David Britt. Santa Monica: Getty Center for the History of Art and the Humanities, 1992.

Le Corbusier and Pierre Jenneret. *Oeuvre complète,* vol. 1, 1910–29, and vol. 2, 1929–34. Zurich: Les Éditions d'Architecture, 1995.

Lhota, Karel. "Architekt A. Loos." *Architekt* SIA 32 (1933): 137–43.

Lipps, Theodor. *Ästhetik: Psychologie des Schönen und der Kunst.* Hamburg: Leopold Voss, 1903–06.

———. "Einfühlung und ästhetischer Genuss." *Die Zukunft* 54 (1906): 100–14.

———. *Raumästhetik und geometrisch-optische Täuschungen.* Leipzig: J. A. Barth, 1893–97.

Loos, Adolf. *Ins Leere gesprochen 1897-1900.* Paris: Éditions G. Crès et Cie, 1921.

———. "Mein Haus am Michaelerplatz" *Parnass,* special issue: "Der Künstlerkreis um Adolf Loos: Aufbruch zur Jahrhundertwende" (1985): ii–xv.

———. "Das Prinzip der Bekleidung." *Neue Freie Presse,* 4 September 1898: 6.

———. *Trotzdem 1900-1930.* Innsbruck: Brenner, 1931.

Lucae, Richard. "Über die Macht des Raumes in der Baukunst." *Zeitschrift für Bauwesen* 19 (1869): 294–306.

Marilaun, Karl. *Adolf Loos.* Vienna: Wiener Literarische Anstalt, 1922.

Muthesius, Hermann. *Das englische Haus: Entwicklung, Bedingungen, Anlage, Aufbau, Einrichtung und Innenraum.* 3 vols. Berlin: Ernst Wasmuth, 1904–5.

———. *Wie baue ich mein Haus?* Munich: F. Bruckmann, 1915; 2nd ed. 1917.

Niemann, George. *Der Palast Diokletians in Spalato: Im Auftrag des k.k. Ministeriums für Kultus und Unterricht aufgenommen und beschrieben von George Niemann.* Vienna: Hölder, 1910.

"Oskar Strnad gestorben." *Neue Freie Presse,* 4 September 1935: 6.

Plischke, Ernst. Interview by author. Vienna, 25 August 1986.

Riegl, Alois. *Historische Grammatik der bildenden Künste.* Edited by Karl M. Swoboda and Otto Pächt. Graz: privately printed, 1966. English ed.: *Historical Grammar of the Visual Arts.* Translated by Jacqueline E. Jung, foreword by Benjamin Binstock. New York: Zone, 2004.

———. *Die spätrömische Kunstindustrie nach den Funden in Österreich-Ungarn.* Vienna: Druck und Verlag der kaiserlich-königlichen Hof- und Staatsdruckerei, 1901.

———. *Stilfragen: Grundlegungen zu einer Geschichte der Ornamentik.* Berlin: Georg Siemens, 1893.

Roessler, Arthur. "Professor Dr. Oskar Strnad—Wien." *Innen-Dekoration* 29 (January–February 1918): 3–22.

Schindler, R. M. "Points of View: Contra." *Southwestern Review* 17 (Spring 1932): 353–54.

———. "Space Architecture." *Dune Forum* (Oceano, California) (February 1934): 44–46.

Schmarsow, August. *Barock und Rokoko: Eine kritische Auseinandersetzung über das Malerische in der Architektur.* Leipzig: S. Hirzel, 1897.

———. *Grundbegriffe der Kunstwissenschaft am Übergang vom Altertum zum Mittelalter, kritisch erörtert und in systematischem Zusammenhange dargestellt.* Leipzig: B. G. Teubner, 1905.

———. *Plastik, Malerei und Reliefkunst in ihrem gegenseitigen Verhältnis.* Leipzig: S. Hirzel, 1899.

———. "Raumgestaltung als Wesen der architektonischen Schöpfung." *Zeitschrift für Ästhetik und allgemeine Kunstwissenschaft* 9 (1914): 66–95.

———. "Rhythmus in menschlichen Raumge-bilden." *Zeitschrift für Ästhetik und allgemeine Kunstwissenschaft* 14 (1920): 171–87.

———. "Über den Werth der Dimensionen im menschlichen Raumgebilde." *Berichte über die Verhandlungen der Königlich Sächsischen Gesellschaft der Wissenschaften zu Leipzig, Philologisch-Historisch Klasse* 48 (1896): 44–61.

———. *Das Wesen der architektonischen Schöpfung: Antrittsvorlesung gehalten in der Aula der k. Universität Leipzig am 8. November 1893.* Leipzig: Karl W. Hiersemann, 1894.

———. "Zur Bedeutung des Tiefenerlebnisses im Raumgebilde." *Zeitschrift für Ästhetik und allgemeine Kunstwissenschaft* 15 (1921): 104–9.

———. *Zur Frage nach dem Malerischen: Sein Grundbegriff und seine Entwicklung.* Leipzig: S. Hirzel, 1896.

———. "Zur Lehre vom Rhythmus." *Zeitschrift für Ästhetik und allgemeine Kunstwissenschaft* 16 (1922): 109–18.

Scott, Geoffrey. *The Architecture of Humanism: A Study in the History of Taste.* Boston: Houghton Mifflin, 1914.

Semper, Gottfried. *Der Stil in den technischen und tektonischen Künsten oder Praktische Ästhetik.* 2 vols. Frankfurt am Main: Verlag für Kunst und Wissenschaft, 1860, 1863.

Sitte, Camillo. *Der Städtebau nach seinen künstlerischen Grundsätzen: Ein Beitrag zur Lösung moderner Fragen der Architektur und monumentalen Plastik unter besonderer*

Beziehung auf Wien (Vienna: Karl Graeser, 1889), 5th ed. 1921. English ed.: *The Birth of Modern City Planning.* Translated by George Rosenborough Collins and Christiane Collins (New York: Rizzoli, 1986).

Specht, Bruno. "Raumkunst." *Deutsche Bauzeitung* 29, no. 81 (1895): 501–4.

Streiter, Richard. "Architektur und Kunstphilosophie." *Centralblatt der Bauverwaltung,* 12 December 1896: 550–53; 27 February 1897: 100–1.

——. *Ausgewählte Schriften.* Munich: Delphin, 1913.

——. Review of *Architektonische Raumlehre* by Gustav Ebe. In *Centralblatt der Bauverwaltung,* 5 December 1900: 588.

Strnad, Oskar. "Einiges Theoretische zur Raumgestaltung" (1913). Typescript, Österreichische Nationalbibliothek, Vienna, published as "Einiges Theoretische zur Raumgestaltung." *Deutsche Kunst und Dekoration* 41 (1 October 1917): 39–68; rpt. "Raumgestaltung und Raumgelenke." *Innen-Dekoration* 30 (July–August 1919): 254–58; 292–93.

——. "Gedanken beim Entwurf eines Grundrisses" in Max Eisler. *Oskar Strnad.* Vienna: Gerlach und Wiedling, 1936: 56–57.

——. "Neue Wege in der Wohnraum-Einrichtung. *Innen-Dekoration* 33 (October *Centralblatt der Bauverwaltung* 1922): 323–24.

——. "Der Palast Diokletians." *Neue Freie Presse,* 24 August 1912: 19–20.

——. "Projekt für ein Schauspielhaus." *Wasmuths Monatshefte* 6, no. 6 (1921): 181–93.

Stumpf, Carl. *Über den psychologischen Ursprung der Raumvorstellung.* Leipzig: Hirzel, 1873.

"Una casa en las proximidades de Viena." *Viviendas* 4 (June 1935): 6–15.

Vischer, Friedrich Theodor. *Aesthetik oder Wissenschaft des Schönen.* 8 vols. Reutlingen and Stuttgart: Carl Mäcken, 1846–57.

Vischer, Robert. *Über das optische Formgefühl: Ein Beitrag zur Aesthetik.* (Leipzig: Herm. Credner, 1873.

Vogel, F. Rudolf. *Das amerikanische Haus: Entwicklung, Bedingungen, Anlage, Aufbau, Einrichtung, Innenraum und Umgebung.* Berlin: Wasmuth, 1910.

Wöfflin, Heinrich. *Prolegomena zu einer Psychologie der Architektur.* Munich:

Dr. C. Wolf & Sohn, 1886.

——. *Renaissance und Barock: Eine Untersuchung über Wesen und Entstehung des Barockstils in Italien.* Munich: Theodor Ackermann, 1888.

——. Review of August Schmarsow, *Das Wesen der architektonischen Schöpfung.* In "Theorie und Technik der Kunst," *Repertorium für Kunstwissenschaft* 17, no. 2 (1894): 141–42.

Worringer, Wilhelm. *Abstraktion und Einfühlung: Ein Beitrag zur Stilpsychologie,* published dissertation, Neuwied, 1907; book, Munich: R. Piper, 1908. English ed.: *Abstraction and Empathy: A Contribution to the Psychology of Style.* Translated by Michael Bullock. Mansfield Center, Conn.: Martino, 2014.

Wulff, Oskar. "August Schmarsow zum 80. Geburtstag." *Zeitschrift für Kunstgeschichte* 2, no. 3 (1933): 207–9.

——. "Zu August Schmarsows Rücktritt." *Zeitschrift für bildende Kunst* 55 (1919/1920): 318–20.

Wundt, Wilhelm. *Beiträge zur Theorie der Sinneswahrnehmung.* Leipzig: Winter, 1862.

——. *Grundzüge der physiologischen Psychologie.* 2 vols. Leipzig: Engelmann, 1873–74.

OTHER SOURCES

Achleitner, Friedrich. "Ein positives Beispiel: Vorbildliche Renovierung der Strnad-Villa in der Cobenzlgasse." *Die Presse,* 14–15 August 1971.

Anderson, Eric. "Beyond Historicism: Jakob von Falke and the Reform of the Viennese Interior." Ph.D. diss., Columbia University, 2009.

Ash, Mitchell G. *Gestalt Psychology in German Culture, 1890–1967.* Cambridge: Cambridge University Press, 1995.

Bablet, Denis, and Marie-Louise Bablet. *Adolphe Appia, 1862–1928: Darsteller–Raum–Licht.* Zurich: Atlantis, 1982.

Bachelard, Gaston. *La poétique de l'espace.* Paris: Presses Universitaires de France, 1957; English ed.: *The Poetics of Space.* Translated by Marie Jolas. Boston: Beacon, 1969.

Beacham, R. C. *Adolphe Appia: Theatre Artists.* Cambridge: Cambridge University Press, 1987.

Behrendt, Walter Curt. *Der Sieg des neuen Baustils.* Stuttgart: Akademischer Verlag Dr. Fr. Wedekind, 1927. Translated as *The Victory of*

the New Building Style by Harry Francis Mallgrave. Los Angeles: Getty Research Institute, 2000.

Beltramini, Guido. "La casa sensibile." In *La casa isolata: dalla tautologia alla banalità: Letture, trascrizioni, variazioni su testi di Wittgenstein, Loos, Frank.* Edited by Giovanni Fraziano, 81–92. Venice: Cluva, 1989.

Benjamin, Andrew. "Surface Effects: Borromini, Semper, Loos." *Journal of Architecture* 11, no. 1 (February 2006): 1–35.

Benton, Tim. *The Villas of Le Corbusier and Pierre Jeanneret 1920–1930.* Basel: Birkhäuser, 2007.

Berry, J. Duncan. "Hans Auer and the Morality of Architectural Space." In *Seeing and Beyond: Essays on Eighteenth- to Twenty-First-Century Art in Honor of Kermit S. Champa.* Edited by Deborah J. Johnson and David Ogawa. New York: Peter Lang, 2005, 149–84.

Bock, Ralf. *Adolf Loos: Works and Projects.* Milan: Skira, 2007.

Bory, Sylvester. "Annäherungen an eine Raumbühne, die nie so bespielt wurde / Approaches to a Space-Stage on Which No One Ever Played." *Daidalos* 14 (15 December 1984): 85–88.

Çelik, Zeynep. "Kinaesthetic Impulses: Aesthetic Experience, Bodily Knowledge, and Pedagogical Practices in Germany, 1871–1918." Ph.D. diss., Massachusetts Institute of Technology, 2007.

Cheng, Anne Anlin. *Second Skin: Josephine Baker and the Modern Surface.* Oxford: Oxford University Press, 2011.

Collins, Peter. *Changing Ideals in Modern Architecture, 1750–1950.* Montreal: McGill University Press, 1965.

Colomina, Beatriz. "Intimacy and Spectacle: The Interiors of Adolf Loos." *AA Files* 20 (Autumn 1990): 5–15.

——. *Privacy and Publicity: Modern Architecture as Mass Media.* Cambridge, Mass.: MIT Press, 1994.

——. "The Split Wall: Domestic Voyeurism." In *Sexuality and Space.* Edited by Beatriz Colomina. New York: Princeton Architectural Press, 1992: 73–80.

Czech, Hermann. "Josef Frank, The Accidental House: The Thirteen Designs in Letters to Dagmar Grill." *Lotus International* 29 (1981): 108–10, 114–15.

——. *Zur Abwechslung: Ausgewählte Schriften zur Architektur.* Vienna: Löcker & Wögenstein, 1978.

——, and Wolfgang Mistelbauer. *Das Looshaus.* 3rd ed. Vienna: Löcker, 1984.

Denti, Giovanni. *Adolf Loos: Villa Müller / Casa Müller a Praga.* Florence: Alinea, 1999.

Domanický, Petr, and Petr Jindra. *Loos-Plzeň-Souvislosti / Loos-Pilsen-Connections.* Pilsen: Západočeská galerie v Plzni, 2001.

Dunn, Richard M. *Geoffrey Scott and the Berenson Circle: Literary and Aesthetic Life in the Early 20th Century.* Lewiston, NY: Edward Mellen, 1998.

El-Dahdah, Farès. "The Josephine Baker House: For Loos's Pleasure." *Assemblage* 26 (1996): 73–81.

Emmons, Paul. "Intimate Circulations: Representing Flow in House and City." *AA Files* 51 (2005): 48–57.

Etlin, Richard A. "Aesthetics and the Spatial Sense of Self." *The Journal of Aesthetics and Art Criticism* 56, no. 1 (Winter 1998): 1–19.

——. *Symbolic Space: French Enlightenment Architecture and Its Legacy.* Chicago: University of Chicago Press, 1994.

Feist, Peter H. "Schmarsow, August Hannibal." *Neue Deutsche Biographie* 23 (2007): 121–23.

Frank, Mitchell Benjamin, and Daniel Allan Adler, eds. *German Art History and Scientific Thought: Beyond Formalism.* Farnham, Surrey: Ashgate, 2012.

Games, Stephen. *Pevsner—The Early Life: Germany and Art.* London: Continuum, 2010.

Gravagnuolo, Benedetto. *Adolf Loos: Theory and Works.* New York: Rizzoli, 1988.

Groenendijk, Paul, and Piet Vollaard. *Adolf Loos, huis voor / house for / maison pour / haus für Josephine Baker.* Rotterdam: Uitgeverij 010, 1985.

Gruber, Karlheinz, Sabine Höller-Alber, and Markus Kristan. *Ernst Epstein, 1881–1938: Der Bauleiter des Looshauses als Architekt.* Exhibition catalogue. Vienna: Jüdisches Museum der Stadt Wien / Holzhausen, 2002.

Hand, Stacy. "Embodied Abstraction: Biomorphic Fantasy and Empathy Aesthetics in the Work of Hermann Obrist, August Endell, and Their Followers," Ph.D. diss., University of Chicago, 2008.

Henderson, Susan R. "Bachelor Culture in the Work of Adolf Loos." *Journal of Architectural Education* 55 (2002): 125–35.

Hnilica, Sonja. "Stadtmetaphern: Camillo Sittes Bild der Stadt im Architekturdiskurs." Ph.D. diss., Technische Universität Wien, 2006.

Hubatová-Vacková, Lada. *Silent Revolutions in Ornament: Studies in Applied Arts and Crafts from 1880–1930.* Prague: Academy of Arts, Architecture and Design, 2011.

Ikonomou, Eleftherios. "August Schmarsow." In *Encyclopedia of Aesthetics,* vol 4. Edited by Michael Kelly. New York: Oxford University Press, 1998, 239–42.

——. "The Transformation of Space in the Architectural Thinking of the Late 19th and Early 20th Century, with Special Reference to Germany." Ph.D. diss., University of Cambridge, 1985.

Jara, Cynthia. "Adolf Loos's Raumplan Theory." *Journal of Architectural Education* 48, no. 3 (February 1995): 185–201.

Jones, Peter Blundell, and Mark Meagher, eds. *Architecture and Movement: The Dynamic Experience of Buildings and Landscapes.* London: Routledge, 2015.

Kern, Stephen. *The Culture of Time and Space, 1880–1918.* Cambridge, Mass.: Harvard University Press, 1983.

Kirsch, Karin. "Franks Doppelhaus in der Weißenhofsiedlung." *Bauwelt* 26 (12 July 1985): 1054–56.

Köhler, Bettina. "Architekturgeschichte als Geschichte der Raumwahrnehmung." *Daidalos* 67 (March 1998): 36–43.

Koss, Juliet. *Modernism after Wagner.* Minneapolis: University of Minnesota Press, 2010.

——. "On the Limits of Empathy." *Art Bulletin* 88, no. 1 (March 2006): 139–57.

Kristan, Markus. *Landhaus Khuner am Kreuzberg.* Vienna: Höhere Graphische Bundes-, Lehr- und Versuchsanstalt, 2004.

Ksandr, Karel, ed. *Villa Müller.* Prague: Argo, 2000.

Leatherbarrow, David. *Architecture Oriented Otherwise.* New York: Princeton Architectural Press, 2009.

——. *The Roots of Architectural Invention: Site, Enclosure, Materials.* Cambridge: Cambridge University Press, 1993.

Lejeune, Jean-François. "Schinkel, Sitte, and Loos: The 'Body in the Invisible.'" In *Sitte,*

Hegemann and the Metropolis: Modern Civic Art and International Exchanges. Edited by Charles C. Bohl and Jean-François Lejeune. London and New York: Routledge, 2009.

Long, Christopher. *Der Fall Loos.* Vienna: Amalthea, 2015.

——. "'Gedanken beim Entwurf eines Grundrisses': Space and Promenade in Oskar Strnad's Hock and Wassermann Houses, 1912–14." *Umění: Journal of Institute of Art History, Czech Academy of Sciences* 49, no. 6 (2001): 520–30.

——. "The House as Path and Place: Spatial Planning in Josef Frank's Villa Beer, 1928–1930." *Journal of the Society of Architectural Historians* 59 (December 2000): 478–501.

——. *Josef Frank: Life and Work.* Chicago: University of Chicago Press, 2002.

——. The Looshaus. New Haven: Yale University Press, 2011.

——. "Wiener Wohnkultur: Interior Design in Vienna, 1910–1938," *Studies in the Decorative Arts* 5 (Fall–Winter 1997–98): 29–51.

Lustenberger, Kurt. "Der Schnitt durch den Plan." *Werk, Bauen + Wohnen* 12 (December 1995): 45–52.

Mallgrave, Harry Francis. *Architecture and Embodiment: The Implications of the New Sciences and Humanities for Design.* London: Routledge, 2013.

——. *Gottfried Semper: Architect of the Nineteenth Century.* New Haven: Yale University Press, 1996.

——, and Christina Contandriopoulos, eds. *Architectural Theory: Volume II, An Anthology from 1871 to 2005.* Malden, Mass.: Blackwell, 2008.

——, and Eleftherios Ikonomou, eds. *Empathy, Form, and Space: Problems in German Aesthetics, 1873–1934.* Santa Monica, Calif.: Getty Center for the History of Art and the Humanities, 1994.

March, Lionel, and Judith Scheine, eds. *R. M. Schindler: Composition and Construction.* London: Academy, 1995.

Mattl-Wurm, Sylvia. *Interieurs: Wiener Künstlerwohnungen 1830–1930.* Vienna: Historisches Museum der Stadt Wien, 1990.

Meder, Iris. "Josef Franks Wiener Einfamilienhäuser." M.A. thesis, Universität Stuttgart, 1993.

——. "Offene Welten: Die Wiener Schule in Einfamilienhausbau 1910–1938." Ph.D. diss., Universität Stuttgart, 2001.

——, ed. *Josef Frank: Eine Moderne der Unordnung.* Salzburg: Anton Pustet, 2008.

——, and Evi Fuks, eds. *Oskar Strnad—1879–1935.* Vienna: Anton Pustet, 2007.

Mundt, Ernst. "Three Aspects of German Aesthetic Theory." *Journal of Aesthetics and Art Criticism* 17, no. 3 (March 1959): 287–310.

Münz, Ludwig, and Gustav Künstler. *Der Architekt Adolf Loos: Darstellung seines Schaffens nach Werkgruppen / Chronologisches Werkverzeichnis.* Vienna: Anton Schroll, 1964.

Neumann, Dietrich. "'The Century's Triumph in Lighting': The Luxfer Prism Companies and Their Contribution to Early Modern Architecture." *Journal of the Society of Architectural Historians* 54, no. 1 (March 1995): 24–53.

Niedermoser, Otto. *Oskar Strnad 1879–1935.* Vienna: Bergland, 1965.

Oechslin, Werner. "Raumplan versus plan libre." *Daidalos* (15 December 1991): 76–83.

Ott-Wodni, Marlene. *Josef Frank 1885–1967: Raumgestaltung und Möbeldesign.* Vienna: Böhlau, 2015.

Ottillinger, Eva B. "Jakob von Falke (1825–1897) und die Theorie des Kunstgewerbes." *Wiener Jahrbuch für Kunstgeschichte* 42 (1989): 205–23.

Panin, Tankao. "Space-Art: The Dialectic between the Concepts of Raum and Bekleidung." Ph.D. diss., University of Pennsylvania, 2003.

Payne, Alina A. "Architectural History and the History of Art: A Suspended Dialogue." *Journal of the Society of Architectural Historians* 58, no. 3 (September 1999): 292–99.

——. *From Ornament to Object: Genealogies of Architectural Modernism.* New Haven: Yale University Press, 2012.

Pevsner, Nikolaus. *Pioneers of the Modern Movement from William Morris to Walter Gropius.* London: Faber & Faber, 1936; rpt. New York: Museum of Modern Art, 1949.

Poppelreuter, Tanja. "Raumplan after Loos: The European Work of Heinrich Kulka, 1930–1939." *Fabrications* 25, no. 1 (2015): 84–103.

Porter, Roy Malcolm, Jr. "The Essence of Architecture: August Schmarsow's Theory of Space." Ph.D. diss., University of Pennsylvania, 2005.

Posener, Julius. *Adolf Loos 1870–1933: Ein Vortrag.* Berlin: Akademie der Künste, 1984.

Prokop, Ursula. *Wien: Aufbruch zur Metropole: Geschäfts- und Wohnhäuser der Innenstadt 1910 bis 1914.* Vienna: Böhlau, 1994.

Rabaça Correia Cordeiro, Armando Manuel de Castilho. "Ordering Code and Mediating Machine: Le Corbusier and the Roots of the Architectural Promenade." Ph.D. diss., Universidade de Coimbra, 2014.

Riesenhuber, Georg. "Josef Frank: Das Haus als Weg und Platz—Eine Textanalyse." Unpublished essay, 2004.

Risselada, Max, ed. *Raumplan versus Plan Libre: Adolf Loos and Le Corbusier, 1919–1930.* New York: Rizzoli, 1988.

Rüegg, Arthur, and Adolph Stiller. *Sechs Häuser: Nach Aufnahmen korrigierte Grundrisse der Wohngeschosse sechs bedeutender Häuser der Moderne im Dreieck Prag-Leipzig-Wien.* Zurich: ETH, 1992.

Rukschcio, Burkhardt. "Studien zu Entwürfen, Projekten und ausgeführten Bauten von Adolf Loos (1870–1933)." Ph.D. diss., Universität Wien, 1973.

——, ed. *Adolf Loos.* Exhibition catalogue. Vienna: Graphische Sammlung Albertina / Historisches Museum der Stadt Wien, 1990.

——, and Roland Schachel. *Adolf Loos: Leben und Werk.* 2nd ed. Salzburg: Residenz, 1987.

Samuel, Flora. *Le Corbusier and the Architectural Promenade.* Basel: Birkhäuser, 2010.

Sarnitz, August, and Eva Ottillinger. *Ernst Plischke: Modern Architecture for the New World.* Munich: Prestel, 2004.

Schafter, Debra. *The Order of Ornament, the Structure of Style: Theoretical Foundations of Modern Art and Architecture.* Cambridge: Cambridge University Press, 2003.

Schwarzer, Mitchell W. "The Emergence of Architectural Space: August Schmarsow's Theory of Raumgestaltung." *Assemblage* 15 (August 1991): 48–61.

——. *German Architectural Theory and the Search for Modern Identity.* Cambridge: Cambridge University Press, 1995.

Semper, Gottfried. *Der Stil in den technischen und tektonischen Künsten oder Praktische Ästhetik.* 2 vols. Frankfurt am Main: Verlag für Kunst und Wissenschaft, 1860, 1863.

Shapira, Elana. "Dressing a Celebrity: Adolf Loos's House for Josephine Baker." *Studies in the Decorative Arts* 11, no. 2 (Spring–Summer 2004): 2–24.

Sheine, Judith. *R. M. Schindler.* London: Phaidon, 2001.

Smith, Elizabeth A. T., and Michael Darling, eds. *The Architecture of R. M. Schindler.* Exhibition catalogue. Los Angeles: Museum of Contemporary Art / New York: Harry N. Abrams, 2001.

Sörgel, Herman. *Einführung in die Architektur-Ästhetik: Prolegomena zu einer Theorie der Baukunst.* Munich: Piloty & Loehle, 1918.

——. "Erwiderung." *Wasmuths Monatshefte,* 20, nos. 11–12 (1919): 86–87.

——. "Über den Natur- und Landschaftsraum in der Architektur." *Wasmuths Monatshefte,* 20, nos. 9–10 (1919): 67–72.

Spalt, Johannes. "Josef Frank und die räumliche Konzeption seiner Hausentwürfe." *Um Bau* 10 (August 1986): 59–74.

——, ed. *Der Architekt Oskar Strnad zum hundersten Geburtstag.* Exhibition catalogue. Vienna: Hochschule für angewandte Kunst, 1979.

——, ed. *Josef Frank 1885–1967: Möbel & Geräte & Theoretisches.* Vienna: Hochschule für angewandte Kunst, 1981.

Stiller, Adolph. "Colored Dots on a Grey Background: Six Key Buildings of Modern Architecture in Central Europe." In *On Continuity.* Edited by Rosamund Diamond and Wilfried Wang, 24–41. *9H,* no. 9. Cambridge, Mass.: 9H Publications, 1995; distributed by Princeton Architectural Press.

Stoklaska, Juliane. "Oskar Strnad." Ph.D. diss., Universität Wien, 1959.

Stritzler-Levine, Nina, ed. *Josef Frank, Architect and Designer: An Alternative Vision of the Modern Home.* Exhibition catalogue. New Haven: Yale University Press, 1996.

Švácha, Rostislav. "The Architects Have Overslept: Space as a Construct of Art Historians, 1888–1914." *Umění* 49, no. 6 (2001): 487–500.

——. "Ke spisu August Schmarsowa o podstatě architektury z roku." *Umění* 49, no. 6 (2001): 561–68.

Szadkowska, Maria, Leslie van Duzer, and Dagmar Černoušková. *Adolf Loos: Dílo v českých zemích / Adolf Loos: Works in the Czech Lands.* Exhibition catalogue. Prague: Muzeum hlavní měsa Prahy / Kant, 2009.

Tanzer, Kim. "Baker's Loos and Loos's Loss: Architecting the Body." *Center: A Journal for Architecture in America* 9 (1995): 76–89.

Ullmann, Ernst. *100 Jahre Kunstwissenschaft in Leipzig.* Leipzig: Karl-Marx-Universität, 1975.

——. "August Schmarsow's Beitrag zur Architekturtheorie." *Künstlerliches und kunswissenschaftliches Erbe als Gegenwartsaufgabe* 1 (1975): 130–39.

——. "Der Beitrag August Schmarsows zur Architekturtheorie." Habilitationsschrift, Karl-Marx-Universität Leipzig, 1967.

"Una casa d'abitazione di Josef Frank e Oskar Wlach." *Casabella* 345 (February 1970): 45.

Van de Ven, Cornelius. *Space in Architecture: The Evolution of a New Idea in the Theory and History of the Modern Movements.* Assen, Netherlands: Van Gorcum, 1978.

Van Duzer, Leslie, and Kent Kleinman. *Villa Müller: A Work of Adolf Loos.* New York: Princeton Architectural Press, 1994.

Varnedoe, Kirk. *Vienna 1900: Art, Architecture & Design.* Exhibition catalogue. New York: Museum of Modern Art / Boston: Little, Brown, 1986.

Vidler, Anthony. *Warped Space: Art, Architecture, and Anxiety in Modern Culture.* Cambridge, Mass.: MIT Press, 2000.

Vladova, Tat'iana. "La pensée de l'art d'August Schmarsow entre corps et configuration spatiale." *Passagen–Deutsches Forum für Kunstgeschichte / Passages–Centre allemande d'histoire de l'art* 41 (2012): 137–51.

Vogt-Göknil, Ulya. *Architektonische Grundbegriffe und Umraumerlebnis.* Zurich: Origo, 1951.

Von Moos, Stanislaus, and Arthur Rüegg, eds. *Le Corbusier before Le Corbusier.* New Haven: Yale University Press, 2002.

Vybíral, Jindřich. "The Architects Have Overslept? On the Concept of Space in 19th-Century Architectural Theory." *Umění* 52 (2004): 110–22.

Wagner, Kirsten, and Jasper Cepl, eds. *Images of the Body in Architecture: Anthropology and Built Space.* Tübingen and Berlin: Ernst Wasmuth, 2014.

Wängberg-Eriksson, Kristina. "Tolvekarna Tyresö." *Form* 80, no. 627 (1984): 49–53.

Weich, Ulla. "Die theoretische Ansichten des Architekten und Lehrers Oskar Strnad." Diplomarbeit, Universität Wien, 1995.

Welzig, Maria. *Josef Frank, 1885–1967: Das architektonische Werk.* Vienna: Böhlau, 1998.

Worbs, Dietrich. "Adolf Loos als Erzieher." *Architekt* 9 (September 1995): 517–22.

——. "Der Raumplan in der Architektur von Adolf Loos." Ph.D. diss., Technische Universität Stuttgart, 1981.

——, ed., *Adolf Loos 1870–1933: Raumplan–Wohnungsbau.* Exhibition catalogue. Berlin: Akademie der Künste, 1983.

Zucker, Paul. "Architektur-Ästhetik." *Wasmuths Monatshefte,* 20, nos. 11–12 (1919): 83–86.

——. "Der Begriff der Zeit in der Architektur." *Repertorium für Kunstwissenschaft* 44 (1924): 237–45.

——. "Formempfinden und Raumgefühl." *Innen-Dekoration* 28, no. 11 (1917): 374–84.

——. "Kontinuität und Diskontinuität: Grenzprobleme der Architektur und Plastik." *Zeitschrift für Ästhetik und Allgemeine Kunstwissenschaft* 15 (1921): 304–17.

——. "Die Unwirklichkeit des Raumes." *Das junge Deutschland* 1 (1918): 233–35.

Zug, Beatrix. *Die Anthropologie des Raumes in der Architekturtheorie des frühen 20. Jahrhunderts.* Tübingen: Ernst Wasmuth, 2006.

INDEX

242

for the architect—one that comes up over and over again—is to determine the size of such joints—what we call moldings. A molding, which has its own separate existence, forms a whole with the courtyard, a single spatial element. A space without joints is like a straw-filled doll, which lies there motionless; the organism is lifeless. The joint can itself be a spatial stimulus, it can contain a host of spatial markers, which lead back to us—that which we call dentils, corbels, or egg-and-dart moldings, and so forth. Their dimensions do not have to be the same as other space-making elements; otherwise the joint will lose its character because the space-making parts of the joint will compete with the space-making parts of the whole, and the joint will cease to be a joint. If they are independently space-forming, then they would become unintelligible, because they would not have any connection with the floor or the ceiling; they would neither rest on the floor nor hang down from the ceiling—and they also would not be attached to the wall as space-making elements. This is usually not recognized, and our schools teach the most incredible and misguided ideas about moldings. Classical, Renaissance, and Gothic moldings are "studied," and one forgets that they were the inspiration of exceedingly keen artistic instincts, which remain intangible, because their premises are so complex and were often unclear even to their creators. The sins of this teaching are evident in most buildings and furniture.

If it is already so difficult to place a pair of flowerpots on a pavement in a courtyard, how difficult is it if we want to put chairs and furniture in our rooms to create a lucid spatial impression? A wardrobe thus becomes more than a storage place for clothing that the cabinetmaker fashions, a chair more than a mere thing one sits on. And a room becomes more than a space with four walls, windows, and doors. Should the floor provide a spatial stimulus? Should the ceiling provide a spatial stimulus? Should the walls? And how should I arrange it all so that I can find unity with the dimensions? That does not work with mere guessing. Because everything needs to be considered. Here the architect should not start with designing the furniture or selecting the

fabrics, but he has to think about proportions, and to find the relationship between these proportions. And if he does not have that ineffable sense, which rests outside of our conscious thinking, of how to find the relationship between these proportions, which is to say to discover the spatial indicators, then, of course, he simply makes walls and designs carpets and furniture in the usual ways with a productivity that is enviable.

Now I ask myself, what should furniture really look like? How should I furnish my rooms? There are so many answers to these questions because there are so many different sorts of spaces, so many different people, so many architects and so many artistic conceptions. But one thing should be clear by now: in any event I can make a restful and strong spatial impression if I make the floor and ceiling readable—in other words, if all of the edges of the floor are visible and they correspond to those on the ceiling. In this way, the spatial impression below and above is set. The wall here, as in the case of the courtyard with flowerpots, plays no role in creating a spatial effect. The wall is placid—an effect which in the case of living spaces is worth striving for.

Here, however, doors and windows have to be placed within the wall. The depth with which the doors and windows are set into the wall is a gauge for the whole sense of the spatial dynamic. All other spatial impressions must conform to this standard if a unified spatial impression is to be maintained. This is often very difficult and seldom achieved in practice. I am reminded of Tyrolean rooms. In most of our dwellings this emphasis on spatial effects is taken into consideration (though with rental apartment buildings, of course, one cannot even speak about space for all those who assume the right to build such buildings have no sense for it at all). Those who do it themselves ignore the spatial premise by draping the rooms with fabric. But fabric does not enhance space—that is the nature of fabric. One can help oneself with doors, in that one can treat them like pictures—which is to say, frame them. Of course, the frame does not have any space-enhancing qualities and has to be handled like a joint—something never done nowadays. But in the time of the Empire, or

for that matter, the Biedermeier, people had a sense for it.

An essential requirement for livable spaces is movement. The changing of one's position relative to various objects (which, by the way, is the stuff of all spatial consciousness) yields a progressive alteration of images, which we receive from the objects in the room. First the chair in front of the armoire is visible, then it is in front of the door, and finally it is by the window. A sense of ease is maintained if I can always see the edges of the floor clearly. Either all furnishings have to have legs, or the room is so large that blurring of the intersections of floor and wall does not happen. If there is a piece of furniture in the room that does not allow me to see where the floor meets the wall, then all of the other furnishings must be so made that there is no other interruption of the view. But the furnishings should also not be so high that one cannot see over them; otherwise they form a wall of their own. They are no longer resting on the floor; they have become something else. The wall then becomes the marker of the space; it no longer relates to the floor, it creates new proportions, which are not found anywhere else in the room, and the unity of the space is destroyed. Something of this sort is only thinkable if it extends up to the ceiling, for it would then become a spatial determinant for the whole room, in which now the other things stand—like our earlier example of the trees in the meadow. I see the feet of the chairs, the tables, the chests, and from them I am able to gauge the depth of the room. In the case of rooms that are not living spaces, a harmonious effect is generally easier to achieve. Pillars or columns with associated beams or lintels, which carry the eye forward, stimulate the spatial imagination. The size of the room establishes the basic spatial image. The establishment of the joints establishes its character. Such rooms also often have different degrees of lighting. It can happen that by altering the light the spatial effect can be diminished. Here color can help. Everything that with normal lighting is in the shadows should be painted blue or black, which will give a sense of calm. Everything that in normal light is bright should be yellow or gold.

the dimensions of a space. If they are spread out haphazardly, like the trees in the forest, then the spatial impression one has will be similar—all cut up—and we will not be able to see the forest for the trees. If we manage to establish relationships between these things—let us call them spatial markers—the nature of these relationships will exercise an impact on our spatial impression. If, for example, columns are placed with standard intervals between them, then we will come away with a sense of a restful, homogeneous space, and movement through the room is formal and regular. For us it is something natural—unified—something we can grasp at first glance. We can strengthen this impression if we put not only on the floor but also on the ceiling something that allows us to read the space—which is to say we combine one set of spatial markers with another. If you imagine one spatial marker and then the next, arranged in an arc, the eye will follow that arc instinctively; it will move up and down, then up and then down again, until it moves all the way back to us. Or imagine this linkage along a horizontal line: the eye will follow the full length of the line, stopping along the way for a moment wherever vertical markers touch horizontal ones. This is a crucial point that has to be indicated especially carefully, so that the eye does not have to interpret something on its own, and so that the spatial impression consequently will become more sure and clear. The less we have to call on our experience to perceive a space, the stronger and more reassuring is our spatial sense. These points at which movement stops, changes, or moves from reading the surface to perceiving depth correspond in some sense with the hinges of the human body in that they provide an opportunity to carry out movement. Let us then call these "joints": in that way we are describing what one would normally understand as a capital, a foundation, or a cornice. With a finely attuned sensibility, one recognizes that there is an alteration here that has to be indicated, and the more precisely this indication is developed, the greater, the more elegant and refined is the whole impression. Instead of the joints of a farmer, those of an elegant lady; instead of the joints of an elephant, those of a

gazelle. The forms of these joints, the recognition of their essential role in fostering affects, and the possibilities they offer are the personal and special domain of the designer, and are among the designer's most challenging and sensitive tasks.

A good spatial conception also requires that one can read the dimensions of the ceiling as well as the floor and recognize their relationships and their proportions. The clearer this relationship is, the clearer the spatial effect. If floor and ceiling convey the same spatial impression, what emerges is a sense of comfort and well-being. What is above me is not other, the space above me is not larger, nor is it broader or more narrow. The first commandment then is under any circumstances to make this line of demarcation, the frame for the floor and the ceiling, as distinct as possible. The more precisely, the more elegantly it is made, the more elegant and precise the effect we get back—very much like the frame of a picture. And the way an object that I place on the floor has a spatial effect—like a tree in a meadow, or a fountain in a courtyard, or a statue on a square—so, too, an object that hangs on a ceiling conveys a spatial effect. There are also quite curious effects, as in the case of an object that extends from the floor to the ceiling. This fosters a remarkably human connection. The affixing of space markers to the ceiling has been common in all epochs. All wooden ceilings and stucco ceilings belong to this category.

There are also methods to apply to the floor or to the wall that aid in clarifying spatial impressions. The way in which that is done, the various ways of discovering the possibilities of spatial markers is a characteristic of an artistic personality. This is something that lies outside our consciousness that is not arbitrary. It comes and goes and is neither graspable nor learnable.

A few possibilities for fashioning spaces: in one instance the flooring might become a medium, for example, in the case of a small square courtyard, which is fully enclosed, surrounded by a wall, which is approximately three meters high. The walls are white. The paving stones here are white, too. The only possibility for sensing the space comes from

the lines of demarcation, where the walls begin, and the line along the upper edge of the walls, where the sky becomes visible.

If, on the other hand, the paving stones are red, then the spatial impression is more evident because the boundary can be more swiftly grasped with the eye. If one erects a pair of flowerpots, one behind the other, to make imagining the space easier, but in such a way that one can see over the top of them, between them the floor is visible and we receive a spatial sense of the floor. Think of a checkerboard pattern of black and white stones that are placed at right angles to each other in a way that enhances the spatial impression. And the flowerpots are placed there as well. Then we have a doubled process of imaging. One receives a certain spatial idea from the flowerpots and another from the checkerboard pattern. But if these two stimuli are not in concert with each other, then the spatial impression is blurred and weakened. The dimensions of the flowerpots must also correspond with the dimensions of the pilasters. But the flowerpots also have their own spatial volume, which we can easily estimate from experience, and their own size, contributing to fostering a certain spatial impression, one that may not correspond with that of the paving stones. Here we have to start to experiment. One might try to reposition the pots, without a successful result. In our example, too, this probably will not work because we have three different standard sizes. In this instance, it would be better to use only red paving stones, or select paving stones and flowerpots with the same dimensions, to find a way to arrange the paving stones, the pots, and distance between the pots in a unified way. There is also another way to clarify the spatial impression, and that is if one would mark the upper edge of the surrounding wall. This is the place that I had earlier described as a joint; here two different directions of movement collide, the verticality of the wall and the horizontality of the sky (the ceiling).

A joint for a space must itself naturally also be spatial. It does not work just to paint a line there. That might work for the frame of a wall, but it would not foster a three-dimensional spatial impression. One of the difficult tasks